THE UNTOLD HISTORY OF
SONORA PASS AND ITS PEOPLE
1860 to 1960

Cate Culver

Manzanita Writers Press
Angels Camp, California
manzapress.com

The Untold History of Sonora Pass and Its People: 1860 to 1960
Copyright ©2020 Cate Culver

ISBN: 978-0-9986910-2-2
Library of Congress Control Number: 2019917460

Manzanita Writers Press
PO Box 460, Angels Camp, CA 95222
manzanitawp@gmail.com
manzapress.com
209-728-6171

To contact Cate Culver to order a book or make a comment, reach her by email at:
sonorapasshistorybook@gmail.com

Front and Back Cover Art: Cate Culver
Title Page: Cate Culver
Book Design: Cate Culver
Book Layout: Joyce Dedini

Dedication

*In memory of my parents, Edson and Ruth
Wells Caldwell, and my sister, Constance
Lucile Fry, who were all history enthusiasts.*

The Caldwell family at their Dardanelle cabin in 1948. Edson, daughter Connie, Ruth and daughter Cathy.
Photographer unknown.

Introduction

Sonora Pass, located north of the famous Tioga Pass that leads to Yosemite, is not well known. Extremely steep, and carved into granite like much of the Sierra, the pass is a hidden jewel. Who were the people who built the roads, established resorts, grazed cattle, constructed dams, made movies, and built cabins on Sonora Pass? A community unto itself, Sonora Pass has a rich history, and Cate Culver has unearthed and recorded the stories and information that would have been lost to time.

In 1944, Cate Culver's family purchased a cabin near Eagle Creek east of Dardanelle. From her earliest childhood, Cate spent summers at breakfast tables and around campfires, listening to the stories and learning the history of Sonora Pass. Getting out old black-and-white photographs often started the conversation. Cate realized that the history and the photographs needed to be recorded and saved. She began several years of research, including interviews with family members and friends of the original Sonora Pass pioneers. Over ninety of the old-timers were interviewed in person and many are brought to life in this remarkable history of the men and women who pioneered Sonora Pass.

The result is the only book of its kind, documenting the history of Sonora Pass from 1860 to 1960. This collection is even more poignant and valuable today, since the Donnell Fire ravaged much of the area on August 15, 2018.

Photograph by Jerry Culver.

Preface

Beginning with the road construction that brought people into the Sonora Pass wilderness, the untold history of Sonora Pass spans one hundred years of development through the 1960s. It revolves around the lives of the people who left their mark on the region. The more I explored the remote little-known area, the place of my childhood and family memories that spanned decades, the more I realized there was a complex and rich history that had not been told. Inspired by David Johnson's book, *Sonora Pass Pioneers*, relating the history of the region up to the mid-1860s, I continued the untold story.

So many people told me, "I am so glad you are doing this." It wasn't that I set out to write a book. It came to me that if I did not tackle the project, who would? As historian with the Calaveras County Historical Society for many years, I had the research skills needed, and I had the passion for Sonora Pass in my blood. What began as an avid interest in collecting historic photos, turned into interviews with elderly locals, and an expansion of the collection of images that told their own stories. I saw the book developing inside the information and knew I had to write it. The book you hold in your hands is the result of five years of meticulous research, poring over documents and photographs stored at the History Center at the Tuolumne County Historical Society and Museum, the Stanislaus National Forest headquarters, newspaper archives, and interviews I conducted with old-timers of Sonora Pass.

I came to write about a century of the area's history in an accidental way. In a Murphys restaurant about eight years ago, I noticed some old black and white photos on the wall. Intrigued by these photos of Sonora Pass, with handwritten captions with dates, I asked the waitress to tell me about them. "Oh, those are Francis Nelson's. He was sweet on one of the waitresses and brought in these framed photos for the restaurant." Fascinated with how the images vividly captured the Pass and had stories to tell, I asked her if she would mind if I took shots of them with my camera, and thus began my collection of historic photos of Sonora Pass.

As sole owner of my family's cabin, owned by my parents since 1944, I knew little about the area's history and the generations of residents who preceded me. To satisfy my historical curiosity, I sought out the older cabin owners to hear their recollections. I showed them my photo collection, and they began reminiscing. I wrote it all down, as was my nature, and I longed to find out more.

As my photo collection grew, I wanted more background information, so I went to see Irving Terzich, a cabin neighbor. He was born in 1916, had lived up there most summers all his life, so I would visit him, bring my notebook, and we would sit for hours. I listened to his stories about the pass, which were reliable and accurate. He had a fine memory. As I was writing the book, and there was information that I needed clarification on, I would ask Irving. At 97, he communicated with me via email from his home in Redwood City if I had any questions. I would email him a photo, and I'd ask him, "Irving, who are the people in this photo and what do you know about them?" or "What about this road on the map? What do you know about it? Or "I heard this story about one of the neighbors. Was it true?"

I lost Irving about midway through the project, and not only felt the loss of untold history, but of a valued friend. He was the backbone of the stories, eager to tell me what he knew, and he supported me every step of the journey. He is listed in the book as one of my History Heroes, for good reason. I began interviewing more elderly residents, and the history just poured out of them, and they loved to talk about the history with me, eager to share their information and to be a part of this project.

The next step occurred when I learned that there were scant published materials of a definitive history about Sonora Pass. I could not let that stop me in what was rapidly becoming a project consuming my attention and imagination, knowing I would need to pursue that history myself. I made a list of questions to ask and returned to interviewing people in earnest, collecting every bit of information possible.

Of course, I cross-checked the validity of this source information by asking multiple individuals, and took particular care in being accurate. I documented what they recalled. By the end of this project, I had interviewed eighty-six people in person, and twelve by telephone.

Unsure of my writing skills, I knew I would need some editorial support. I met Rob Gordon, researcher with the Tuolumne County Historical Society, and his assistance in poring over records and online sources was invaluable to me. I asked him to be my editor on the project and was pleased when he said yes. I attended Manzanita Writers group meetings where I met Suzanne Murphy. Knowledgeable about Sonora Pass, and a writer and teacher, she offered to assist in editing, as well. Towards the end of the project, I met Alan Haack, who knew the area since boyhood, and offered to read my chapters with an editorial eye. With their support, I was able to accomplish something I never thought would be possible, an enormous undertaking that consumed my life for several years.

I would like to thank all the people I interviewed, acknowledged throughout, who brought the Sonora Pass history to life. They are my History Heroes. Also, thanks goes to my editors, who I refer to as my Editorial Angels. In addition, I would like to express my gratitude to the Tuolumne County Historical Society, who published my article "Daughter of Dardanelle" in their quarterly publication, *CHISPA*, and invited me to be a guest speaker for the Tuolumne County Museum at their programs.

I am blessed for my husband Jerry Culver's enduring support and his love of Sonora Pass, our summer retreat at the primitive family cabin that has become an integral part of our life together. And when we nearly lost it to the Donnell Fire in August last year, we realized that it's not just the cabin that we love, but the entire wilderness area.

The loss of the Dardanelle Resort in 2018 and the cabins in the area is heartbreaking. We used to have a cabin tucked into a lush forest. Now, we have a view of granite bluffs on one side, and in another direction, burned trees. The new view is spectacular. One day, the trees will return, but not in our lifetime. Jerry and I are marking the tiny, baby seedlings about three inches high, with stakes—eight cedars and two pines, so far. We watch their progress and marvel at nature's ability to renew and heal itself. I have had to heal my own loss as well, knowing this is a huge change, and that I need to accept it.

I now realize I have preserved this precious past not only to pursue my own passion, but to capture an era before it slips away. Now, all has changed due to the fire, and it gives me great satisfaction that I stepped forward and wrote this book to be archived in the annals of history.

Table of Contents

IV. Kennedy Meadows Gateway to the Emigrant Basin

V. The Back Country Grazers

VI. The High Country

VII. Protectors of The Land

CHAPTER 1

Crossing the Sierra

Lower Relief Meadow.
Acrylic painting by Cate Culver.

It was an amazing accomplishment to come to California over the Sierra. The state's first emigrants from the Midwest had only a vague notion of how to reach California. Before the Gold Rush, settlers were enticed by the dream of being at the forefront of creating a future state. The travelers often had optimistic expectations of reaching California's Central Valley in a matter of days, once they crossed the high desert of Nevada. When they reached the imposing mountains of the Sierra Nevada, they discovered that the 10,000-foot peaks loomed yet higher as they followed the range south.

The range extends approximately 400 miles north to south and boasts the highest peak in the continental United States, Mount Whitney. Massive formations of rising granite and volcanic rock break away at their bases in fields of wagon-sized talus. Windswept conifers root themselves to the edges of the talus and grow in increasingly thick forests as the terrain dips and winds through canyons and steep river gorges. Weather systems created by the mountains themselves give birth to the river rapids that charge through the landscape and eventually meander to the Sacramento-San Joaquin River Delta.

This mountain range remains a barrier between east and west, granting limited winter passage even in modern times. Yet for all its wildness and unforgiving granite cliffs and rivers, the Sierra has a soothing sense of peace and stillness.

Despite the seeming inaccessibility of the mountain range, the emigrants were not the first people to explore the area. Indigenous people had been spending summers in the Sierra for thousands of years. They considered white men to be interlopers and usually did not engage with the newcomers. Communication was difficult and often led to serious misunderstandings. Few pioneers consulted native people to guide them across the range.

No maps or knowledge of the terrain existed in 1841 when the first emigrants, known as the Bidwell-Bartleson party of 32, were confronted with crossing the Central Sierra. The pioneers had already experienced so much hardship that to make better time, they abandoned their wagons west of the Great Salt Lake. With only mules and oxen, some of which they later ate out of desperation, they traversed the mountains free of their wagons. Eventually after summiting the crest out of Antelope Valley on the eastern slope, the party found their way along the Clarks Fork of the Stanislaus River, one watershed north of Yosemite National Park. Following the often-treacherous Stanislaus River canyon, they arrived by foot in the Central Valley, ragged and starving, to begin their new lives in the West.

No other emigrants attempted to reach western California over the Sierra this far south until the Gold Rush was wildly romanticized. Eleven years later in 1851, after California had become a state, fifty optimistic gold seekers from the Midwest organized themselves into the Clark-Skidmore party. By the time their wagon train approached the western edges of Nevada, they were dangerously low on provisions. They naively believed that riches beyond their dreams lay only a few days' journey away where they could resupply themselves. With limited rations, in the mid-August summer they elected not to follow the Bidwell-Bartleson path, but headed southwest, following the Walker River. The farther south they traveled, the higher the mountain range seemed to appear. Breaking new trail was hard work up to the large and lush Pickle Meadow. However, surrounding the meadow, ominous 11,000-foot peaks jutted into the blue-black sky. Before reaching the crest, they realized

more provisions were needed and sent a relief party of eight men to locate the booming Gold Rush town of Sonora on the western slope. They were unaware of the difficulties ahead for them, the seemingly endless sea of granite ridges and steep canyons that lay before them, and expected to reach Sonora that evening. Two and a half days after their departure, the relief party was expected to return with more provisions, but the eight men became lost, and six days later reached Sonora.

Meanwhile, the party of hapless Midwesterners abandoned their thirteen wagons and pressed onward to cross the summit at 9,780 feet, seven miles south of present-day Sonora Pass. Many struck out on foot across the granite cliffs, through thick forests and unyielding rock terrain. At a meadow under East Flange Rock, delirious and starving, they were finally met by the relief party. The landmark became known as Relief Meadow. They eventually found their way to Sonora and Columbia where they were greeted with a brass band and a fine dinner in their honor. The extremely difficult Walker River Trail continued to be improved and used intermittently, until the Sonora-Mono Wagon Road was finally built.

SOURCES
Allpine, T. "Seeing Things along the Old Sonora-Mono Road." *Union Democrat,* 10 Aug. 1912, p.A1.
"Gateways to California, Sonora Pass." *PG&E Progress*, Jan. 1966, edition #9. Newsletter.
Johnson, David. *Sonora Pass Pioneers*. Tuolumne County Historical Society, 2006.
Tuolumne County Historical Society, "The First Emigrant Crossing of Sonora Pass." *CHISPA*. Vol. 14, No. 4, Apr.-Jun. 1975.

CHAPTER 2

Building the
Sonora-Mono Wagon Road

Meadow near the summit where the Mi-Wuks and Paiutes would meet during the summer and trade.
Photograph by Cate Culver, 2017.

Conceived as early as 1852, a serviceable road was needed instead of the existing dirt wagon trail, but it would be close to one hundred years before a truly functional paved road would be built. The terrain was raw and untraveled by most adventurers until a rough wagon road was punched through the granite skeleton of the Sierra. It was a monumental task, frequently underestimated.

Indigenous peoples of both the western and eastern slopes of the Sierra had their traditional trails to navigate across the mountains. The western slope trails were used by the Mi-Wuks, the eastern slope trails by the Paiutes. The Paiutes would regularly meet up with the Mi-Wuks in the summer at a large meadow near the crest of the summit. There they would socialize and trade. The Mi-Wuks traded acorns and paint, while the Paiutes offered pine nuts and obsidian.

The merchants of Sonora and Columbia were interested in attracting more miners and settlers to the southern mines. Once the Gold Rush started, transportation to California was of significant concern. The rich mining communities of the eastern Sierra and the Nevada Territory were dependent on California for their supplies. They

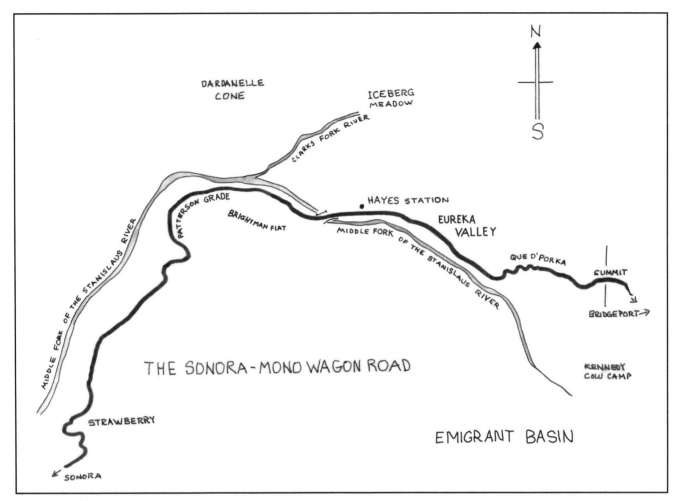

Map by Cate Culver

needed essential fruit and vegetables and mining equipment. The Indian trails were inadequate. It was soon apparent that one of the old Indian trails needed to be improved. Construction of a wagon road was needed from Sonora over the Sierra to the Nevada Territory.

David Johnson, author of a Tuolumne County *CHISPA* publication, *The Sonora and Mono Wagon Road,* writes, "Credit for the discovery of today's Sonora Pass has gone to Andrew Fletcher, superintendent of the Columbia and Stanislaus Water Company. Fletcher and others discovered the route in 1862 while on a hunting and fishing trip."

Fletcher was the founder of Sugar Pine City, where he owned a sawmill. Fletcher guided the commissioners over his route in hopes that the new road could bring more business to his sawmill.

Representatives from Mono, San Joaquin, Stanislaus, and Tuolumne counties met in 1863 to propose the road and arrange financing from each county. Commissioner L.H. Brannock, from San Joaquin County, who explored with the other commissioners, found the route through Rattlesnake Creek to be the best in his judgment. This route eventually won out and the creek was renamed Deadman Creek. The plans for the new road launched a land rush for choice property along the route. The road commissioners themselves were eager to acquire prime land and began filing claims on parcels.

William A. Clark, a road commissioner, had proposed a route along Saint Mary's Pass near the present summit. A river forms from the watershed flanked by Sonora Peak, and fed by Boulder Creek, Disaster Creek, and Arnot Creek. Fletcher, to gain favor with the commissioner, named it Clarks Fork. It joins the Middle Fork of the Stanislaus River. Out of self-interest, Clark tried to maneuver the road's planned route to pass by his land between Sonora and Strawberry.

Road through Brightman Flat in 1942.
Photograph courtesy of Jo Spicer Danicourt.

Expressman Fredrick A. Brightman, thirty-eight years old in 1863, carried secured freight and mail on the new Sonora-Mono Wagon Road. He observed the huge flat that extended several miles along the river. It was beautiful property along the new road. With shrewd foresight, he perceived the possibilities of developing the prime location. Brightman claimed one hundred and sixty acres that straddled the Stanislaus River. There is no evidence that he constructed a building or had a residence there. By 1866, Brightman moved down the mountain to Summerville (the town of Tuolumne), and then moved to Yosemite, where he was a saddle train guide, escorting tourists by horseback into the outback of Yosemite. Beautiful Brightman Flat, populated now with a summer home tract, still bears his name.

On June 12, 1863, guided by published road surveys and maps, Tuolumne County Assessor David Hayes staked a claim to a ranch on Clarks Fork, which he called Onion Valley. At the same time, though, two of the new road commissioners, James P. Allen and William G. Heslep, were exploring an alternate route for the new road on a route up the Middle Fork of the Stanislaus in Eureka Valley that would bypass Clarks Fork and Hayes' land. Five days later, Heslep and chief engineer H.P. Handy purchased choice sections of land in Eureka Valley.

While others grumbled about the road commissioners' abuse of office, David Hayes simply packed up and shifted his claim, planting it defiantly on Allen's and Heslep's Eureka Valley property. Sensing the futility of attempting to dislodge Hayes, the two road commissioners abandoned their claim

even though Hayes had no legal right to the land. Later, this site was called Camp Abraham and was used during the construction of the Sonora-Mono Wagon Road. Andrew Fletcher, William A. Clark, John Danforth Patterson, James P. Allen, H.P. Handy, David Hayes, and Fredrick A. Brightman had knowledge about the new road and hoped to profit from its passing by their property.

The proposed road was approximately one hundred and thirty miles long. W.S. Cooper was the Tuolumne County Surveyor who charted the final plans for the route. The road construction would be from the town of Sonora to the mining community of Aurora in Nevada. John Wallace had an excellent reputation as an engineer and was chosen to partner with Cooper. The two men were able to take advantage of some existing trails.

The road was built through this canyon.
Courtesy of the Tuolumne County Historical Society and Museum.

There was an old Indian trail near Sugar Pine, used by the Mexicans in 1850 to pack ice down to the mining towns of the Mother Lode. This trail was eventually widened into a wagon road and known as the "Ice Trail." Some of this trail may have been used in constructing the new road. There was already a road from Sonora to Confidence, built in 1852 by the Tuolumne County Water Company, to bring water in a ditch from the South Fork of the Stanislaus River to the gold-bearing placers in the Columbia District. The primitive trail and road needed to be altered to meet 1860s standards. New specifications were for grades not to exceed a fourteen-foot rise in a one-hundred-foot length of elevation. The roadbed was sixteen feet wide.

Its function was to be an adequate road on which mules, oxen, and horses could pull a wagon. To meet these challenges, significant financial support was crucial.

On June 21, 1851, John Danforth Patterson, Tuolumne County Water Company secretary, participated in a preliminary survey to find a route for a water ditch. Once the crew located a favorable route and the ditch was completed in May of 1852, the town of Columbia sprang to life. As a result, Patterson, considered a founding father of Columbia, was elected County Supervisor.

John Danforth Patterson, born in Vermont in 1827, came to California as a pioneer in 1849 or early 1850, and settled in Columbia. On a spring day, May 21,1860, J.D. married Mary Louisa Markham, age eighteen, in Columbia. He was a mature thirty-three. His political alignment was with the southern states. As his popularity grew, he was elected to office as county sheriff in 1859 and then again in 1861. Patterson was also a contractor, owned the Patterson House saloon in Columbia, and was credited in 1851 with laying out and naming the streets in Columbia.

Sheriff Patterson had an unruly population to keep under control. In March 1861, he hanged four murderers. Patterson built the county jail, which is now a part of the Tuolumne County Museum. By 1863, Patterson's term as sheriff had ended, and he was awarded the main contract for the construction of the Sonora-Mono Wagon Road. If anyone could tackle the imposing road project, it would be the sheriff. He was a confident and well-respected man who could lead men to build a one hundred and thirty mile-long road over the Sierra.

The California legislature in 1862 and in 1864 passed various acts provided funding and issued $53,000 in bonds for the Sonora-Mono Wagon Road. Locals feared it might become a turnpike with tollgates. However, State Senator Leander Quint of Tuolumne County called for it to be a free road financed by property taxes.

Road construction began in 1863. To build the Sonora-Mono Wagon Road, Patterson took advantage of a labor force of gold miners experienced with blasting rock and working with picks and

View of Patterson Grade with the canyon below.
Cate Culver photographer 2016

shovels. Mule skinners with wagons hauled rock to level the roadbed. Huge sugar pines, firs, and cedars had to be cleared, bridges built, and culverts dug. He set up his base camp at Niagara Creek.

Carlo De Ferrari writes, "The road was to be built in sections. The first would traverse between River Hill and Cascade Creek, and the junction of Clarks Fork and the Stanislaus River at Fletcher's Flat, where Fletcher had promised a ferry station.

"Patterson, an ex-commissioner, owned several choice lots along the route and needed this venture to succeed.

"The second section was to connect Cascade Creek to the head of Sugar Pine Creek at Bald Mountain, with the third to spread easterly from Fletcher's Flat as far as the approaching winter would allow the work." Carlo De Ferrari continues, "There was one period where Patterson ran completely out of money, but with glib talk and pleasing promises, he kept most of the men working when their pay was months overdue. For the first time the construction crews were run tightly, without liquor."

PATTERSON GRADE
5 MILES LONG

Old highway sign found in the Dardanelle dump by Cate Culver's father, Edson Caldwell, in the 1950s.

Historian David Johnson writes, "J.D. Patterson's crew began work on the difficult River Hill section first. Three-and-a-half miles from Niagara Creek down to the junction of the Clarks Fork, blasting a path along the granite cliffs and building up high rock embankments to support the narrow roadbed. That section of the road became known as Patterson Grade. In the years to come, Patterson Grade was legendary for its fragile grip on the side of a sheer granite canyon. The engineering of the road was praised by noteworthy road builders of the time. Not for the faint of heart, one misjudged turn had dire consequences, sending the traveler head-over-buckboard into the brush, boulders, and cliffs below. The *Union Democrat* newspaper in November of 1863, printed, "The Sonora Mono Road is being pushed vigorously. About 250 men are employed."

By 1863, the bond funds had been entirely spent. In March of 1864, county supervisors, pressured to have the road completed, advertised for bids. The former road superintendent, James P. Allen, who owned considerable property from Cow Creek to Strawberry, wanted the road completed and put in his bid. J.D. Patterson, who had already invested his time and labor, was also forthcoming

with a bid. The county accepted the bids, and the pair reorganized and set to work, calling themselves the Sonora and Mono Wagon Road Company. They planned to finish the lower parts of the road first, and collect tolls for that segment of road to finance the mountain sections. The building of the high mountain road over the summit continued. Despite setbacks, the Sonora-Mono Wagon Road was completed in May 1864.

After constructing the difficult Patterson Grade, the roadbed was not much of an effort. The route followed grassy sand flats, strung together alongside the river. Locals know them as Brightman Flat, Pigeon Flat, Douglas Flat, the Eureka Valley, and a large flat at Baker Station.

In May of 1864, the *Union Democrat* newspaper reported, "The Sonora Mono Road is now open to Mono, and pack trains and travelers are passing daily over it. On account of the shortness of the route, heavy travel is expected during the summer, while the scenery is magnificent. There will soon be a line of regular stages running, connecting with pack trains on the summit."

However, the *Union Democrat* article of July 9, 1864, printed a different story: "Work on the Sonora-Mono Road progresses finely. About

Eureka Valley with the wagon road winding through the Jeffrey pines. The Stanislaus River out of sight at the left.
Photograph courtesy of the John Snyder family.

The Sonora-Mono Wagon Road heading down toward Kennedy Meadows and Baker Station.
Courtesy of the Tuolumne County Historical Society and Museum.

200 men are employed and the road will soon be completed to Hayes' Valley at the foot of the Sierras." The article also reported, "The first crossing of the 9,624-foot elevation summit was recorded as B.O. Marston and M.M. Rumbly by crossing in a horse and buggy in October of 1864."

Historian David Johnson, in the Tuolumne County Historical Society publication, *CHISPA* continues, "Patterson and Allen continued to work on the road through 1865, widening the track and repairing damage caused by the spring runoff. Although the contract called for the completion of the road by the end of 1865, the contractors were granted a two-year extension. Traffic on the road was not nearly as high as anticipated, because the mining boom in Esmerelda and other parts of Nevada faltered in 1865."

Judging the road to be a lost cause, at the end of 1865, Patterson abandoned the backbreaking project and returned to Sonora where he found work as a contractor.

After four years in Sonora, Patterson moved to White Pines County in Nevada, a booming mining area with an unruly population. On November 8, 1870, he was the first elected sheriff of that county.

Two years later, he was re-elected. In 1881, his wife Mary died in San Francisco, and a year later J.D. himself died of pneumonia in Eureka, Nevada, at age fifty-five. To this day, Patterson Grade remains a beautiful yet imposing stretch of highway.

Historian David Johnson, writes, "James P. Allen continued on struggling to meet the terms of the contract. With only meager tolls from stations at Sugar Pine and Hayes Station at Eureka Valley, to sustain his work, Allen had only completed about forty miles of widening the road to a double track by the summer of 1866."

One of the most difficult sections of the road was the steep climb to the summit, where the road crossed Deadman Creek eight times. Hillsides of loose decomposed granite and huge boulders sliding onto the road were a constant problem. The roadbed wound around granite outcroppings that defined the treacherous roadway. Through the rock-lined canyon at the higher elevations, the pathway followed Deadman Creek, which frequently washed over the road.

Hayes Station served as a mail relay station for mail to Sonora, Bridgeport, Bodie, and Aurora. These mail carriers and their stations were as follows:

Major Lane at Strawberry, John Welch at Niagara, Fredrick A. Brightman at Brightman Flat, David Hayes at Eureka Valley, James Leavitt at Leavitt Meadows, and Sam Fales at Fales Hot Springs.

As the roadwork was nearing completion, the Civil War was drawing to a close. On April 9, 1865, Lee surrendered to Grant at the Appomattox Courthouse. Five days later, the nation was plunged into grief as news of President Lincoln's assassination spread and quickly reached the West.

Stations to accommodate travelers, pack trains, and wagons sprang up along the road. In 1877, a stage line operated between Sonora and Bodie. Six horses pulled the coach with relays at Sugar Pine, Cow Creek, and later Baker Station, then Leavitt Station, Fales Hot Springs, Bridgeport, and Mormon Ranch, ending at Bodie.

In 1878, miners in Bodie again struck rich veins of gold, and traffic on the wagon road increased. Soon stage lines were operating again, and a stream of freight wagons and mules trains packed with supplies brought the wagon road back to life.

In 1879, Greenbury Columbus Baker built a station for travelers along the wagon road. He situated it on a large flat before the turnoff to Kennedy Meadows. It was the last of any services before the long grades up to the summit, eight miles farther on.

By 1881 the gold mines in Nevada played out, and the traffic on the road dwindled. Baker hung on, and for a few months in 1897, took over the contract to keep the road repaired.

Between 1885 and 1895, men from Sonora, Shaw's Flat, and Columbia hauled fresh fruits and vegetables to the thousands of miners and their families in Bodie. The road was not much more than a trail. To withstand the ride, the teamsters used the heavily-built Concord stagecoach, pulled by four horses. The roads were rough. To handle the fruit as carefully as possible, thorough braces were employed. These braces were strips of leather cured to the toughness of steel and strung in pairs to support the body of the coach and enable it to swing back and forth.

On reaching the landmark, known as the Que de Porka, the wagons came to a stop. Here

Road along Deadman Creek known as Blue Canyon.
Courtesy of the Tuolumne County Historical Society and Museum.

Sonora-Mono Wagon Road as it approached the summit.
Photograph courtesy of the John Snyder family.

The author Cate Culver exploring the old Patterson Grade in 2017. Photograph by Jerry Culver.

The Que de Porka landmark.
Photograph courtesy of Tuolumne County Historical Society and Museum (Fred Leighton collection).

the wagon road squeezed between granite rock formations. The road was so steep that logs were placed between the rocks for traction. Usually two wagons accompanied each other. At the foot of steep grades such as the Que de Porka and Deadman Creek, drivers would unhitch one team and add it to the other, using eight mules on one wagon.

By July of 1898, Baker gave up on maintaining the Mono County part of the road. Herds of sheep and cattle continually tore up the road, and constant repair was overwhelming. By August, discouraged, Baker relinquished the Tuolumne County side of the road as well, but the county stepped in and temporarily put Baker's segment of the road "in very good order." Knowing it could not sustain the maintenance, county officials looked to the State of California to assume responsibility.

In March of 1901, the governor of California signed legislation which made the old Sonora-Mono Road a part of the state highway system. It became State Route 13, from Long Barn in Tuolumne County to Bridgeport, in Mono County.

SOURCES

Angel, Myron, ed. *History of Nevada: 1881.* Oakland: Thompson and West, 1881. P. 651.

Buckbee, Edna Bryan. "The Enterprising Ditch Diggers." *The Saga of Old Tuolumne.* New York Press of the Pioneers, 1935. P. 265.

"The Douglas Station." *CHISPA,* Tuolumne County Historical Society Quarterly, Vol. 37, No. 2 Oct.-Dec. 1997.

Elliott, Joe, Jr. "Early Stanislaus Recollections." Stanislaus National Forest Service.

"Fales Hot Springs." Mono County Historical Society, *The QUARTERLY,* Vol. 8 No. 3 Jan.-Mar., 1969, 2011 newsletter.

"Fruit Wagons from Sonora to Bodie." *CHISPA,* Tuolumne County Historical Society Quarterly publication Vol. 19, No. 2. Oct.-Dec. 1979.

Johnson, David H. "The Sonora and Mono Wagon Road," *CHISPA,* Vol. 37, No. 3, Tuolumne County Historical Society. *Quarterly publication.* Jan.-Mar. 1998. p. 148 and p. 1301.

"Rusticating in the Mountains." Tuolumne County Historical Society Quarterly publication *CHISPA,* Vol. 38, No. 2, Dec. 1998.

"The Sonora and Mono Wagon Road," *Sierra Heritage Magazine,* May/Jun. 1996.

"Notes from Carlo M. De Ferrari." Tuolumne Heritage Publication. 28 Mar. 1969. Reprint. 2013.

Redneh, A. "Out of the Past." *Union Democrat,* Feb. 1883, Reprint, 7 Jun. 1951.

Rutherford, Lenore. "Neighbors Find Their Place in the Snow." *Union Democrat,* 21 Jan., 1993 Long Barn, Slide Inn, p.9.

Snider, Jim. Telephone interview. *Yosemite Historian.* 15 Nov. 2017.

Wright, Patty. Personal Interview. Oct. 2014.

CHAPTER 3

Sonora-Mono Wagon Road
Becomes State Route 13

A family stops for a break at the summit in their Dodge automobile.
Photograph courtesy of Bill Coffill.

The wagon road was a continual maintenance problem. After Greenbury Baker stepped away from the road repairs, Tuolumne County stepped in and temporarily put Baker's portion of the road "in very good order." Much repair and maintenance was needed when the state acquired the road. Above Baker Station, the road had washed out in places, bridges were unsafe, and culverts needed replacing. Loose gravel washed giant boulders down that had cracked off the cliffs and rolled onto the highway.

A report from the Department of Highways in 1902 printed, "The sixty-one miles of this road from Long Barn to the junction of Highway 395, was in July of 1901, in a very bad state of repair. The

twenty-two miles over the granite formation was nothing more than a creek bed, while all the bridges on the route were either in a rotten condition or else fallen down. The bridge over Middle Fork of the Stanislaus River and the one over Eagle Creek, both large structures must be rebuilt."

In 1901, Michael J. Curtin, 39, was appointed to the position of road supervisor. His brother was State Senator John Curtin and Tuolumne County District Attorney, who had aspirations to become governor of California. Michael, before he was appointed, was a teamster, hauling freight from Oakdale to Sonora.

He set up his headquarters at the abandoned Baker Station building. What was usable at Baker

Michael J. Curtin, first road supervisor of State Route 13.
Photograph courtesy of Tuolumne County Historical Society and Museum.

View down the grade.
Photograph courtesy of the Gary Haigh family.

Bridge over the Middle Fork of the Stanislaus River in 1906.
Photograph courtesy of Pacific Gas and Electric Company.

Station was a sixteen-foot by twenty-foot single room cabin made of sugar pine shakes over a framework of debarked poles with a planked floor. The walls were generously scribed with the initials of visitors. For a summer work crew this was adequate, and most workmen were housed in tents. No evidence of Greenbury Baker's establishment remained.

The work to repair bridges and the roadbed began. With a crew of about ten men with picks and shovels, and liberal use of cedar bark to fill in the ruts, Curtin gradually made progress. In 1905, twenty thousand dollars was appropriated for the construction of bridges, culverts, and for road grading. A maintenance fund of $5,000 per annum was established to support the entire seventy-five miles of road.

Four years later, in August of 1905, the *Union Democrat* newspaper printed, "The Sonora and Mono Road is now in excellent condition for the lighter class of traffic, while the heaviest of vehicles would have the best of going were it not for the fact that an old and unsafe bridge spans the main Stanislaus River which is to be replaced the coming fall or spring by one of steel. Superintendent of construction M.J. Curtin and his force of eleven men and five horses have done an immense amount of work on this highway. State commissioner Ellery, under whose orders Curtin is acting, insists that nothing but stone and cement be used whenever possible."

The road was in such bad shape up to Baker Station that the workers building the Relief Dam had

The Sonora-Mono Wagon Road near the summit.
Photograph courtesy of the Tuolumne County Historical Society and Museum. (Fred Leighton collection).

Lewis C. Chase in 1913, standing on the road as it turns up the grade near Blue Canyon, somewhat below the summit.
Photograph compliments of the Tuolumne County Historical Society and Museum. (Francis Nelson collection).

to take over rebuilding thirty-eight miles of the road, as the state was too slow in making repairs. Some of the company's road crew set up at Baker Station with Curtin where they had a Standard Oil gas station.

In 1907, the *Calaveras Weekly Prospect* newspaper on July 13 printed, "The Sonora-Mono Road is positively not open for the passing of vehicles. Up near the summit, in addition to slides, there remain snow banks fifteen feet in depth. However, twenty-five men or more are camped in the vicinity of Douglas Station, who are working to clear the old Emigrant road, and thus get across into Mono County."

In 1913, an investigative committee recommended the road be abandoned. There was just not enough traffic to justify all the maintenance. Michael Curtin resigned, and a search for a new superintendent continued, despite the committee's findings.

On June 7, 1913, the *Union Democrat* newspaper reported, "The Sonora-Mono State Highway superintendence has been given to L.C. Chase, of Big Oak Flat, a gentleman of ten years experience in road building and repair work on the Tioga and Big Oak Flat roads. The position of a dozen years past has been filled by M.J. Curtin, and under his personal supervision much work of permanent character has been done and the highway is rated as one of the best in the State. The change of management was not brought about because Mr. Curtin was not performing his full duty, but simply to remove from State employment a man who was not in sympathy with the policy of the

State administration." The report continued, "The new superintendent plans to cut down the work force from five to three men. Hired on were John Smith and William Gray, of Groveland, and Lee Wentworth, who has been employed on the road for the last six years, will be the third."

In May of 1914, Chase purchased supplies and provisions and set up his maintenance station at Mill Creek. Chase was considered a very capable man, older and more experienced than the younger Curtin he replaced. He was a good bridge builder who knew how to use cables and all kinds of blocks and tackles to handle large logs and rocks, and build with cement.

The *Union Democrat* newspaper announced on August 31, 1912, "Twenty-six autos have gone over the summit, eleven coming from the Mono side. The bulk of the traffic is represented by ordinary conveyances, pack animals, and considerable bands of sheep, horses, and cattle."

Ranger Joe Elliott, Jr. wrote, "Travel was slow and difficult: normally more time was spent trying to travel rather than moving. Boiling radiators and tire troubles resulted in frequent delays. In the teens, it might take four hours from Sonora to Strawberry and probably another four hours to reach Brightman Flat. When radiators and tires were not the problem, burned out bands or fouled spark plugs might be the cause of delay. When anyone went any considerable distance without such delays, he was considered to have been very lucky. Most of the travel was at speed of less than twenty miles per hour."

By 1916, travel to the high Sierras was becoming popular. Outdoorsmen wanted to challenge their driving skills with a test of their automobile to reach the summit. The primary test was to dare travel on the notorious Patterson Grade. Most travelers of the day carried a block and tackle, a supply of tires and tools, and needed some mechanical skills. Few made it to the summit.

Bruce Woods, the fire warden at Brightman Flat Ranger Station, noted that during the first twenty-two days in July of 1916, he counted 274 people who had passed his station. That count included nineteen autos, eleven trucks, seventy horses, and 420 head of cattle. Most of the travelers in autos made it as far as Baker Station and did not attempt the notoriously steep grade to the summit.

In 1918, on June 9, from the Ceres Garage in Ceres, California, in the San Joaquin Valley, the *Oakland Tribune* reported that two young men decided to scout out the Sonora-Mono Wagon Road. "An attempt was made to surmount the Que d' Porka grade Sunday afternoon was abandoned, but successfully accomplished Monday. The grade is only about two miles but the roadway is composed of decomposed granite, and this car has the record of being the first automobile to reach the top under its own power, an accomplishment requiring three hours of effort. The road from Douglas to the summit pass and hence on to Bridgeport is impassable, and will be for some three weeks yet. It requires fording Deadman Creek eight times, and the warm weather is melting the mountain snows so rapidly the creek banks are full."

Old bridge over the Middle Fork of the Stanislaus River at Bone Springs, near Dardanelle, California. The bridge abutment and remains of the old Sonora-Mono Wagon Road still exist. *Photographer unknown.*

Three years later, the *San Francisco Chronicle* reported on Sunday, August 21, 1921, "In order to get first-hand information about the Sonora Pass country, the Chronicle recently sent a scouting party to the region. The trip was made in a Chandler touring car furnished by the Peacock Motor Sales Company distributor. Arrangements for the scouting expedition with the forest service headquarters in Sonora were completed, and Deputy Supervisor Elliot acted as guide and host for the Chronicle representative.

"From Baker's Station to the summit of the pass a distance of approximately nine miles the route of the road is probably the most terrifying and atrocious in the west. It is absolutely unfit for motor travel and over many places cannot be made without aid of at least a saddle horse.

"Not only is the roadway steep, but it is filled with sand and sharp granite boulders that defy

Wooden bridge over the Clarks Fork in 1932. *Photograph courtesy of Matt Bloom (Gerald French collection).*

Travelers pause for a break before attempting the Que de Porka grade in 1925.
Photograph courtesy of the Tuolumne County Historical Society and Museum.

Road maintenance crew at work on the pass in 1927, above Deadman Creek.
Photograph courtesy of the Haigh family.

traction, and if attempted will tear the casing to ribbons." The highway department continued to struggle every year to keep the road passable. In 1923, the California Highway Commission established its highway maintenance station site at the old Baker Station. It was just an acre and a half on the flat.

By the early 1920s, automobile travel was gaining over horse and buggy. The roads had to be maintained and the road workers lodged near their work. Lewis Chase had retired, and Ed Harris became the new road superintendent. By September of 1924, the *Oakland Tribune* stated, "The state road crew which has been working the last three months on the summit grade of the Sonora-Mono road has taken off for the season. Extensive improvements to the grade have been made under the direction of superintendent S.E. Harris.

"The floor of the dreaded Que d' Porka roadway has been lowered, making the steep grade and the highway widened in many places. This will be good news to the hosts of automobile drivers who have dreaded this grade."

Through the 1920s, a considerable amount of WWI surplus government equipment was made available to the states for road maintenance and construction. The modern equipment was welcomed and gave the crew renewed enthusiasm for their work ahead, although much of the work was still done with horse teams using block and tackle.

Ed Harris and his crew of twelve men continued through the summer of 1924 to work on State Route 13. They were consigned a war surplus air compressor and two power drills. The road crew made extensive

Highway Superintendent S.E. Harris in June 1924.
Photograph courtesy of the Tuolumne County Historical Society and Museum. (Francis Nelson collection).

improvements and were able to blast some of the obstructive granite outcroppings to widen and level the roadbed.

An avid fisherman, Ed Harris enjoyed living at the road maintenance headquarters at the old Baker Station. Harris chose the site because he liked the nearby fishing across the road. Lewis C. Chase, his predecessor, had set up a few tent cabins for the men working on the grades up to the summit, but no usable buildings remained.

CAL STATE HIGHWAY CAMP AT BAKER STATION

Baker Maintenance Station.
Cate Culver postcard collection.

The Maintenance Station was built over a period of three years, from 1929 through 1931. When work began in 1929, the state hired a construction crew of skilled carpenters. No expense was spared, and the buildings were well made, probably some of the best-built structures on the pass. They were never open year round as the road would close at first snow and open when the crew cleared the highway and made repairs after the winter storms. The crew at Baker was responsible for a 47.4-mile section. It began at Long Barn and ended at the summit of the highway.

The newly-built Baker Station in 1934.
Photograph from the A.A. Gourley collection.

Great thought was given to the position of the buildings to make Baker a workable station. The living quarters for the superintendent and foreman, and the bunkhouse buildings, were all grouped together and included a dining hall, social hall, and bathhouse. The truck shed, oil and gas shed, blacksmith shop, pumps, and loading platforms were placed for easy road access. Feeding the road crew during the summer required a lot of planning. Food staples were purchased and stored for use throughout the season. Located behind the dining hall was a sawdust-lined six-foot by eleven-foot cold storage

icehouse. Workers gathered snow and ice from the high elevations and packed it in the building so that meat and dairy products were refrigerated. Elbert Miller routinely stopped with his produce truck on his route over the pass. His truck had fresh vegetables, fruit, and sundries, even candy bars. Also, food was available at the nearby Kennedy Meadows Resort which kept a reliable stock of supplies.

The station site overlooked the dirt road, a small meadow, and the river. Great granite cliffs towered over the back of the site. Since they had their own building, superintendents and foremen frequently

A crew at work on the road. *Photograph courtesy of the Tuolumne County Historical Society and Museum.*

brought their families for the summer to swim, fish for trout, hike, and relax. It was a time the family looked forward to each year.

In the spring of 1933, the road crew arrived to find that the bridge over the Middle Fork by Dardanelle had collapsed. This was a major problem, because there was no other route up to the pass, so the bridge had to be replaced immediately.

By 1937, there was a spurt of new work on State Highway 13. Several new bridges were built and a new road bypassed the old Strawberry Resort by the river. More and more of the road became realigned and oiled. By the 1940s, much of the road was paved.

Sometime in the 1940s, Lloyd Haigh took over as highway superintendent for the highway, which had been renamed State Highway 108. Born in 1902 of Scotch-Irish descent, he lived in Coulterville and graduated from Humphreys College in Stockton with a degree in engineering. His wife Emma came with him in the summers to the Baker Station Maintenance Camp, where they kept their little cabin

New bridge built across the Middle Fork in 1933.
Photograph courtesy of the Tuolumne County Historical Society and Museum.

Road crew at work on stretch of road in Blue Canyon in 1927.
Photograph courtesy of Haigh family.

immaculate. He was always called Mr. Haigh. No one ever called him Lloyd despite the fact that he was outgoing and friendly.

In the early 1950s, the Patterson Grade was cut anew above the old grade. It required much blasting through the granite cliffs and the project took four long years of hard work. By the 1960s, however, the Maintenance Station fell into disuse. Long Barn, about 40 miles to the west, was seen as a better, year-round base of operations for that portion of Highway 108. In 1959, Highway 108 was included in the California Freeway and Expressway system by the California Legislature.

Sonora Pass, Highway 108, is still seen as a remote path across the Sierras. Not as well-known as Donner or Tioga passes, it remains a road less traveled and the locals like it that way. It endures as a scenic treasure.

Road maintenance crew at work July 21, 1940.
Photograph courtesy of the Stanislaus National Forest Service.

SOURCES

Conners, Pamela A. "Historical Overview of Recreational Residences on the Stanislaus National Forest," Report. 1993.

"Ceres Sends Motor Into Stanislaus." *Oakland Tribune*. 9 Jun. 1918. p. 52.

Haigh, Gary. Personal interview. 4 Aug. 2016.

Haigh, Lloyd H. *Baker Station*. Stanislaus National Forest Service.

"Need Funds." *San Francisco Chronicle*. 21. Aug. 1921, p. 2.

Oakland Tribune 9 Apr. 1922 p. 24.

"Relocate Sonora Pass Road Deadman Creek." *Union Democrat,* 10 Apr. 1926. Front page.

"The Sonora Road." Report of Department of Highways, 1902, Bulletin. 17.

Union Democrat. Short Local News Items and Personal Mention. 27 Jul. 1912. Front page.

"Sonora-Mono Road Grades Cut, Widened." *Oakland Tribune*. 3 Sep. 1924, p. 32.

Stoll, Kendra, M.C., MLIS, History Reference Librarian, Transportation Library and History Center. California Department of Transportation (Caltrans). N.d.

The newly-graded road in 1934.
Photograph from the A.A. Gourley collection.

CHAPTER 4

The Que de Porka

Que de Porka postcard, copyrighted by Ed Hess, 1938.
Jerry and Cate Culver postcard collection.

The landmark, Que de Porka, translates to "tail of a pig" in Portuguese. The famous landmark was named in the 1880s by a Portuguese immigrant, Matt Marshall, whose name was anglicized when he came through customs.

This part of the road up the Sonora Pass was extremely steep and twisty. Marshall brought produce in his wagon from the Ratto Ranch, and block ice from the Standard Dairy over the Sonora Pass to Bodie. The round trip took one week. He traveled this section of the road often, and it reminded him of looking at the curly tail of a pig, and so it was named.

No history remains as to who hung the sign over the road that read, "Que de Porka," but it came down when Paramount Pictures was filming

For Whom the Bell Tolls in 1941. The movie includes a scene of army tanks creeping down the grade and shots of the famous landmark. The director had the sign removed for the scene in the film. The film crew never put it back.

During the 1950s, local forest ranger John Spicer led a drive to have the sign put back, but unfortunately nothing came of his requests. The only good thing about the sign's absence is that it is helpful in dating old photographs. If the sign is in the photograph, the shot was taken before 1941.

As one drives the road to the summit, the landmark suddenly looms ahead. Passing through the towering rock above, the road dwarfs any vehicle. The road through the landmark used to be so steep that small logs and scrap lumber were placed in the roadway to give the wagons more traction. At some point, the road crew lowered the roadway, which made the grade less steep. However, it remained extremely narrow. The local highway patrol officer in the 1940s frequently had to arrive with a crowbar to pry a car from between the rocks. At the Dardanelle Resort, a block and tackle were on hand for the same purpose. Even in the 1950s, when a passenger car stopped in the narrow gap, the driver could reach out the window and touch the rock, and the passenger could reach out and touch it as well.

The narrow, steep landmark was known to every early traveler, mainly because it was such a steep grade to pull wagons up through the passageway and beyond. It offered many picture-taking opportunities, for often travelers wanted their photograph taken at the landmark.

SOURCES

Danicourt, Jo Spicer. Personal interview, 2015.
Davis-King, Shelly. Personal interview, 2018.
Leonard, Norene Sardella. Personal interview, 2015.
Terzich, Irving. Personal interview, 2015. (Helped Mr. Huff collect the insects in 1926).
Wright, Patty. Personal interview, 2014. (Descendant of Matt Marshall).

The landmark of Que de Porka in September 1921, with logs and lumber to help with traction through the steep grade.
Photograph courtesy of Chris Robinson.

A ride through the landmark in 1928 in Ed Burgson's car.
Photographer John Balestra, courtesy of Chris Robinson.

The car is a Rio Flying Cloud. License plate 1923. Car owner William Nelson of Douglas Station stands next to the car. This picture was taken before the road was cut down about ten feet to lower the grade incline, and then widened.
Photograph courtesy of Tuolumne County Historical Society. (Francis Nelson Collection).

Early Que de Porka photograph.
Courtesy of the Tuolumne County Historical Society and Museum. (Gerald French collection).

Car drives down the Que de Porka grade.
Photograph courtesy of the Stanislaus National Forest Service. (Photograph from the Marjorie Fontana Collection).

A ride through the landmark in 1928.
Photographer John Balestra, courtesy of Chris Robinson.

Frank Burgson in the cart, Ed Burgson in the car, and Mr. Huff with the horse. Headed to Fales Hot Springs in 1928.
Mr. Huff was an entomologist who collected and studied local insects. He would put them in a jar with ether to kill them, then dry and mount them. He had a large collection of beetles, butterflies, and other insects.
Photographer John Balestra, courtesy of Chris Robinson.

Early traveler through the narrow rock formation.
Photograph courtesy of the Tuolumne County Historical Society and Museum. (Leonard Ruoff collection).

A couple pause for a photo at the Que de Porka landmark.
Photograph courtesy of Tuolumne County Historical Society and Museum. (Fred Leighton Collection).

Lady standing in the narrow roadway at the Que de Porka.
Photograph courtesy of the Stanislaus National Forest Service. (Photograph from the Marjorie Fontana Collection.)

CHAPTER 5

The Clarks Fork Road
and Why It Was Built

The Clarks Fork of the Stanislaus River is a beautiful river flowing through a canyon floor with several gorges, large flats of green grass, and pines at the river's edge. The river forms the boundary between Tuolumne and Alpine Counties. A large meadow under the granite iceberg landmark marks the end of the canyon.

For years, cattlemen had used the area. For example, brothers Chester and Walter Murphy from Telegraph City, cattlemen who owned Wheats Meadow located on the north side of the river, grazed cattle there from the 1920s to 1960s. They built a cabin on the land. The Murphy brothers subsequently sold Wheats Meadow to the Forest Service. When it acquired the meadow, the Forest Service also built a cabin. A telephone line was run to Brightman Flat Ranger Station for fire protection.

Charlie Wagner drove his cattle in the 1870s to the Clarks Fork on the Sonora-Mono Wagon Road, to graze them in the high meadows during the summer. In 1875, he had a cabin built beside the Sonora-Mono Road, on a long flat bench with a view of the Middle Fork of the Stanislaus River below. In 1926, Antone Airola took over Charlie's grazing rights.

By the late 1920s, the Stanislaus National Forest management realized the recreational opportunities of the area. To achieve this goal, a road was constructed entirely on Forest Service land, with no entanglements from other entities. Local Stanislaus forest officials saw the road as a gateway to new favorable building sites that would not be conspicuous from the roadway. They foresaw the building of cabins, campgrounds, and maybe a new ranger station.

Early bridge over the Clarks Fork River.
Photographer Charles Thompson. Courtesy of David Thompson.

By 1931, plans were put in motion to build a seven-mile low standard road. It would, for the most part, follow an old cattle and sheep herding trail up the river canyon. This new primitive road opened and the public poured in to explore, hike, fish, and camp.

By 1937, the perspective of the Forest Service changed. Now there was a movement to build roads in the Sierra Nevada that would primarily accent the beauty of the mountains and be strongly sensitive to the aesthetics of the Sierra. The idea evolved to build a scenic road linking Lake Tahoe to Yosemite Valley called the "The Sierra Way." The State Chamber of Commerce, particularly its Stockton and San Joaquin Valley divisions, and the California State Automobile Association, lobbied hard for the Sierra Way. The proposed road would shorten travel time for motorists while opening places of spectacular scenic wonder.

Bridge over Clarks Fork in 1923.
Photograph courtesy of the Stanislaus National Forest Service.

The Iceberg rock formation above the meadow.
Photograph by Cate Culver.

Bridge across the Middle Fork of the Stanislaus River in 1937.
Photograph courtesy of the David Thompson family.

When the Forest Service started building the Clarks Fork road, Sierra Way promoters saw it as a link from Sonora Pass to Ebbetts Pass Highway. The Forest service was likewise interested in the Sierra Way and how it would promote tourism. In 1933, regional forester S. B. Show expressed interest in cooperating with the conversion of this road to a high standard highway.

The new Clarks Fork link from Highway 108 to Ebbetts Pass would be twenty-one miles long. Reconstruction of the Clarks Fork Road as part of the Sierra Way began in 1937. It was to improve the existing road along Clarks Fork to Iceberg Meadow. The new section would follow the trail along the east side of Disaster Creek, past Adams Camp, through Gardner Meadow to Highland Lakes and Tryon Meadow, and hitting the Ebbetts Pass Highway about a mile west of the pass.

A large construction camp was built at the Wagner Cow Camp site, a large flat above the Middle Fork of the Stanislaus River. It consisted of housing for the road crew and their families, a large kitchen and dining hall combination, and even a small schoolhouse. The camp was in use for three years.

The giant Matson Navigation Company heard about the new road and sent a scout up for a look and to speak with Stanislaus Forest Supervisor J.R. Hall about the possibilities of establishing a camp for its employees. The company had plans to build a hotel, ten housekeeping cabins, a swimming pool, and other accommodations as an initial step.

A Civilian Conservation Corps crew, previously set up at Strawberry, moved its camp to the Clarks

Fork to work on building bridges and campgrounds. Along the road, huge rocks left from blasting out the roadway were used to build several rock retaining walls.

Construction began, with great consideration given to the beauty of the road and how it would wind through the canyon, accenting views of the mountains and river. The bridge across the Middle Fork of the Stanislaus, with its arching design, is a fitting gateway into the Clarks Fork in keeping with the Sierra Way theme. The road continued under construction until 1941 when it reached Iceberg Meadow. Then the whole project fell apart and the road continued no farther.

Alpine County, over which the majority of route miles would run, was in favor of such a road. Later, the county officials came to realize that the county's highway maintenance funds would be

---

The stone retaining wall was built by the Civilian Conservation Corps in 1942. The rocks were obtained from the road construction. *Photograph by Cate Culver 2013.*

overwhelmed in maintaining the new high elevation road. Alpine County backed out.

The forest supervisor for El Dorado County, north of the Stanislaus National Forest, opposed the Sierra Way and the Clarks Fork section, on the grounds of maintenance costs for such a short use season.

In December of 1941, the United States entered World War II and the national focus shifted to the war effort. It became evident that although it was a great idea, the high costs of a road intended for pure pleasure was not what the taxpayer needed. The Sierra Way came to a halt at Iceberg Meadow beneath the view of the iceberg-shaped monolith.

In 1945, the Forest Service realized that Clarks Fork Road had recreational possibilities and took another look. Plans developed to make the Clarks Fork a major recreation area. The plan provided for a resort site, summer home tracts, and a campground with water diverted from the river for a swimming pool. The resort would be built on the abandoned Civilian Conservation Corps site located slightly above the road. The resort would include a store, restaurant, pack station, and other services. This major recreational area would have a ranger station with an office, workshops, storage area, and a barracks for work crews and rangers living quarters. Once the war ended, none of these plans came about.

New bridge for the "Sierra Way" across Clarks Fork. *Photograph courtesy of the Tuolumne County Historical Society and Museum.*

Young Alice Foletti poses under the bridge across Clarks Fork of the Stanislaus River in 1940, accessing Horse Camp, where her father, "Swiss," and brother, Pete Foletti, had just finished construction of all the stone work.
Photograph courtesy of Alice (Foletti) Hardin.

During WWII there had been speculation about continuing the road over to Nevada as a secret pass in case the Japanese attacked the West Coast. Once WWII ended, those plans were also put aside. Thus, the Clarks Fork Road remains as it has been since 1931, a lovely road along the Clarks Fork of the Stanislaus River.

SOURCES

Brandt, Hazel Perkin. *Wagner Camp, Stanislaus National Forest, A Brief History*: 1923-1993. Pinecone Press, N.d.

Conners, Pam. "A Century or so of Land Use on the Central Stanislaus Watershed Analysis Area: 1848-1958." Report. Stanislaus National Forest Service. N.d.

Gibson, James H. "Plan of Development for the Sonora Pass Road Recreation Area.

Harrison, Aubrey. Personal interview, 2015. Eyewitness to the building of the rock walls by the CCC boys.

"Matson Navigation Co. May Establish Employee Camp in Local Forest: Clark's Fork Bridge." *Union Democrat* August 16, 1940. Front page.

"Stanislaus National Forest." Report. Feb. 1945.

Whittle, Donnie. Personal interviews, 15 Sep. 2016 and 5 Feb. 2017.

"Tuolumne CCC Camp Moved to Near Strawberry." *Union Democrat,* 30 May 1941. p. 5.

CHAPTER 6

Early Cattlemen on the Clarks Fork

During the heyday of cattle ranching in Tuolumne and Calaveras Counties, there were a number of notable cattlemen who ranched at low elevations and had summer grazing allotments in the high country. One such individual was Charles Wagner. Wagner's allotment was in the Clarks Fork area, and his activities there formed the basis for all the subsequent development in the area.

Charles Wagner, of German heritage, owned ranches near Oakdale and Lake Tulloch area in the 1870s. Starting out from these ranches, Wagner drove his cattle up to the Clarks Fork area to graze in the high meadows during the summer. It took several days to move the cattle slowly through the hills to the mountains.

In 1875, Wagner constructed a cabin at his Clarks Fork cattle range. He selected a building site on a long, flat, granite bench formation alongside the Sonora-Mono Wagon Road affording a lovely view of the Middle Fork of the Stanislaus River. He hired Henry Menson of Sonora to build the cabin. Menson arrived with all his tools, and on the site, he cut and milled the lumber for the little cabin.

The primitive building was sufficient for a summer stay. It included a narrow kitchen and sleeping quarters. Water was obtained from a nearby spring. Later construction included a barn constructed of logs, a bunkhouse, and a corral built of log poles. The corral was essential for keeping the horses and cattle confined to a manageable area.

Wagner's allotment extended from the cabin through Iceberg Meadow and into Wheats Meadow. This area was essentially canyon land, with the Clarks Fork descending through granite ravines until

The family comes to visit Charlie at the Wagner Camp. Left to right: Charlie Wagner, Herman Molton, Aunt Lizzie Molton and Myrtle, Irma N., Harold, Charles Lewis, Ben and Lillie Valverde. August 24, 1918.
Photograph courtesy of Sonny Upwall and the Wagner family.

merging with the Middle Fork of the Stanislaus River. Small spring-fed meadows lined the upper benches of the canyon.

Charles Wagner remained a well-liked bachelor his entire life. Because he had no immediate family to help with the cattle drives, he relied on his sisters Lizzie and Julia, their husbands, and his nephew Charles Lewis.

Typical of these cattle drives was the one that took place in the spring of 1904. In this instance, about five hundred head of cattle were driven from the O'Byrnes Ferry Bridge in Calaveras County to Clarks Fork in a total of four days. Care was taken to not push the cows too much to prevent them from getting sore hooves. Charlie Lewis drove the chuck wagon with its assortment of pots, pans, plates, and food staples. It was his responsibility to build a

The original Wagner cabin still standing in 1940.
Photographer Charles Thompson. Courtesy of David Thompson.

nightly fire pit and cook the dinner. The food was a basic camp menu, mostly a mulligan stew made from potatoes, meat, and vegetables. Beans and bacon with biscuits were offered up for dinner too.

The first day found the group camped just outside Sonora, near Mrs. Elsbree's Saloon. This establishment was operated by Mrs. Elsbree and Philip Elsie. Philip was Wagner's nephew. The family looked forward to this stop each year so they could visit and catch up on news. They were up early the next morning guiding the cattle uphill to the Coffill Ranch in the Confidence area. The third stop was at the Long Barn boarding house. In addition to providing lodging, this business had the added benefit of serving meals.

The last stop was the famous Conlin Hotel on Strawberry Flat. Here they could camp in the meadow alongside the South Fork of the Stanislaus River. The Conlins always made them feel welcome. The following morning it was off to their destination, the Clarks Fork camp. They arrived with dust billowing from hundreds of cattle, sounds of dogs barking, and young Charles Lewis perched in the chuck wagon bringing up the rear. Now they could prepare food in a real kitchen and settle in comfortable beds.

After decades of long cattle drives, Wagner became too infirm to continue and retired from the stock raising business in 1926. He sold the Clarks Fork grazing rights to the Airola family of Calaveras County. Charles Wagner died in 1935.

During the mid-1920s and 1930s, changes came to Clarks Fork. The Ghirardelli family of San

Francisco chocolate confections fame would arrive on the flat for the summer and set up an elaborate camp. Owners of the few cabins built at that time on the flat found the Ghirardellis to be good neighbors. In the late 1930s, construction began on the Sierra Way road. The road crew and their families occupied the site for three years and had a large dining hall and kitchen combination, and even a small schoolhouse.

In early 1926, Antone Airola acquired the Iceberg Meadow grazing allotment which had been previously used by Charles Wagner. Airola took over the old fifty-one-year-old Wagner cabin for his mountain headquarters.

Wagner bunkhouse at his Clarks Fork cow camp in 1954.
Photograph courtesy of Bill Airola.

Antone's father Manuel was a goldminer at Melones on the Stanislaus River in Calaveras County. His mother was Charlotte Figaro, both parents being native of Italy. At Melones, they raised their family. Antone was born on the ranch on February 20, 1866, in Calaveras County.

During the summer months in Melones, Antone and his brothers helped a neighbor on his ranch. The neighbor was Jean Yfol, a Frenchman who owned a ranch up on the Stanislaus River. Antone worked herding cattle, branding, putting up hay for the winter, and gathering the cattle to take to the mountains for summer grazing. The Frenchman had his headquarters at French Camp, between Vallecito and Robinson's Ferry. At the end of each season, the Frenchman gave each of the boys a cow as payment for their work. This became the start of Antone Airola's cattle herd and his life as a cattleman.

In 1890, Jean Yfol decided to sell his land and return to France. He favored Antone, age twenty-four, and sold it to him. Newlywed Antone and his wife Louise now had their own ranch and moved to French Camp.

1925 wedding photograph of Fred and Irene Airola.
Photograph courtesy of the Airola family.

Antone Airola at the Wagner cabin on the Clarks Fork.
Photograph courtesy of the Airola family.

Antone and his wife, Louise De Martini, had three children: Adeline, born in 1887, who married Archie Stevenot; Fred, born in 1890; and the youngest, Sidney, who was called "Babe," born in 1902. Antone and his sons Fred and Babe became prominent cattlemen in Calaveras County.

Manuel had about 300 cows and amazingly, he had named each cow, and they say he had a little notebook in his shirt pocket that he would make notations about each of the animals. As Manuel grew older, he knew he needed to pass on the cattle business to his sons. Both were capable. Fred took the Iceberg allotment, while Babe set up at Cow Creek and Bumble Bee on the Sonora-Mono Wagon Road beyond Strawberry.

Fred married Irene Thompson in 1925. He was thirty-five and his bride was twenty-one. Fred and his wife Irene had no children. Irene and Fred acquired the Wagner grazing rights in 1926. They took over the old Wagner cabin and set themselves up in the cattle business. They added on to the old cabin and made it a comfortable summer headquarters for their mountain cow camp.

Irene, a new bride, would often ride the range checking fences and looking for stray cows with Fred. She always rode a beautiful horse. Irene usually rode a Tennessee Walker and turned heads with her exceptional horse. The Airolas were always particular about breeding their cattle and horses, selecting only the best stock.

Irene became acquainted with her only neighbor, Hazel Brandt Truex. Both women were often alone at their cabins during the summer, and they became close friends. They would join each other for meals and play a lot of gin rummy. Sometimes the women walked all the way to Dardanelle Resort for the mail. On weekends, the two would go to the resort for whist parties and dances put on by the Bucknams, owners of the resort. By the mid-1940s, other cabins were built on the flat, and they welcomed new neighbors.

Fred died of a heart ailment in San Andreas on November 20, 1955, after an extended illness. He was sixty-five. Irene was left a widow at the age of fifty-one. In 1956, the grazing allotment passed to John William "Bill" Airola, son of family member Tone Airola.

In 1973, Bill Airola and his wife Betty knew it was time for a new cabin. They decided to incorporate the old Wagner cabin into their new plans and enlarge the original building. The new Airola cabin became designated Lot 7 in the Wagner Summer Home Tract. Bill died at eighty-one and is buried in the family cemetery near Angels Camp in Calaveras County.

The Airola family cattlemen have continued throughout the decades to keep the grazing allotment at the historic Wagner Cow Camp. Each generation brings new life to the old ways of their ancestor, Antone Airola, who had loved the mountains and acquired the Clarks Fork cattle range in 1926.

The site of the little Wagner cabin on the flat overlooking the river eventually grew into what became known as the Wagner Summer Home Tract. Surveyed in 1931, the tract's need for an adequate water system was always a problem, and it wasn't until the mid-1940s that a majority of the seventeen cabins were built.

Most likely, Charles Wagner had no idea that his cow camp would someday become a popular summer destination and that a colony of cabins would populate the flat.

As an update, sadly, on August 5, 2018, the Donnell Fire burned all of the Wagner Tract, with the exception of two cabins.

SOURCES
Airola, Bill. Personal interview, 1, Mar. 2017.
Brandt, Hazel Perkin. *Wagner Camp, Stanislaus National Forest, A Brief History 1923-1993.* Pinecone Press, Jul. 1993. Earlier edition, 1983.
Brooks, Roy. "Cattle Driving By." *CHISPA,* Tuolumne County Historical Society. Vol. 13, No. 3, Jan.-Mar. 1974, p. 448.
Findagrave.com.
Hamilton, Jack. Personal interview, 15 Jun. 2017.
US Census, 1920.
US Census, 1940.
Wood, Coke. "Tales of Calaveras." *Prospect,* 4 Aug. 1966. (from his book *Old Tales of Calaveras*).

The old Wagner cabin acquired by the Airolas, photographed in 1952. *Photograph courtesy of the Airola family.*

The corral at the Airola cow camp, west of the cabin. *Photograph courtesy of the Airola family.*

The Airola "Cow Palace" remodeled in 1973. *Cate Culver photograph taken in 2016.*

CHAPTER 7

Hayes Station
In Eureka Valley

During 1864 to 1865, David Hayes, with his partner John Welch, built Hayes Station alongside the new wagon road. It was situated in Eureka Valley, a large, long grassy flat, with granite cliffs to the north, and the Middle Fork of the Stanislaus River within walking distance.

This building measured twenty-four feet wide by fifty feet long and had a split-shake roof. The building was constructed of hand-hewn logs with neatly mortised corners, and it was designed so that a second story could be added later. The timber pieces were about twelve-by-twelve inches thick and fifty feet long. It had a combination dining room and kitchen with a large fireplace used for cooking and for heating the building. In the middle was a store, and on one end, a storage room. This was a stopping place for travelers, teamsters, pack trains, and stage and mail carriers traversing the Sonora-Mono Wagon Road.

Gold mining in the Nevada districts sputtered, and the wagon road traffic was not what Hayes had expected. In 1869 Hayes decided to sell the station. However, he didn't own the property, so on November 19, 1869, he filed a claim before selling it. He sold out to Henry C. Schultz for the sum of $250. Hayes moved to Bridgeport where he went into business with his older brother Henry.

Then gold mining in Nevada picked up again and fees from the tolls poured in. Henry C. Schultz, who had the road contract, was amazed at the turn of events. Although the heavily-traveled road was taking a beating, he could afford the maintenance since business was very good.

The next year, though, Schultz sold the land to Henry A. Douglass for $250, who used it for his summer cattle range headquarters. It became known as the Douglass House. On June 29, 1891, Henry's daughter, Frances Rolleri, received a patent for one hundred and sixty acres on the land in Eureka Valley, and it became known as Douglas Flat, dropping the last "s." Rolleri subsequently sold the property to Edward V. Burgson in the 1930s. It then passed to William Alhouse of San Jose in 1966.

David Hayes, early pioneer who built Hayes Station.
Courtesy of the Mono County Historical Society.

Hayes Station, about 1918, when the Nelsons leased it.
Photograph courtesy of Tuolumne County Historical Society and Museum. (Fred Leighton collection).

By 1925, the old Hayes station, its porch gone, was in a state of collapse. An attorney bought the building thinking he might want the old hand-hewn logs to build a fancy lodge. He had it torn down, and the logs were numbered so that the building could be reconstructed. Most likely, nothing came of his plans.

Today a monument marks the site of the first building on the old Sonora-Mono Wagon Road. It stood for over sixty years, giving shelter to passersby.

Barns built against granite cliffs in Eureka Valley.
Photograph from the A.A Gourley collection.

SOURCES

Johnson, David H. "Rusticating in the Mountains." *CHISPA*, Tuolumne County Historical Society. Vol. 38, No. 2 Oct.-Dec. 1998.

---. "The Sonora and Mono Wagon Road." *Sierra Heritage Magazine.* May/Jun. 1996.

Nelson, Francis. "The Douglas Station." Tuolumne County Historical Society, *CHISPA*, Vol. 37, No. 2, Oct.-Dec. 1997.

Robinson, Chris. Personal interview. Jun. 2017.

CHAPTER 8

Baker Station
and Greenbury Columbus Baker

At the base of Sonora Pass, before the steep climb to the summit, is an area known as Baker Station. Along the entrance to Kennedy Meadows is Baker Campground. This early pioneer's name is a familiar landmark in the Central Sierra, yet today, little is known about the man himself.

Greenbury Columbus Baker was born in Missouri in 1845. In 1862, at the tender age of seventeen, he enrolled in the Missouri Militia on the Union side in the War Between the States (known as the Civil War). When he was discharged two years later, Baker had attained the rank of sergeant. Throughout the war, he had heard men talk of the West, its gold, and the beautiful land of California.

After serving in the militia, Baker headed west by mule team, leaving his Missouri home in March, arriving in San Joaquin Valley in July. It had been a great adventure for this young man to cross the prairie, the Rockies, and the Sierra. He had encountered all kinds of men and heard their stories of failures and dreams. Baker had endured hardship, matured, and knew his own mind and what he wanted.

At age twenty-two he situated himself in Empire City, on the Tuolumne River in Stanislaus County, a popular port for steamboats, where he was exposed to commerce and the business world. Four years later, he was living in Snelling, in Merced County, a small gold mining community along the Merced River. He moved to Modesto and bought a small ranch west of the city, engaging in stock raising and finding work as a carpenter.

Greenbury Columbus Baker, with his bride Mae Elsie Carter in 1873, married at Center Mills, a logging community.
Photograph courtesy of the Tuolumne County Historical Society, and Museum.

In 1873, Greenbury met and married Mae Elsie Carter at Center Mills. Baker was twenty-eight, and his bride just eighteen. Mae was the daughter of John Beach Carter, a pioneer and lumberman with profitable mills at Center Mills, near Confidence, and another mill at Columbia.

In 1875, a daughter was born. They named her Cora Mae and affectionately called her "Queenie." Other children followed: a daughter Laura, who died as a toddler, and sons John Beach and Henry Newton. The 1880 census record lists Baker as a hotelkeeper in Columbia, where he probably operated during the winter months.

The new Sonora-Mono Wagon Road opened in 1864, offering business opportunities. The Sonora-Bodie stage line was open and busy with passengers traveling to the gold strikes in Mono County. The road was heavily used by pack trains full of supplies, freight wagons hauling heavy equipment, and gold-seekers.

Greenbury traveled the new road and looked over the area. He found a wide, long flat area alongside the Stanislaus River. A lush meadow spread out on one side of the road near the river, and granite monoliths rose up behind the flat on the other side of the road. Two miles up the road wound the popular trail leading to Kennedy Meadows and Kennedy Lake, where outdoorsmen liked to pack into the mountain lakes. Farther up the road began the steep climb to the Sonora Pass summit. While snow prevented wagon and stage travel during the winter and early spring, a stage stop and hotel could be a profitable business for an enterprising individual at this location during the summer season.

In 1879, Baker, then thirty-four and an experienced hotelkeeper, decided to construct a station for travelers where they could have dining, accommodations and a stable for their pack animals. He was an experienced carpenter and set to work on three buildings. One, described as fifty to sixty feet long and perhaps thirty feet wide, was the hotel. The second, a barn across the road in the meadow by the river, was constructed of poles with shake sides and a roof, plus a corral. It measured approximately eighteen by twenty feet, with mangers on the river's side.

The third building was a one-room bunkhouse near the hotel. It had no window glass, only shutters that opened for light, and screens to keep insects out. It was constructed of poles with shakes, and no ceiling. Primarily used as a bunkhouse, it contained a wood-burning cook stove.

Importantly, early on, the place was recognized for its recreational values, and Baker advertised these qualities in the Sonora newspaper articles.

Sometimes called Baker's Resort, fishing, scenic beauty, hunting, and relaxation were among its selling points. It was also a day and a half horseback ride from Sonora to Baker's, and a day's ride to Bridgeport to the east.

By 1881, mining played out in the Bodie and Esmeralda mining districts. Due to a lack of passengers, the Sonora to Bodie stage stopped running and travel on the road became infrequent.

Greenbury Columbus Baker in 1884, wearing his Ancient Order of United Workmen badge.
Photograph courtesy of the Tuolumne County Historical Society and Museum.

In 1883, the Tuolumne County Board of Supervisors granted the road franchise to prominent lumberman John Beach Carter, Baker's father-in-law.

In 1888, in an attempt to bolster business, his father-in-law started a weekly stage run to Baker Station, leaving Sonora every Monday and returning on Saturday. The stage brought passengers who wanted to enjoy the fine hunting and fishing. They could also rent a horse to ride to the popular Kennedy Lake to fish for trout. During the winter

Section of the wagon road near Blue Canyon. *Photograph courtesy of Tuolumne County Historical Society and Museum. (Fred Leighton collection).*

months when the pass was closed, Baker must have run another hotel elsewhere as he is listed on record as a hotelkeeper in Confidence, a lumber and mining town near Miwok and Sugar Pine.

In 1897, Baker took over the road maintenance of the Sonora-Mono road. He desperately needed the road to be in good repair for his business to thrive. In his contract, he could charge a toll to pay for his maintenance expenses.

The grade to the summit of the Sonora-Mono Wagon Road being extremely steep, it was difficult to get mules and equipment up the primitive dirt road and make repairs. Maintenance costs on this part of the road were substantial from the start, with heavy snow and seasonal flooding causing repeated washouts, erosion, and blockages from fallen trees and boulders. In June 1898, Baker and his crew worked on the road and repaired a bridge between Strawberry and Baker Station.

By July, Baker gave up on maintaining the Mono County part of the road. Then, by August, discouraged, he relinquished the Tuolumne County side of the road as well. Road travel had diminished. There was little income from the toll he charged.

His hotel and resort were failing, so he abandoned Baker Station, leaving all his hard work behind. Greenbury returned to Confidence and the comfort of his in-laws, and added a saloon to his existing hotel in that town.

Later, in 1907 at sixty-two, he began drawing his Civil War pension. Records do not show what happened to his wife Mae. A distant family member states that she died in 1928.

Baker moved to Santa Ana in Orange County, and married Ida Mitchell in 1910. That marriage lasted two years. Then, on the rebound, he married Lizzie Fabun. He was sixty-six and Lizzie forty-nine. Eight years later, the census records list him as being divorced and living in a boarding house.

Baker died February 18, 1921, at age seventy-six, at the home of his daughter Cora Mae Gordon, in Venice, California. He is buried at the Fairhaven Memorial Park in Venice.

Baker Station, although no buildings remained, became a road maintenance station and kept the Baker name. The popular campground along the Stanislaus River has taken on his name as well.

SOURCES

Baker, Greenbury C. Obituary. *Modesto Evening News*, 21 Feb., 1921, P. 3, Column 4.

---. Memorial #8722201. *findagrave.com*

Blake, Sherry. Personal interview, 2018.

Buckbee, Edna Bryan. *The Saga of Old Tuolumne*. Press of the Pioneers, 1935.

California Great Register, Voter Registration, Greenbury C. Baker, 1867.

California Great Register, Voter Registration, Greenbury C. Baker, 1871.

California Great Register, Voter Registration, Greenbury C. Baker, 1875.

Civil War Veterans Pension Records. Orange County, California. Submitted by Gordon Bricken, Searchable Database, http://www.cagenweb.com/orange/civilwarvets.htm.

Conners, Pam. "Baker Station: Historic Context." Tuolumne County, California, Stanislaus National Forest Report.

Family Search California, County Marriages, 1850-1952.

Great Register 1866, John Beach Carter, Lumberman, ID Archive 1398.

Great Register 1892, John Beach Carter, Road Superintendent, ID Archive, 1401.

Greenbury Columbus Baker. Family Search.

United States Civil War and Later Pension Index, 1861-1917.

US Census, 1860.

US Census, 1880.

US Census, 1920.

Patterson Grade.
Photograph courtesy of Tuolumne County Historical *Society and Museum.*
(Fred Leighton collection).

CHAPTER 9

Camping in the Forest

Ladies camping at Kennedy Meadows in 1907.
Photograph courtesy of Shelly Davis-King.

After the Sonora-Mono Wagon Road was completed in 1865, farmers from the San Joaquin Valley packed up the farm wagon and went to the mountains to camp. They longed to relax in the upland forests alongside the rivers and enjoy the cool breezes. Since the road was in poor repair with ruts, potholes, and thick dust, it was a slow and plodding journey. A few people stopped at Strawberry Flat and camped alongside the South Fork of the Stanislaus River. For those who continued on to the higher elevations, there was the dreaded five-mile-long Patterson Grade. The road was built on the edge of a sheer canyon. It was steep and extremely narrow—a cause for anxiety for any traveler—but with a horse and wagon, it was

possible to pull up the mountain to Brightman Flat where a crude one-lane road cut through the sandy meadow for several miles. It was the first nice place to camp along the Middle Fork of the Stanislaus River. Ideal campsites were numerous along the river. Huge ponderosa pines provided ample shade, and the large granite boulders scattered about the open flat offered attractive campsites.

Families camped where they wanted and stayed as long as a month. This type of outdoor living was called "household" camping. Simple primitive canvas tents or lean-tos provided shelter. Folding tables and chairs were a necessity. Makeshift shelving was wedged between trees for the kitchen. Large nails were driven into trees for hanging tools and utensils.

Campers strung ropes between trees to hang blankets for privacy, and hammocks swung between tree trunks. Cooking was done over an open campfire. Few housekeeping chores were needed, allowing time for relaxation and visiting. You were in God's country, surrounded by nature.

Excited children played in the sparkling creeks, built dams, and waded, while adults fished for trout in the river. The time was passed with the simple pleasures of dreamy days, relaxing under the tall pines with the rushing river nearby. Most who came returned year after year to be rejuvenated in spirit and health. Many campers planned their trip to coincide with the opening of the trout season, the last Saturday in April.

Fishermen, nearly elbow to elbow, lined the Stanislaus River. With baited hooks, each cast into the best deep pools. Rainbow trout were plentiful, and the limit in 1913 was a generous fifty fish per day. Each camper desired to provide fish for breakfast for the gang. Throughout the camps, the smell of sizzling trout lingered in the morning air.

Deer hunting season in the fall also attracted great numbers of outdoorsmen. The backroads were overrun with hunters' canvas tents and assorted hunting gear. As most outdoorsmen did not hunt alone, it was a great time for male companionship, and the backcountry filled up with eager hunters.

When the Stanislaus Forest Reserve was established in 1897 the rangers mostly built trails and enforced laws concerning sheep passing through the forestlands. There were no official campgrounds or regulations. Camping was free and unrestricted.

In the early 1900s, the state took over the Sonora-Mono Wagon Road and appointed a road supervisor. However, funding was not adequate and few improvements were made on the old road. Still, the public came to the mountains in droves with their horses and wagons, which were eventually replaced by automobiles. Auto-camping in the Sierras exploded as modern doctors promoted the benefits of being in nature. The fresh air and tranquility of hikes in the woods were a cure for the soul. The forest filled with these automobile campers. The government saw the national forests as a "safety valve" for relief from blue-collar urban life.

Car Camping at Pinecrest.
Photograph courtesy of Matt Bloom. (Gerald French collection).

Lee Gibb and his wife camping in 1936.
Photograph courtesy of the Tuolumne County Historical Society and Museum. (Fred Leighton collection.)

By 1916, Ranger Thraves reported that "the area's popularity for summer camping along the Mono Highway for those who use the flats along the river as camping places, has been steadily increasing each year."

On July 26, 1919, the *Union Democrat* in Sonora printed, "The Forest Service and Department of Agriculture is endeavoring to bring about a full public realization of what the forests offer," and the newspaper quotes one of several booklets issued by the Forest Service that invites visitors, "You will encounter no 'Keep Out' signs on the forests," as it reassures further, "They are not fenced against the public, but invite your presence and use. The only signs you will find are those which point you on your way to ask your co-operation in preserving the beauty and value of these free recreation grounds and their resources. Firearms are not barred, and hunting and fishing are restricted only by the requirements of the State game laws."

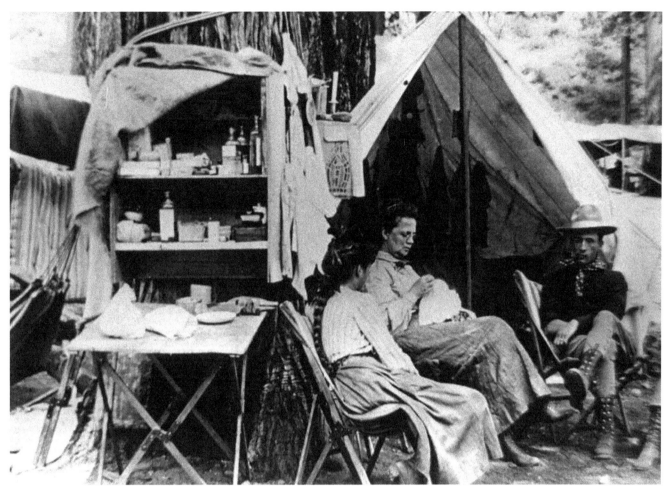

Camping at Kennedy Meadows. *Courtesy of the Tuolumne County Historical Society and Museum.*

The article continues encouraging would-be campers to take advantage of the mountain forests: "You are welcome to all the necessary firewood and to forage for your saddle and pack animals: and, so far as possible, the grazing of commercial stock is regulated in such a way as to save an accessible supply of forage for the campers' use. You may camp where you like and stay as long as you please. The Forest Service asks that you look only to the proper sanitation of the camp and that you be careful with fire. Information on the forests will be furnished to all who apply to the forest supervisors, the district foresters, the Forest Service at Washington, D.C."

This promoting of the forest for rest and recreation was so successful that the local paper reported in September of 1920 that at one period during the summer, in a ten-mile stretch along the Stanislaus River, there were estimated to be fully five hundred people camped, either in a rough forest cabin, in a canvas tent, or out in the open under the starlit heavens. Their initial call for individual campers to handle their own sanitation issues was inadequate. By 1921, sanitation became a huge problem due to campers polluting the river water. Rules for the regulation of automobile camping were adopted at a meeting of the State Board of Health. The regulations specify that a caretaker must be placed in charge of campgrounds to see that grounds and equipment are kept in sanitary condition. That summer, Dr. W. L. Hood, the county health officer, made a trip to inspect the conditions.

With the advent of automobile travel, the Forest Service built roads to access campsites along the creeks and rivers. By 1935, free campgrounds reserved by the Forest Service for recreational use were located at Pinecrest, Cow Creek, Lily Creek, Cascade Creek, Mill Creek, Niagara Creek, Clarks Fork, Brightman Flat, Pigeon Flat, and Deadman Creek on the Sonora-Mono Road.

Campers at Deadman Creek.
Photograph courtesy of Cynthia Mc Carrie.

In 1948, the Forest Service experimented with a program of fee-based campgrounds, which was readily adopted by the public. The *Union Democrat* reported in 1949 that "charging a fee for camping at Pinecrest will be continued in a similar manner as first tried in 1948. Plans have also been announced to start charging camping fees in other regions of the Stanislaus Forest. The schedule of charges authorized are as follows: Camping—Fifty cents per day per car not carrying more than six persons, or $3.00 per week. For parties of more than six persons, an additional ten cents per day per person will be charged. Group picnic fees will be handled at the flat rate, set by the Regional Forest."

By 1957, Summit Ranger Station had forty-three campgrounds and two hundred and twenty family unit camp sites. Throughout the years and into the present, many campgrounds have been added, and the public continues to seek out recreation at Sonora Pass. Today, campgrounds abound along each fork of the Stanislaus River, and campers continue to enjoy the simple pleasures of the sound of the river and smell of the fresh mountain air.

SOURCES

Ayers, Robert. "History of the Stanislaus." Feb. 1911 Report. *CHISPA* Tuolumne County Historical Society quarterly publication , Vol. 40, No. 4 Apr.-Jun. 2001.

Conners, Pam. "A Century or So Of Land Use On The Central Stanislaus Watershed Analysis Area: 1848-1958." Report. *Stanislaus National Forest Historian,* 1993, p. 90.

Union Democrat. "An Ideal Home in the Mountains." 26 Jul. 1919, p. 4.

Union Democrat. "Observations in the Mountains." 18 Sep. 1920. Front page.

Union Democrat. 17 Feb. 1949.

CHAPTER 10

Sonora Pass Roars to Life

The 1920s marked a period of vigorous economic expansion throughout the country. The nation's total wealth more than doubled. The rapid development of the automobile brought on the growth of the suburbs, and cities expanded. More families had leisure time. Professional sports, tourism, and recreational activities became major businesses. People traveled to California to see the awesome Yosemite Valley and Lake Tahoe regions, and to explore the Sierra Nevada Mountains.

In central California, the Stanislaus River, coursed down though granite bedrock from the highest mountains, relaxing as it reached the lower flats. It is always a beautiful river of mesmerizing blue-green pools, deep rushing gorges, and calm clear water flowing over water-worn granite boulders. The road hugged the river, creating a mountain paradise.

The Sonora-Mono Wagon Road, once it reached Brightman Flat, was a good road for several miles. The road edged the river and provided excellent campsites. The ability to drive to Sonora Pass in a few hours, instead of days, brought campers who crowded into the timberlands. Sonora Pass became a summer destination and the forests were abuzz with summer activity as the pass sprang to life.

With the press of campers everywhere, the Forest Service reacted by setting up summer home tracts, allowing the public to build cabins on Forest Service land. Cabin ownership boomed as people from the valley leased lots from the government and built cabins. Resorts sprang up and the forest rang out with hammers and saws used in building hotels and primitive summer homes. Lumber was hauled

J.D. Bucknam and helper at work building a rental cabin.
Photograph courtesy of Jerry and Ruth Howard.

from Hales and Symons Lumber Yard in Sonora and other small private sawmills. The road was alive with trucks hauling building supplies, along with new tourists in their Fords exploring the mountains. Businessmen took note, realizing opportunities to provide services for the public. Plans were set in motion to build resorts and accommodate tourists.

In 1923, George Conlin, who owned and operated the Strawberry Hotel along the South Fork of the Stanislaus River, remodeled his property to serve the deluge of travelers. He added a sitting room, dining room, and ten upstairs bedrooms, plus

Trucker hauling building supplies gives children a ride. The truck is a Model "T" Chevrolet one-ton pickup with 36 horsepower, a workhorse in its day.
Photograph courtesy of Jerry and Ruth Howard.

a general store and saloon. Six housekeeping cabins were built to rent to guests. Conlin added a barn, plus a stable, a generator, and two gasoline pumps out front.

At Douglas Flat, farther up the mountain, the Nelsons did business at Hayes Station, an early stage stop built of logs. They sold provisions and provided a few rooms for rent. Seeing others profiting from the '20s boom, Bill Nelson decided to abandon Hayes Station in 1922 and move a short distance up the road to build a new hotel that included a restaurant, tents cabins to rent, and riding stables.

In addition, at Douglas Flat, J.D. McCarty, a sheep rancher from Copperopolis, built a first-rate dance hall for the public to enjoy, complete with a wind-up phonograph. From the cabins, campgrounds, and resorts, people came out in the evenings and danced the night away to the latest jazz music and popular older tunes.

At Dardanelle, in 1923, the Bucknams built a simple cabin with a lean-to for a store. By 1926 they opened their large hotel with a restaurant, tent cabins, gas pumps, and pack stables.

At Kennedy Meadows Pack Station, the last outpost before traveling over the pass, Charles Ledshaw expanded in 1927 by opening a store, building tent cabins to rent, and installing a filling station.

Everyone wanted to take advantage of the influx of tourists to the high country, but the roar

of the building boom of the 1920s fell to a whimper by the 1930s when the country plunged into the Great Depression. Sales of cabin lots from the Forest Service quickly came to an end. Throughout the 1930s, with the country gripped in economic despair, the public had little money for recreation, and the resorts on the pass languished. By the early 1940s, World War II had started, and the nation became occupied with the war effort. The luxury of a family trip to the mountains was dampened by gas rationing. Few people left their home towns.

Throughout the 1930s and '40s, Dardanelle Resort and Douglas Resort remained in business, as did Kennedy Meadows Resort, which burned down in 1940, but was soon rebuilt. Both resorts struggled but were able to attract customers and did fairly well.

In 1937 a new highway was built that bypassed the Strawberry Hotel, causing the business to suffer. At Hayes Station the old building had crumbled into a pile of logs. The McCarty dance hall languished.

The flood of building and expansion in the 1920s was never repeated, with two exceptions. At Strawberry, Richard and Mary Carter built the Strawberry Inn and a store in the early 1940s. Pinecrest Resort built new facilities and thrived, with stores, sports rentals, an art gallery, marina, restaurant, motel, and RV park accommodating thousands of tourists every summer season. Nearby campgrounds attracted a large number of campers every year, as they still do.

At Pinecrest shoreline, summer home tracts sprang up in the '20s and '30s. In 1938, the last cabin was built at Pinecrest. Only a handful of cabins along the Sonora Pass highway were built after the 1940s. No new resorts were ever constructed.

CHAPTER 11

Strawberry

In years gone by, "Old Strawberry" was a popular stopping place for mountain travelers. Located at a convenient spot on the South Fork of the Stanislaus River, it has largely disappeared to history. Only one diminutive outbuilding remains in a large meadow once brimming with activity.

There were three distinct places called Strawberry that had the abundant wild strawberries. Early pioneers, traveling east and west on the old Walker River Trail, came to a place thirty miles from Sonora on the North Fork of the Tuolumne River. This was the first Strawberry, called Strawberry Flat House. Here, in a meadow in 1853, the first accommodations for travelers were furnished by Henry Palmer of Knights Ferry who provided a hot meal and a night's rest. In a diary entry, Joseph Williams wrote, "On Monday, October 10, 1853: Here is a ranch and boarding house. We got our breakfast here. Had onions and cucumbers, meat, coffee and molasses and good bread: paid three shillings for each. Lay here today to wait for wagons."

From this outpost, a traveler heading east followed Indian trails or just navigated his own way to cross the backbone of the Sierras on the Walker River Trail. At the time, Strawberry Flat House was the last taste of civilization.

When the Sonora-Mono Wagon Road was being built in 1863 through 1865, it was rerouted with the road passing through a meadow along the South Fork of the Stanislaus River. Here, a second place came to be called Strawberry Flat. On this flat, at the rivers' edge were lush grasses, wildflowers, and a forest of pines and firs in the background. It was a stunning piece of nature's mountain glory.

Strawberry Flat in 1910, view from the sawmill.
Photograph courtesy of Tuolumne County Historical Society and Museum. (Fred Leighton collection).

As new activity from the building of the road drew attention to the area, men in charge of the new road, having inside information, became land speculators. The area was first claimed by William A. and Jemina Boyce as a homestead on November 4, 1861. A year later C.H. Esmond and Augustus D. Lascelle purchased the land in a sheriff's sale. Then, in 1863, John McDonald claimed a portion of the land and established a small wayside inn beside the road. Within a year, Lascelle sold his half-interest to James Allen, a merchant in Knights Ferry, who had been appointed road commissioner for the building of the new road. Then, McDonald sold to Allen as well. Washed out from Knights Ferry in the Great Flood of 1862, Allen and his partner Henry Palmer now owned some of the best land along the new road. By 1865, they sold out for a handsome profit to David Tulloch, who operated a flourmill at Knights Ferry. In 1875, Thomas W. Lane, another

George F. Conlin's Strawberry Resort alongside the old Sonora-Mono Wagon Road. The photograph was taken in 1915 a year before he died. His son George Thomas, and daughter Mary, then continued to operate the resort.
Photograph from an old postcard. Courtesy of Bill Coffill.

Knights Ferry resident, purchased the property from Tulloch. Lane constructed a new hotel on the edge of the meadow.

The road brimmed with the activity from gold miners and their pack animals, cattle drives, and sheep herders. The Bodie Stage Line and freight wagons loaded with produce for the Nevada mining boom passed through. They all stopped at the inn to water and feed the livestock, and have a meal and a drink. Some would bed down for the night.

Ed Parsons, a popular Sonora saloonkeeper and Tuolumne County Treasurer, took over the property in 1886. For more than a decade, he, with his wife Mary Jane (Bradford), and their seven children, operated the inn from spring to fall. Their Chinese cook, Sing, attracted a following for his skill as a chef.

George F. Conlin passed through the area on the wagon road and admired its beauty. He approached Ed Parsons and, in 1897 acquired a 360-acre parcel on Strawberry Flat. Conlin saw great potential in having an inn with a river view alongside the road.

Bridge across the South Fork of the Stanislaus River, built in 1910 by Lewis C. Chase, then superintendent of the Sonora-Mono Wagon Road.
Photograph courtesy of Tuolumne County Historical Society and Museum.

George F. Conlin, born in 1870, was one of eleven children who grew up at Shaw's Flat near Sonora, attending school in Columbia. He set up a sawmill across the river near the forest, hauled logs using ten huge oxen, and started a small lumber business. He was twenty-seven, ambitious, and a single man.

Seeing the opportunity to expand the inn and having an abundance of lumber, he hired carpenters

The new Strawberry Store, built in 1923. The photograph was taken during deer hunting season as hunters displayed their bucks. *Photograph courtesy of the Tuolumne County Historical Society and Museum. (Gerald French collection).*

and built the Strawberry Hotel with rooms for guests and a restaurant. George built a huge barn and other buildings on his property in the meadow. The wagon road passed in front, so it was easy for travelers to refresh, visit, and exchange local news.

George was the only one of his siblings to marry. Around 1904, he married Nellie Grace Robertson. They had two children, George Thomas, born February 21, 1905, and daughter Mary. The children spent their summers at the hotel and helped with chores. In the summer of 1916, George became ill and Nellie tended him at their home in Columbia. His health worsened and he died before Christmas on November 22, 1916, at age forty-six. Conlin was held in such esteem by his community that the well-attended funeral cortège left his home, and an hour later arrived at Saint Patrick's Catholic Church in Sonora. It

then proceeded to the cemetery. Left with young children, Nellie decided in 1920 to move the family in with her father, Christopher Columbus Robertson, in Columbia.

By the 1920s, families in the valley who had automobiles came up the mountain to the hotel, eager to relax on the porch in the shade and view the meadow. They came to the mountains for relief from the summer heat. Recreation took over Strawberry Flat as families of campers and fishermen came and stayed for several weeks.

Nellie continued to operate the Strawberry Hotel, assisted by her son George and daughter Mary. Soon they realized business was so good they needed to provide more accommodations. To finance the expansion, they subdivided the original 360-acre homestead and sold off lots to private parties.

In 1923, Nellie and her children decided to move the hotel twenty yards from the original site. The old building was remodeled to include a sitting room, dining room, and ten upstairs bedrooms, plus a general store and saloon. Up on the hill

Conlin's Strawberry Resort gas pumps, store, and dance hall.
Photograph courtesy of Tuolumne County Historical Society and Museum.

behind the hotel, they had six housekeeping cabins built to rent to guests during the summer. A barn with a stable and two gasoline pumps were added out front. The installation of a generator brought electricity to the compound. A new dance platform erected in the meadow brought young folks out for Saturday night dances. Just sitting on the porch to escape the summer heat was a welcome way to relax and socialize. George put a long watering trough in front of the store, in which he kept about a dozen fifteen-inch rainbow trout. Little boys visiting for the summer delighted in feeding the fish grasshoppers and chunks of bread. Of course, fishermen had to stop and admire such beauties.

A tram was built to cross the river for more fishing access. More families and campers came for trout fishing, horseback riding, and numerous hiking trails. George was a skilled fisherman and a guide for deer hunters who came every fall to bag a deer.

George married Miriam, an Indiana native. In 1936 they had a son they named Daniel T. Conlin. In the 1930s, George sold off his water rights from the Stanislaus River to Pacific Gas and Electric

IN THE HEART OF THE SIERRAS

Strawberry Resort

is situated 30 miles above Sonora on the Sonora-Mono Highway at an elevation of 5240 feet. Ideally situated for a cool delightful summer vacation along the South Fork of the Stanislaus River.

HUNTING AND FISHING GROUNDS
are readily accessible and pack animals are available at reasonable rates for trips into deeper forests.

FREE CAMP GROUNDS   GENERAL MERCHANDISE STORE
Excellent Meals Served

HOTEL AND COTTAGES
A Modern Hotel of Perfect Accommodations
Hotel per day, $4.00. Per week, $22.50
Cabins per week, $15 to $20. Per month, $50 to $60

GEORGE AND MARY CONLIN   ADDRESS VIA SONORA, CALIF.

Company for $100,000. He did, however, retain his water rights on Herring Creek in order to supply water to Strawberry Flat. With the money from the sale, George installed water culverts to drain water away from the hotel complex to prevent flooding.

In 1937, the main highway was realigned and climbed the hill above the flat, and a new bridge was built across the South Fork of the Stanislaus River. The new road bypassed Strawberry Flat, which devastated the historic business.

In the 1940s, Miriam asked her sister Mazie Pierson to come out from Indiana and manage the old Strawberry Hotel on the flat for the

View of Strawberry Hotel from the river. *Photograph courtesy of Matt Bloom. (Gerald French collection).*

summer. It had become a place of quiet leisure. The housekeeping cabins had been sold off and traffic was now diverted to the new Highway 108. Business was slow and came to a halt after the barn burned in 1946.

In 1952, a new surge of activity surrounded the place when the Morrison-Knudson Company contracted to build the Beardsley and Donnell dams. The company selected the Strawberry Hotel as their headquarters and leased it from 1952 through 1957. After the dams were built, the Strawberry Hotel settled back into a quiet community. The old Strawberry Hotel had been owned by the Conlin family for sixty-one years at the location in the flat. George and his son had built up the travelers' rest stop into a thriving business until 1937, when the fortunes of time changed.

When the newly aligned main highway bypassed the lovely resort, the resourceful Conlins knew they had to move their business to the new route intending to build the year-round Strawberry Inn, the third place called Strawberry. George T. and his sister Mary decided that, if they were going to stay in business, they needed to move close to

the new Sonora-Mono Road. The new road meant they could be open year-round and offer all types of rental equipment for skiers on their way to the new Dodge Ridge Ski Resort, near Pinecrest.

George's sister Mary Conlin married Richard Carter, and they decided to build a resort complex by the new road. They selected a site near the curving bridge across the South Fork of the Stanislaus River. The resort building cost $12,000, and the original building was constructed during the summers of 1938 and 1939. This was during the Great Depression and the Carters, to save money, used lumber left from the construction of the Strawberry Bridge. They named the complex Carter's Strawberry Café and Resort Hotel, later called the Strawberry Inn. The interior was knotty pine with hardwood floors throughout, and included a spacious forty- by- forty-seven-foot ballroom for entertainment. The Grand Opening was Saturday evening June 28, 1940. The Carters went all out, hiring an eight-piece orchestra from Modesto to play music for a public dance to celebrate the occasion.

The hotel had all the modern conveniences and included a bar, lunchroom, and gas station

Carter's Strawberry Inn overlooking the South Fork of the Stanislaus River.
Photograph courtesy of Bill Coffill.

with a bay for repairs. In the basement, they built two rental rooms with perfect views of the river flowing below. They added two storage spaces in the back of the basement. Little cabins for rent were built nearby. Needless to say, they were always booked. The restaurant overlooking the river was added in the late 1950s. The mounted deer heads over the bar were reputed to have been shot by famed television producer Ralph Edwards, who created, produced, and hosted *This Is Your Life* and *Truth or Consequences*. As the Dodge Ridge Ski Resort expanded and the roads improved, business was steady in summer and winter at the family resort.

On the other side of the new highway, Miriam and her husband George T. Conlin built a grocery store with living quarters upstairs in 1939. Rental cabins were built out back. George died in 1958 and Miriam died in 1969. George and Miriam left their property to son Danny, who owned a logging business.

The grocery store and cabins were sold to Mike and Jackie Sparrow. They lived upstairs year-round with their daughter and son. At the uphill end of the store, they added a little fast food restaurant. It was just a counter where a person would order a hamburger or hot dog and fries. Customers sat on the lawn and ate under the grove of cedar trees out front.

After Mike's death, Jackie leased the store to Tony Ferraro. Jackie married Paul Stetler, one-time owner of a boat dock at Pinecrest. The couple managed the ten rental cabins and a heated swimming pool, which became known as Sparrow's Resort.

The year 1955 brought great changes to Strawberry. The Tri-Dam project, which included Donnell, Beardsley, and Tulloch dams, moved into the small community to start construction of Beardsley Dam.

The chief engineer of the Oakdale Irrigation District, Russell E. Hartley, had packed in by horseback as a young man in 1924, so he was familiar with the area. He recognized its great potential for water storage. In 1955, his vision became a reality and construction on the dams began.

To accommodate the added population of Tri-Dam workers, the Carters added a fourteen-foot extension to the dining room and kitchen facilities. The new dining room was dedicated in August of 1955 and named the Hartley Room, after the engineer. The event was attended by over one hundred people, including Russell Hartley.

On the Conlin property across the South Fork, twenty or more two-bedroom houses were built to house the contractor's personnel. At the conclusion of the project three years later, the Conlins repurchased the houses.

In the meantime, back at the flat and the old Strawberry Hotel there, the operation languished. The road bypass decimated the business. In 1955 the store was razed, which further affected their ability to attract tourists. Then, George died in 1958, so Miriam moved to Sonora. She sold the old hotel and property to John and Germaine Firth of Berkeley that same year. The Firths had plans to re-zone and build condos and a commercial complex, but the Strawberry property owners wanted their privacy and opposed any changes.

In 1963, the Firths leased the old hotel to Mary Lou Scott, who opened a pizza parlor and offered live music and dancing. The neighbors objected to the traffic, loud music, and were concerned that sewage was polluting the river. By the late 1960s, hippies moved in and drugs became an issue. Germaine resumed management in 1969, with the intention of offering moderately priced meals and housing for hikers, hunters, and skiers.

Sparrow's Store at Strawberry. *Photograph courtesy of Tuolumne County Historical Society and Museum.*

The old hotel and the rest of what was left, burned to the ground March 6, 1970. The building was unoccupied and the cause of the fire was undermined. Germaine sought to gain a permit to rebuild a new hotel, restaurant, and dormitories on the old hotel site. The Tuolumne Board of Supervisors turned her down twice when petitions were signed by eighty Strawberry property owners and one hundred and eleven Strawberry Home Owners Association members, against Firth gaining a permit to build. After the hotel burned, Germaine lived for years in a back shed with no heat, water, or plumbing. Hop vines grew over her porch in the summer.

At the new location on the main highway, that new Strawberry Inn fared much better. Even so, in 1959, Richard Carter sold the Strawberry Inn to Ken and Judy Sneed who added a service station. Judy became upset with all the feral cats that went after birds near the river. She sat on the deck with her slingshot loaded with marbles and became a

very good shot by thumping preying cats. By the time the Sneeds sold the inn on June 2, 1975, it included thirteen rooms, a ninety-seat dining room, bar, car repair garage, trailer park, and fourteen acres straddling the South Fork of the Stanislaus River.

Today, Strawberry consists of mostly two large buildings near the bridge over the South Fork of the Stanislaus River. These buildings and their complexes have maintained businesses since 1937. The views of the river entice travelers to stop for a meal or an overnight stay. Winter sportsmen frequent Strawberry, since it is open year-round. Yet few travelers realize that hidden in the forest by the river are summer home tracts. Roads wind through the pines with cabins that have their own community of homeowners who stay through the winter months.

Any history of Strawberry is always largely about the industrious Conlin family. Their foresight to build along the bend in the river established a place in local history for generations.

One of the remaining buildings at Old Strawberry. *Photograph by Cate Culver 2017.*

SOURCES

Berry, Ron. Personal interview. 16 Aug. 2016.

Cross, Merrit. "Early Days at Strawberry." An unfinished manuscript, unpublished, found in a historic collection.

"Diary of Joseph Williams." Stanislaus National Forest files. Pg. 2.

Hender, Art. "Exoteric." *Union Democrat.* 23 May 1953.

Johnson, David. "The Sonora-Mono Wagon Road." *CHISPA,* Quarterly publication. Vol. 37, No. 3 Jan.-Mar., 1998.

Miller, Elvira. Personal interview. 26 Nov. 2017 and 11 Jan. 2018.

"Mountain Metropolis, Tri-Dam Constructors Set Up Shop." *Union Democrat.* 11 Aug. 1955. Front page.

"New Strawberry Resort to Open This Saturday." *Union Democrat.* 21 Jun. 1940. p. 6.

Reveal, Jack. "A History of the Summit District, Recollections of the Years 1948-1960." Unpublished manuscript.

"Strawberry Inn." *Union Democrat.* 2 Jun. 1975.

"Strawberry Hotel Blaze Sweeps Rapidly Through Wood Structure." *Union Democrat,* 6 Mar. 1970.

"Strawberry, Mono Road's Historic Stopping Place Still Bustles with Visitors the Year Round." *Union Democrat.* 3 Sep. 1992. p. 7C.

Union Democrat. 2 Jun. 1975.

Union Democrat. "Strawberry Flat House." 19 Aug. 1977.

Union Democrat. 16 Jun. 1955.

CHAPTER 12

Pinecrest
The Jewel of Sonora Pass

Cowboy pauses to view Strawberry Lake.
Photograph courtesy of Tuolumne County Historical Society and Museum.

In the era prior to the appearance of settlers in the Stanislaus National Forest, there existed an expansive granite basin rimmed by towering peaks. Situated at 5,600 feet in elevation, this basin was several miles above the present community of Long Barn. It was an area of striking natural beauty. From this location, the Pinecrest Recreation Area was born.

In 1852, engineers from the recently organized Tuolumne County Water Company built a road to the area they called Strawberry Flat. It was the aim of the water company to provide water needed for gold mining in the lower elevations of the Mother Lode during the summer months. A dam was built on the South Fork of the Stanislaus River, filling the meadow. It was called a "crib" dam, built entirely of stone and logs. Goldminers who had timbered the mine tunnels were familiar with interlocking logs and completed this sturdy dam by 1858. It reached a height of sixty feet. From the resulting lake, water was diverted to a series of ditches and flumes to the mining claims and towns in and around Columbia and the foothills. Two other dams at higher elevations were part of this complex. Two caretakers were employed to maintain the dams and these men were housed in a cabin at the edge of the lake.

By 1912, with growing populations in the towns of Sonora, Columbia, and Jamestown, there was a need for more water and electrical power. The water company decided to replace the log crib dam, which held water for fifty-five years, with a rock and cement one. Once the workers began blasting

Overview of the granite basin and Strawberry Lake, later renamed as Pinecrest.
Photograph courtesy of Tuolumne County Historical Society and Museum.

The Strawberry Dam (Pinecrest), a crib dam, from logs, completed in 1858, supplied water to the gold mining towns of the Mother Lode. *Photograph courtesy of Bill Zurnstein.*

out the canyon floor for the dam footing, the area became infested with rattlesnakes. The workers reported that they killed thousands! Rock from the canyon walls was dynamited and crushed to be used as a filler material. Mortar was applied to the final face of the dam. The new dam was 170 feet high and 125 feet wide. In November of 1916, after three years of construction, the dam was complete, creating Strawberry Lake. The operation was transfered to the Pacific Gas and Electric Company in 1923.

During the three years that the dams were being built, workers were lodged in a large, two-story crew house at the edge of the lake. James Diamond, a worker during the construction of the dam, saw the

The new dam under construction in 1913. *Photograph courtesy of Bill Zurnstein.*

The Diamond Hotel, also called the Diamonds' Hotel, sat tucked against the forest and overlooked the lake.
Old postcard courtesy of Bill Coffill.

possibilities of the structure. With his wife Catherine, he decided to develop the building into a hotel. In 1918, his daughter Rosalie Diamond secured a permit for the area and it became the Pierson-Diamond Resort. Pierson was the postmaster and Rosalie's husband. By 1920, Rosalie divorced Pierson and ran the hotel with her parents. A man named Dupree Reed Averill, an engineer, came into Rosalie's life and she married a second time. That marriage ended as well. Rosalie took back her maiden name and ran the hotel by herself for many years.

When the hotel was completed in 1918, the view of the lake was not attractive as it was filled with logs and debris. Old shacks surfaced from their moorings and floated in the water, and trees projected out from the lake. Over the years, locals worked on cleaning it up. The hotel created an image as a grand hotel with fine dining on white linen tablecloths. An expansive porch provided visitors a superb view of the lake. It was the heart of the community where business was discussed and plans made. Through the years, the original building was enlarged and rental cabins built, including a sport shop, a service station, boat dock, and the local post office. The hotel was a labor of love, and the

Rental cottages near the hotel.
Old postcard courtesy of Bill Coffill.

Later addition to the Diamonds' Hotel.
Courtesy of the Pinecrest Art Gallery.

Advertisement for the Pinecrest Resort in 1931.
Courtesy of Sam Yancy Discovers Twain Harte Again.

Automobiles park on the shoreline.
Photograph courtesy of Bill Zurnstein.

Diamonds worked hard to maintain its reputation as a prime vacation spot.

Many visitors enjoyed spending hours on the porch. One could start the day sipping a cup of hot coffee in the still of the morning, when there wasn't a ripple on the lake, and watch the smoke rise from the wood stoves in the cabins ringing the lake. Later in the evening, a visitor could relax with the breeze of the mountain air, a fine dinner, and a cocktail to end the day. This is what the tourists came to experience year after year.

Rosalie Diamond, demure and sweet, continued on with the hotel and took charge after her parents had passed, even hiring a three-piece band from Modesto to play every Saturday night for dances. She took great pride in her flower garden out front and tended it regularly.

Once the new dam was in place in 1916, the Forest Service laid out one hundred lots around the lake for the purpose of providing summer home sites. The lots averaged one hundred feet, running along the lakeshore, and two hundred feet extending inland. The only restrictions placed on prospective permittees were that each lot was to have a fly-proof sanitary outhouse in accordance with the specifications of the State Board of Health.

Many of the lots were covered in brush or heavy vegetation and there was very little interest from the public in leasing a lot to build a cabin. There was only one primitive road along the west shore. The north shore tract of twelve lots had no road at all and was the last to be laid out. Lots were held as long-term land permits from the Forest Service. The entire Pinecrest area is owned by the United States Government, and is administered by the U.S. Forest Service.

One of the first to build a cabin was Rosie Costa, a registered nurse who wanted a cabin for her mother, Adeliade Costa, seventy-five, who suffered from asthma. Rosie and her family had camped in these mountains for years. She thought the mountain air would be a good for her mother's lungs. Rosie, forty-two, figured a summer cabin would benefit the whole family. In 1918, she went to the Forest Service office in Sonora and looked over the new maps of available lots, selecting Lot 27. She went to the lake to see what she had selected and found no road. Rosie walked to locate her lot and discovered it was covered in brush. It was not what she expected, although her lot was right at the water's edge on the southern shoreline.

Even with help from her family, it was a huge undertaking to clear just enough brush and debris to haul in lumber on a wagon. She had a small primitive cabin built. Her sister Katherine and husband Archie Stevenot joined them during the summers.

The only access to water for domestic use was the lake. Rosie hauled water in buckets up the shore to her cabin. Six years later, the water problem became even worse when the lake receded, and it was even farther to walk to the shoreline and transport water to the cabin.

At the Diamond Hotel, the spring went dry and the Diamonds became discouraged. The Forest Service had no funds for a water system, and the new permittees saw no future in the situation. As the summer went by, the lake level continued to drop and eventually it was only half full.

By 1924, there were forty lots with cabins, and something had to be done about the lack of water. Archie Stevenot came to visit and saw how desperate the situation had become and took charge. Archie knew there was a spring about two miles up the canyon and led Charles H. Segestrom, Sr. and brother Eric to see if it might resolve the water situation. They measured the water flow at about five gallons a minute and decided it was enough.

Cabin owners formed a committee headed by Charles H. Segerstrom. They figured it would cost about $15,000 to put in a water system. If each cabin owner paid one hundred dollars toward a reliable water system, then that money would be a start. Archie contacted the cabin owners and raised the money, convincing them that it was a good idea. Then the committee was able to persuade a local bank to lend them eight thousand dollars.

By June of 1924, Archie led a crew of twenty-nine men working on the project. Through connections with Pacific Gas and Electric Company, they were able to borrow equipment. The electric company was very generous and did what it could to help. The men laid ten thousand feet of water pipe and installed two holding tanks. Motivated by the need for a water system, the crew had it completed within about ten days. The water system accommodated a Forest Service house and the campground.

Pinecrest Lodge in the 1930s.
Photograph courtesy of Bill Zurnstein.

Pinecrest Lodge, also known as Diamonds' Hotel, on the shoreline overlooking Strawberry Lake in 1932.
Photograph courtesy of Bill Zurnstein.

In the late 1920s, the road to Pinecrest was still primitive. It took three and a half hours of driving time from Sonora. Archie Stevenot, a man of vision and influence, set to work on improving the road. He contacted his brother Fred G. Stevenot, Director of Natural Resources, Bert Meek, Director of Public Works, and even Governor C.C. Young. With the help of these officials, the funds for road improvement appeared. With the upgraded road and available water, Pinecrest blossomed with newly built mountain cabins. Most cabins on the lake were accessible by boat only. Owners would park and wheelbarrow their supplies in on the trail or use a boat to cross the lake.

By the mid-1920s, the Forest Service had developed a small campground near the lake. Despite being primitive, it was popular with campers and their tents. Each camper strung ropes from trees and hung blankets to create some privacy.

Many of the early families at Pinecrest came from large farms in the Stockton and Modesto area. They built comfortable cabins and kept them well maintained. In these early days of Pinecrest, the cabin owners were people of some means. They all knew each other and socialized. Often they brought their housekeepers for the summer. Children ran free about the cabins and owners looked after each other's property. There was no crime or any thought of it. Pinecrest was their Lake Tahoe.

Although Pinecrest was just a small community, on September 13, 1923, the town celebrated California's Admission Day. During the afternoon, entertainment included races and games. Later at the Diamond Hotel, a dinner was served at 6 pm, followed by a program of dancing in the new dance pavilion for the remainder of the evening.

During the 1930s, the Civilian Conservation Corps Company No. 923 set up a camp on the outskirts of Pinecrest. They built a trail around the lake, but the primary task was to put in a campground for the lake visitors. Once completed, the public discovered Pinecrest and poured into camp to fish, swim and sail. By the mid-1940s, the summer population had exploded to about 5,000 visitors. By 1940, there were 354 summer homes.

In 1938, the last cabin at Pinecrest was built. In August that year, cabin owners organized their own association. The following year, residential electric power was introduced; however, the cabins around the lake had to wait to get electricity. With no road, it would be some time until they all had power.

At the north end of the lake, the cabins were of a different sort. Water lapped against terraced granite outcroppings. From the ledges, the views of the windswept water were stunning. Remote, with no road, a dozen hardy families chose to build their mountain retreats on these rocks.

Twelve cabins were constructed in a ten-year span from 1925 to 1935. Despite the Great Depression, families with established employment or those who owned successful farms had extra savings to build a simple cabin. The magnificent granite cliffs became cabin foundations, and primitive structures emerged above the lake and through the pines. But transporting the building materials wasn't

Harold Matthews and his son Harold Jr. unload lumber in the summer of 1933 to build their cabin on the north shore.
Photograph courtesy of Kirk Patterson.

so simple. Every family needed a boat to transport their tools, lumber, nails, windows, doors, bundles of sugar pine shakes, and a wood stove. Once at the water's edge, it all had to be hauled up the rocky shore to the building site.

Building on granite had major drawbacks. An indoor toilet was out of the question. There was no way to penetrate the rock for a septic system. All the cabins had outhouses, and garbage had to be transported across the lake for disposal. Water had to be carried up the cliffs from the lake. It was impractical to haul gasoline by boat for a generator, or propane gas for a refrigerator or stove, so heating and cooking were accomplished using the wood on site.

These twelve families, secluded from tourists, bonded together and socialized through the generations. Common topics of conversation were often rattlesnake sightings, big fish caught, new boats, and family news. They relished their intimate world.

In 1938, the north shore residents discussed the need for a clean water system to serve all the cabins. After some exploring, they decided to bring water from Herring Creek. It was some distance away

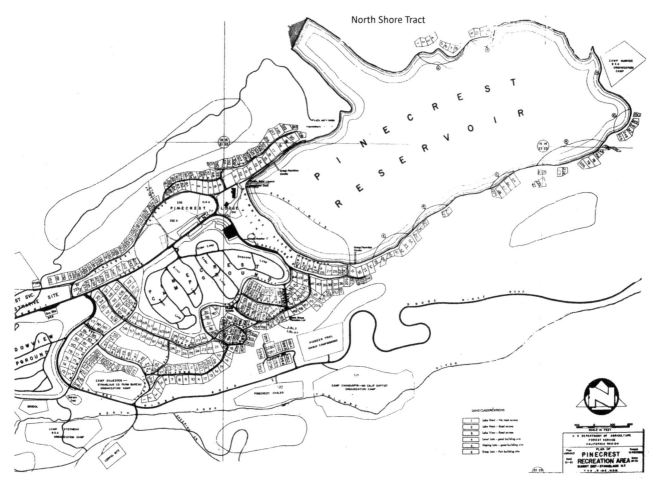

Early map of Pinecrest.

cross-country, a mile and a half downhill, but worth the effort. Everyone chipped in for materials. Jim Buckley designed the system, and his son Meredith with Vernon Dunleavy, Jr. set to work laying pipe and installing a holding tank. The new gravity-fed water system was a success. Water pipe had at last reached the kitchen sinks at Pinecrest. However, the system was stressed if too many cabins were using it at the same time.

Karl's Place.
Photograph courtesy of the Tuolumne County Historical Society and Museum.

As time went by, further development came to the area. Karl's Place, located by the lake, began as a bakery sometime before 1940, and expanded to a general store with soft drinks and ice cream. Operated by Karl DeFiebre, who also ran a bakery in Tuolumne City, it was close to the shoreline and catered to day-use visitors and campers. Karl's Place continued to expand and consisted of a general store, winter sports shop, modern bakery, dining room, lunch room, kitchen, barber shop and beauty shop, butcher shop, spacious lobby, and an office, plus some limited sleeping quarters. Karl's Place, though not as upscale as the Diamond's lodge, provided healthy competition.

In November of 1948, a fire of undetermined origin burned swiftly through Karl's Place. No equipment or personal belongings were saved, and it was never rebuilt. But the legendary taste of his delicious donuts remained on the lips of patrons for many years. According to Ranger Jack Reveal, the Forest Service did not renew Karl's permit.

Early postcard of sunbathers at the beach. *Cate Culver postcard collection.*

During WWII, gas rationing made it difficult for families to vacation any distance from home. Pinecrest remained a nearby getaway, and although trade was a bit slow, business owners managed. Young men who had worked the summer jobs were drafted, and high school boys now stepped into larger shoes and found welcome summer employment.

The teenaged boys on the north shore heard their parents complain of making so many boat trips across the lake for daily supplies. The teens came up with a clever idea of a daily delivery service, taking orders for a small fee, then boating across the lake to obtain and then ferry supplies back. They would make the rounds to each cabin and take orders. Typically, the order included milk, ice, a stop at Karl's Bakery for fresh bread or a pastry, and the delivery of messages. Off the boys would speed in a boat across the lake to fill the shopping list. They would return and scramble up the cliffs with arms loaded to distribute the orders. Their little business provided them with welcome income for the summer. The delivery service lasted from 1938 to 1945.

Local stonemason Bill Fredrick made the rounds to cabins under construction and offered to build cabin owners a stone fireplace for fifty dollars. He used local granite rock. Fredrick built a good half of the fireplaces at Pinecrest.

In 1935, local resident Art Rude saw an opportunity to provide evening entertainment for families. He set up his screen and projector on a section of the beach, and roped off an area for people to come and sit on blankets and watch movies once a week. Within five years, an outdoor amphitheater was built, and by 1964, a new one complete with benches took its place.

Pinecrest continued to grow in popularity. Visitors from the central San Joaquin Valley and the San Francisco Bay Area filled the campgrounds every summer. In 1937, on that Fourth of July Sunday, some 7,000 visitors came to the lake. In preparation, new improvements were made for safety, including a new outboard motor boat for the lifeguards, and a telephone line around the lake to aid the lifeguard station. A new ordinance was passed that no dogs were allowed on Strawberry Lake beach.

In 1944, Pinecrest Lodge, formerly known as the Diamond Hotel, built a lovely outdoor wooden

Strawberry Lake. Later, the name was changed to Pinecrest Lake. *Photograph courtesy of Tuolumne County Historical Society and Museum.*

dance floor. It was edged with a railing and the floor was waxed for easy dancing. The music came from a phonograph and the fee was twenty-five cents to dance. Wafting through the night air came the popular music of Frank Sinatra, Judy Garland, and the Mills Brothers. Swing dancing had become popular and the dance floor was a big hit for evening entertainment.

In 1948. Pinecrest had five telephones: two at Pinecrest Lodge, one being a public pay phone, and two at the ranger station. The fifth was for Johnny Sardella, who worked for Pacific Gas and Electric Company.

The Dodge Ridge ski area opened in 1939. Then, in the 1940s, there was an explosion of popularity in winter sports, especially snow skiing. Ski areas were developed and the public flooded into the Pinecrest area to enjoy winter sports. Karl's Place had a small hill for a rope tow.

By the 1950s, the national economy was booming with post-war prosperity. Rationing ended and consumer goods became available again. It was the age of Ike Eisenhower, the President who lowered taxes, balanced the federal budget, built the Interstate Highway System, and expanded Social Security.

Cheap domestic oil kept the engines of industry running. The soldiers were off to college with the GI Bill and returned to the work force as educated men. Families were snapping up new cars and houses.

Great change came to Pinecrest in 1938. Powerlines had at last reached all the cabins, originating from the Pinecrest parking lot and continuing around the lake. On the south shore, the postholes had to be drilled and blasted into the granite, and the poles, crossarms, wire, insulators, and transformers had to be ferried across the lake.

Cabin owners expanded their cabins, remodeling kitchens and adding bedrooms. The burlap metal-frame cooler was now replaced with an electric refrigerator, and wood burning cookstoves were abandoned for electric ones. Washers and dryers were installed and an electric vacuum cleaner stood in the closet. No longer did they have a cabin in which they swept the floors and shook out the rugs. Now they owned a second home.

Throughout the decades, on the north shore, ownership of the original twelve cabins had mainly been kept in the families. Only five had changed hands over the years. To this day, the families continue every summer season to launch their boats,

Sailboat ride on the lake.
Photograph courtesy of Bill Zurnstein.

hike around the lake, and climb the cliffs to enjoy their mountain retreat. They swim in the lake, sail, fish, and hike, delightfully isolated from the rest of Pinecrest, just as in earlier days.

In the post-war years, further changes came to Pinecrest. The Pinecrest Stables were operated by the Sanguinetti brothers. Ray Sanguinetti was mostly in charge with brother Marion helping as needed. They packed tourists in to Emigrant Basin, but most of their income came from hour-long rides, which were popular with the private organizations. In 1952, Reno Sardella took over the operation of the pack station and stables.

The Free Library was organized in 1948 by Arlene Reveal, wife of the local Forest Ranger Jack Reveal. The little library was located in the lobby of Karl's Place and had a collection of several hundred books. The shelving was built by volunteers and staffed by ladies who took turns at the librarian's desk. During the winter months, snowbound residents frequented the library for reading material and social interaction.

After Karl's Place burned in the winter of 1949, firemen retrieved the books. They were moved to the lobby at Pinecrest Lodge. In 1952, the library moved to the firehouse.

Pinecrest changed when the Forest Service announced to many cabin owners that they had to tear down their cabins at their own expense because the land was needed for a public beach and campground. The new Forest Service philosophy was that the forest should be accessible to all people. This became quite a public controversy.

Shockwaves tore through the community of cabin owners. They had thought the Forest Service agreements were carved in stone. This takeover made them feel insecure about their cabin ownership. Many wanted nothing to do with having their cabin on leased Forest Service land.

Congressman Harold T. "Bizz" Johnson created enough noise in the 88th Congress to make the Forest Service feel obliged to drastically scale back their plans and offer at least a new lot for displaced cabin owners in the Crestview Tract.

Harry Hoefler had the answer. He owned a cattle ranch below Pinecrest and decided to develop

Bathing beauties on the shoreline.
Photograph courtesy of Bill Zurnstein.

it for private lots. He named it Mi-Wuk Village. He advertised private lots for sale in the scenic mountains. Displaced Pinecrest cabin owners fled the Forest Service land for the secure private ownership of a lot at Mi-Wuk Village.

In 1954, the Meadowview Campground at Pinecrest was improved with oiled roads, parking spurs and regulation barriers, and new picnic tables. This campground was generally used by short-term campers, many of whom were introduced to the beauty of the area. Many were able to become cabin owners. To date, Pinecrest has hundreds of cabins.

Pinecrest cabin owners continue to enjoy a community of people who love the mountains and come for the summer to enjoy the lake and the weather. Today, Pinecrest has a strong Permittees Association. The association represents the homeowners, and provides a water and sewer system, a volunteer fire station, and snow removal.

Over the years, Pinecrest has grown in popularity and remains a jewel of Sonora Pass.

SOURCES

Conners, Pamela. "Historical Overview of Recreational Residences on the Stanislaus National Forest," Report. *Historian,* Apr. 1993.

Fisher, Carl T. *Pinecrest Past and Present.* 1986. Unpublished manuscript.

Haack, Alan. Personal interview, 10 Jul. 2018.

Hart, Rich, and Deanne Hart. Personal interviews, 3 Jul. 2018.

Patterson, Kirk. Personal interview, 9 Nov. 2018.

PG&E Progress, Newsletter published by Pacific Gas and Electric Company, Vol. XV Nov. 1938

"Record Crowd at Pinecrest Fourth." *Union Democrat,* 9 Jul. 1937. Front page.

Reveal, Jack, District Ranger. "A History of the Summit District: Recollections of the Years 1948-1960." Loose pages in a historic collection, unpublished.

Union Democrat, 13 Sep. 1973.

Union Democrat, 23 Jul. 2010.

HOTEL, PINE CREST, LAKE STRAWBERRY, TUOLUMNE CO., CAL.

Shoreline of Pinecrest Hotel
Cate Culver postcard collection.

CHAPTER 13

Leland Meadows

A short distance above Pinecrest, below Cow Creek, a small road winds three miles to Leland Meadows. In the early days, this small meadow was thought to be one of the prettiest in the mountains. Its story begins with Benjamin Shaw, who lived above Phoenix Lake and brought his dairy stock to the mountains, summering at what is now Leland Meadows. The land was not surveyed at the time, and he owned it by "right of use." He built a log cabin and used the land for fifteen years. Shaw milked fifty-four cows, and he and his wife Louisa made 1,400 pounds of butter one summer. They stored the butter in oak casks called firkins. Each firkin held eleven gallons of butter. In the fall they sold the butter to buy necessities. One year the Strawberry Hotel bought 300 pounds.

During this period, large herds of sheep were driven through the area. Frustrated with the influx of "hoofed locusts," as John Muir called them, Benjamin Shaw sold out to G.A. Leland, Jack O'Neil, John Greenley, and a man named Bohler. Leland was issued a patent on the land on April 24, 1900. Later in 1927, Leland went into partnership with his neighbor Jack O'Neil.

Gustavus Adolphus Leland was a baker in Jamestown, where he lived with his children and wife Frances. At some point his son John took over the cattle business.

By the late 1950s, new interest was shown in the meadow, but this time cattle was not what they had in mind. Raymond and Earl Voorhees, who owned a cabin on Leland Creek, operated the La Follette Dairy in Oakdale, where they sold milk and ice cream. The two brothers were exploring up the creek and came upon a beautiful meadow with an

Benjamin G. Shaw in 1854.
Photograph courtesy of the Tuolumne County Historical Society and Museum.

old barn and cabin. Inside the barn were yellowed newspapers from the 1870s and 1880s stuffed in the wall for insulation. After the discovery of the nearby meadow, the brothers spoke of nothing else. What if they could buy that land and build condos to rent or buy? They could escape the grind of the dairy business and could live full time in the mountains.

After some research, they found that the forty acres that contained the meadow was for sale. G.A. Leland had homesteaded the property in 1896 and partnered with Jack O'Neil in 1927. The Voorhees brothers purchased the forty acres from Ike O'Neil. The planning commission gave them the go ahead in 1964 to build by the meadow. After selling off the dairy, they built a one and a half-mile road into the meadow and named it Leland Meadows after the pioneer. The road was given to Tuolumne County, so the county would take over its maintenance.

The brothers, serious about their investment, got their contractor's licenses. They first made plans to move their families to the area and build homes for themselves. Each brother built a house at the edge of the meadow, and by 1966, the families had taken up residences. The children attended the Pinecrest School.

They bulldozed the soggy meadow, making it deeper. Soon it filled in to become a fine lake, and the brothers planted trout. The lake added beauty to the land.

The Voorhees decided to start with thirty-two townhouses, two to six units per building. The townhouses were built on a hillside overlooking the meadow below. To preserve the natural beauty of the area, utilities were put underground. To quickly start a business, they brought in trailers and set up a "snow play" area and rented out skis and sleds. Their wives helped with the rentals on the weekends. When nearby Bumblebee Resort went bankrupt in 1976, they moved a few of the buildings to their resort.

In 1968, Raymond's wife, Evelyn, opened a beauty shop at Pinecrest Lodge. Earl's wife, Alice, became a teacher's aide at Pinecrest School, and they became members of the Pinecrest community.

Eventually, Leland Meadows consisted of an outdoor heated swimming pool, lighted tennis courts, a sauna, and a bathhouse.

The one-time cattle range with a lush meadow where milk cows produced great quantities of milk is long past. In modern times, there is a small lake and a subdivision of condominiums.

G.A. Leland and wife Frances at their home in Jamestown.
Photograph courtesy of the Tuolumne County Historical Society and Museum.

SOURCES

"Interview with Louisa Jane Foster Shaw." *Union Democrat*, 28 Nov. 1925. Front page.

Voorhees, John Earl. Obituary. *Union Democrat*, 23 Jul. 2007.

Voorhees, Raymond. Personal interview, 16 Aug. 2016.

CHAPTER 14

The Dardanelle Summer Home Tracts
and the People Who Built Cabins

People in the past have often fantasized about the pleasures of having a little cabin in the mountains, a retreat from the bustle of the city or the chores of the farm. But the mountain land was owned by the government. After requests from the public, in 1919, the Forest Service said yes, they would provide a space for you to build a cabin in the forest. People came and built simple dwellings that came to be prized for generations. On July 26, 1919, the *Union Democrat* in Sonora printed an invitation in an article with the headline, "AN IDEAL HOME IN THE MOUNTAINS." Then, it read, "The U.S. government offers ideal sites for summer homes in the national forest. The people are invited to select some congenial spot in the forests and make it their 'ideal vacation land.' A few people in Tuolumne County have accepted the government's offer and above Strawberry have built homes in the summer time for rest and recreation. There is room for hundreds more, there being many ideal spots along and adjacent to the Sonora-Mono Road."

Emil Coffee's cabin in 1925 at Brightman Flat, with young neighbor Francis Cottle.
Photograph courtesy of the Francis Cottle family.

A handful of people started building cabins without consulting the Forest Service. They were not discouraged that snow prevented access to the road six months of the year. Due to concerns about water and sanitation, the Forest Service took action. It was decided that if campers had their own cabins, they would become stewards of the land and come to the aid of the Forest Service firefighters. Between 1916 and 1927, summer home tracts were laid out. Forest officials indicated that summer homes were to be well-maintained and must harmonize with their environment. It was generally understood that they were to be rustic and simple.

The lease for a lot from the Forest Service cost $5.00 annually and required renewal each year. Permits were issued to anyone wishing to build and own a cabin, and were good for ninety-nine years. By 1949, the Forest Service began issuing twenty-year leases, and the fees for the lease increased through the years.

In 1918, Brightman Flat Summer Home Tract was surveyed by Ranger Joseph E. Elliot. Brightman Flat was a very large area bordered by the Stanislaus River on one side, and a mountain slope on the other, ideal for summer cabin sites. Brightman Creek flowed through the sandy flat draining into the river, and multiple springs were located at the base of the mountain. The lots were grouped together, leaving open undeveloped space.

Sixty-two one-acre lots with plentiful water and flat land were laid out. Ranger Elliot only surveyed the front two corners. Later the cabin owners placed the back two corners wherever they pleased, enlarging their lots. Campers at Brightman Flat could now build their summer home on their favorite campsite.

Typically, a new permittee at Brightman Flat would bring a wagon load of lumber, often salvaged from torn down buildings or taken from the ruins of the San Francisco earthquake. With just this wagonload, a small primitive cabin was built. The carpentry usually was what the owner could manage with help from relatives. The cabin was mainly used for storage. The families erected "tent cabins" for sleeping quarters.

Chrittendon Hampton, a Sonora attorney and

Chrittenden Hampton, a well-known Sonora civic leader, was one of the first to build on Brightman Flat. He finished his cabin July 4, 1921, and of course, a big celebration followed.
Photograph courtesy of Janet Krogh (Cornell).

Crittenden Hampton with his wife and friends at their Brightman Flat cabin site. Here they slept in the tent, and cooked and stored supplies in the little cabin.
Photograph courtesy of Janet Krogh (Cornell).

civic leader, finished his cabin on July 4, 1921. The cabin was small, held cooking supplies, and folding tables and chairs. The family slept outside in canvas tents.

Brightman Flat cabin owner Judy Duncan recalls, "My grandfather Hans Eriksen came to America from Norway. He would come summers with the family and camp at Brightman Flat. In 1921, with the help of relatives and the Cottle brothers next door, Hans built the family cabin. It had no windows, just shutters. Drinking water came from a spring up on the mountainside. There was a cooler built on a wood frame covered with burlap, which was placed on slats over the nearby creek that kept their food cold. A crock set in the creek held butter and milk. The Eriksens would pitch their canvas tents behind the little cabin and that is where they slept. The one-room cabin was used to store the camping equipment so they would not have to transport it at the end of the season. In front of

The Cottle cabin in about 1938. Sign above the door reads "Whispering Trees."
Photograph courtesy of the Francis Cottle family.

The Arnold children playing with broomsticks. Little Patsy, Arthur, Darlene, and Timmy Arnold in 1941.
Photograph courtesy of Art Bjorge.

The Bledsoes were from Missouri, and in 1868, homesteaded in the valley, where they raised grain and livestock. They built this cabin in the early 1920s.
Photograph courtesy of Jeanette Barnett.

the cabin by the road was a communal campfire, a gathering place in the evenings for the Norwegians."

Judy reminisces, "Parents would set up beside the creek which ran in front of the cabins, to watch the children play in the water, as the nearby river was too dangerous for the little ones. My grandfather Hans loved children and would carefully select a chip of wood and carve little boats for the neighbor children. They delighted in floating them down the little creek. This simple entertainment would last for hours as the older adults were content to keep a watchful eye, visit, and just enjoy the mountain air."

Cabin owner Kandis Roen Schmidt remembers, "In the early 1930s, Albert Sigvert Roen was visiting his friend Lee Prouty at his Dardanelle cabin.

Impressed by the beauty of the mountains, he gave some thought to having a cabin, too. Albert attended a game of pinochle at the resort and he asked a local ranger at the game how he could get a lot for a cabin. The head ranger said, 'Meet me at 10 a.m. tomorrow morning.' The next morning Albert followed the ranger up the hill above the Flat. The ranger asked, 'How many lots do you want?' Surprised by this offer, Albert said five, thinking of his Norwegian relatives."

The Norwegians primarily were grain farmers from the Central Valley who had settled in Waterford, Oakdale, Valley Home, and Eugene. The Dardanelle area reminded them of home in Norway. In late July, after harvesting their oat, wheat, and barley crops, they frequently came and camped for a month. Eight Norwegian families built cabins at Brightman Flat. They all knew each other and were often 'shirttail' relatives. After breakfast, when the men were gone, the women would gather mid-morning, taking turns making pastry and visiting at each other's cabins. They would speak Norwegian and watch the young children over coffee and treats. In the evenings, they would gather for potlucks followed by card games. Pedro and Whist were favorites.

Of course, not all of the cabins at Brightman Flat were owned by farmers or Norwegians. Six Italian families, many from the Bay Area, built cabins. They would rotate from cabin to cabin to play cards in the evenings while the children excitedly roasted marshmallows over the campfire. The old folks spoke of the past in Italian and shared homemade wine.

Ed Burgson stands in front his cabin at Bone Springs in 1922. The cabin was built by his father Frank on the Old Sonora-Mono Road near the bridge that crossed the Middle Fork of the Stanislaus River. *Photograph courtesy of Chris Robinson.*

Other cabin owners built their cabins just for deer hunting season. In the fall, they would arrive with a large group to hunt for deer in the high mountains. It was not a family cabin, but built ruggedly just for the men. The cabin owners at Bone Springs Summer Home Tracts were a different sort. The tract was small, just nine cabins at the base of a mountain. A few were built along Sonora-Mono Road. There were numerous springs and no special view, no river frontage, just an area tucked into the forest. The Stanislaus River was a short walk away, as was Eagle Creek. Not one was Norwegian or a farmer. Their cabins were well-built and not used just for storage.

In 1922, Frank Burgson, who operated a restaurant in Sonora, built his cabin alongside the road. He kept horses in a corral in a nearby meadow. After he retired from owning the restaurant, he cooked at the Dardanelle Resort. His son Ed and his friends used the cabin as a headquarters to hunt and fish.

Mitchell Terzich, the owner of the Terzich Soda Works in Sonora, built a little cabin in 1916 at Brightman Flat. But water was a problem at this location, so he relocated to Bone Springs alongside the Sonora-Mono Wagon Road. Terzich humorously

The original Mitchell Terzich cabin.
Pat Perry photographer. Photograph courtesy of the Tuolumne County Historical Society and Museum.

named the spring based on a male joke. Enough said. In 1922 he built a larger cabin, and by 1925 he had built an even larger third cabin. His son Irving started coming to the cabin at age ten in 1926. He became an expert fly fisherman and returned many

The Bromley women relaxing on the cabin porch in 1928. Fannie Bromley on the left, Aunt Marion Bromley, center, and Fannie's daughter Mae on the right. (She married Edwin McMahon). *Photograph from the Mae (Bromley) McMahon collection.*

summers with his wife June and their family. They would stay most of the summer, well into their eighties. Irving, a local historian, had a fine memory and was well-known in the area.

Innis Bromley, a well-respected Sonora doctor, also desired a cabin in the area. The Bromley cabin was built in about 1917. The carpenter was a Mr. Burns who built the cabin and all the furniture. The interior contained a master bedroom, kitchen, washroom, a narrow pantry, and inside stairs leading to upstairs bedrooms. A screened sleeping area was added to the south side. The doctor devised an electrical system on the west side of the cabin. Designed with glass batteries, one could see the acid inside. The battery system produced hot water that

The Frank Ralph cabin about 1940.
Photograph courtesy of the Bashford York family.

flowed through copper pipe into the cabin.

The original one-room cabin belonging to Frank J. Ralph sat close to the edge of a granite cliff. Frank was a longtime supervisor for Tuolumne County, serving from 1921 to 1941. During his service, he was chairman of the county hospital, courthouse, memorial hall, county jail, and Courthouse Square committees. Ralph grew apples near Tuolumne City, a big business at the time.

In 1944, Bashford York purchased the Ralph cabin and built a new one. "Bash," a well-known historian in Tuolumne County, was active in the Historical Society and was writing a history of Sonora Pass. In 1994, while traveling on the Patterson Grade, she lost control of her car, plunged over the cliffs, and perished in the terrible crash.

"Swiss" Foletti, a stonemason who owned a saloon in Sonora, often came up with his family to the Dardanelle area. He selected a lot in the Bone Springs Summer Home Tract. He built his cabin in 1926 with whatever scrap lumber he could find, much of it salvaged from remodeling jobs where there was a window or door left behind. A spring above the cabin provided ample water. Set on the side of a hill, the little cabin had a nice view of the Dardanelles rock formation. His wife Angie was a well-respected business woman who owned a millinery shop on Washington Street in Sonora. Angie tutored new Italian immigrants and made space at the back of her store for them to study English.

Their daughter, Alice Hardin, recalls that they came for the entire summer in the early days. For supplies, they brought 100 lbs. of flour, 5 lbs. of syrup, and live chickens. They planted an Italian herb garden in a patch of sun beside the cabin. Out back, "Swiss" built an earthen oven where every week Angie baked fourteen loaves of French bread.

William Barron, a Soulsbyville blacksmith, and farmer, built a primitive cabin among the huge cedars in the early 1920s. He located a wet area above Eagle Creek and developed a spring.

Watercolor of Fleishhacker cabin by Cate Caldwell Culver, 2009.

William Barron on the cabin porch in mid-1930s.
Barron family photograph collection, courtesy Bill Remick.

The Barron and Remick women relaxing in the shade at the cabin. At left, Pat Remick in rocking chair, little brother Bill standing by Selina, his grandmother's sister, Lottie Barron, Loyda Remick in pants, and Clara Remick, circa 1943.
Barron family photograph collection, courtesy Bill Remick.

This cabin, covered with sugar pine shingles, had an open kitchen and living room, with an enclosed screened-in sleeping porch. The cabin had no indoor plumbing except cold water piped to the kitchen. William Barron and his wife Lottie both loved the mountains and came often.

Mortimer Fleishhacker, a philanthropist and prominent San Francisco banking and paper tycoon, built his two-story cabin at Bone Springs in 1934. It was the talk of Dardanelle, such a luxurious cabin built from redwood by professional carpenters who spared no expense. Builders blasted out granite boulders for the building site. The front porch of the cabin had a marvelous view of the Dardanelle Cone, a local landmark. Situated next to Eagle Creek, it sat in a prime location. Cabins were restricted

The caretaker's cabin. Owned by Edson and Ruth Caldwell, parents of the author. Photograph taken in 1947.
Photograph courtesy of Cate Caldwell Culver.

Kitchen of the caretaker's cabin, owned by the Caldwells, with the wood burning cook stove, old teakettles, and antique chair.
Cate Caldwell Culver photograph collection.

Edson Caldwell on the cabin terrace with daughter Cathy (Cate Culver) in 1950 and her cat Puskit, that ran free.
Cate Caldwell Culver photograph collection.

Sheriff Dambacher's cabin at Bone Springs.
Photograph by Cate Culver 2013.

from being built so close to the creek, but with his influence, this one was allowed. Fleishhacker built a small cabin nearby to house a caretaker or extra guests. He also put in a water system with a redwood holding tank from the Barron Spring, with pipes to the neighboring William Barron cabin. Unfortunately, his wife became ill, and after two years, he sold it all.

The small Fleishhacker caretaker's cabin, constructed in 1934, was built of redwood and included a large living room, a small kitchen with a wood burning cook stove that had a built-in hot water tank, and a small bathroom. Edson Caldwell, a college professor at Sacramento State University, and his wife Ruth, purchased the cabin in 1944 for $700, a year before the author was born. They both loved to fish and hunt. On a personal note, the author still enjoys her hot water heated up in that wood stove as she cooks breakfast on its cooktop, with hot water at the ready for the rest of the day.

The Dambacher cabin was built in 1923 by John Henry "Jack" Dambacher. Jack was elected Sheriff of Tuolumne County in 1922, and was re-elected five times. In 1946 he retired from public office.

Five other summer home tracts were carved out in the area of the Dardanelles, a prominent rock formation silhouetted on the mountain above the Middle Fork of the Stanislaus River. All the tracts were fed by local springs and had access roads.

The Twin Buttes Tract was laid out in 1925, and had eight cabins. It was located near the Bone Springs tract. Just a few cabins had views of the river.

The Buena Vista Tract, surveyed in 1920, consisted of just two cabins situated on cliffs overlooking the Stanislaus River.

The Cedar Grove Tract, laid out in 1922, had only four cabins located on the mountainside above the highway beyond the Stanislaus River bridge.

Pearl Coffee's cabin at right. Behind it is the Francis Cottle cabin. Hampton barn at left. Brightman Flat.
Photograph courtesy of Patty Charles.

The Riverside Tract with its five cabins was laid out in 1922. On the uphill side of the road, it overlooked the river from some height. The pine and cedar trees blocked any expansive view.

The Wagner Tract, named after a cattleman, was situated off the Clarks Fork Road above the Middle Fork of the Stanislaus River. The tract was laid out in 1931 and included seventeen cabins built on a flat, but only a few had a view of the river some distance below.

Many of these cabins in the tracts are still in use.

By the end of the 1920s, the Forest Service was starting to realize the demand for recreational cabins was far greater than it had expected. There were no guides for cabin builders and the architecture left much to be desired. After a few hard winters, many looked like rundown shacks and were an eyesore on the landscape. By 1927 the Forest Service provided guidelines with a set of standards, and required approval of rough plans for all cabins

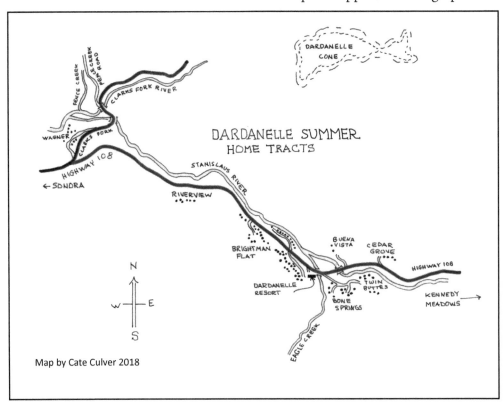

Map by Cate Culver 2018

Pearl Coffee's cabin in the foreground. Hans and Clara Eriksen's cabin in the background (currently owned by Judy Duncan). Behind the cabin, Glen Duncan can be seen shaving. Brightman Flat.
Photograph courtesy of Patty Charles.

prior to construction. All cabins were to be painted or stained, and no "loud' colors permitted. All buildings were to be permanent in nature and of a neat appearance. Permit holders were required to remodel their cabins to current standards.

By 1940, the last lot was available at Brightman Flat. Attilio Bacigalupi obtained a permit and built his cabin. His family was from San Francisco, and it took eight hours to travel to the cabin. When they came, the family stayed all summer.

The era of building one's primitive cabin in the forest had come to an end. As the years passed, many owners upgraded by adding more rooms, a larger kitchen, and indoor plumbing. The old cast iron wood burning cook stove was replaced by a propane stove, and a generator was added for electricity. However, some have remained exactly the same with few improvements. Many cabin owners have passed their permit to own a cabin down through the family generations or to a family friend. Rarely do cabins come up for sale.

SOURCES

"Camp Sanitation to be Good in Mountains." *Union Democrat*, 23 Jul. 1921. Front page.

Coffill, Bill. Personal interview, 8 Jul. 2017.

Conners, Pamela. "Stanislaus National Forest: Recreational Residence Overview." 1993 Report.

Conners, Pamela A. and Linda Marie Lux. "A Kingdom For A Song." *Summer Homes in the National Forests.*

Cornell, Janet. Personal interview, 2014.

Duncan, Judy. Personal interview, 2014.

Hamilton, Jack. Personal interview, 15 Jun. 2017.

Hardin, Alice. Personal interview, 2014.

"New Rules for Automobile Camps." *Union Democrat*, 1 Jan. 1921. P. 4.

"Observations in the Mountains." *Union Democrat*. 18 Sep. 1920. Front page.

Poag, Lorraine. Personal interview, 2014.

Schmidt, Candis Roen. Personal interview, 2015.

Terzich, Irving. Personal interview, 2014.

Tuolumne County Historical Society Quarterly publication, *CHISPA*, Vol. 40, No. 4 Apr.-Jun. 2001.

Union Democrat, Personal and Brief Items of Interest. 26 Jul. 1919. p. 4.

AUTHOR'S NOTE:

As lifestyles have changed, many of the cabins sit empty and are infrequently used. Usually the older generation is in residence and the younger folks locate elsewhere. As I notice a cabin sitting idle all summer, I wonder, "What could be more important than visiting your mountain cabin?"

Historic Recreation Residence Tracts
Sonora-Mona Road Recreation Area

Tract	Tract Survey Date
Pinecrest	
Lower Strawberry Lake	1916
Lower Strawberry Lake Addition	1926 (c.)
North Shore	Unknown (past 1926; pre 1938)
Brightman Flat	1918
Fern Dale	1920 (consolidated with Brightman Flat)
Buena Vista	1920 (consolidated)
Bone Springs	1921
Bumble Bee	1921
Deadman	1921
Douglas, West	1921 (compass survey)
Baker's Station	1922
Cascade Creek	1922
Cedar Grove	1922
Cow Creek	1922
Mill Creek	1922
Riverside	1922
Leland Meadow	1923
Niagara	1923
Douglas, East	1925
Twin Buttes	1925 (resurveyed)
Perryman	1927
Wagner	1931 (compass survey)
Hells Half Acre	Unknown (pre 1945)
Chinchilla	1940

CHAPTER 15

J.D. Bucknam
and the Dardanelle Resort

When he was a boy, J.D. Bucknam camped at Brightman Flat. When he returned as a man, he built the Dardanelle Resort. Camp Dardanelle celebrated its grand opening on July 1, 1923 at Brightman Flat. At that time, the camp itself was a dirt-floored cabin with living quarters in the back of a small store. However, J.D. Bucknam had big plans to build a large resort. At 48, he saw the potential in the area and set to work establishing his place among other enterprises along the Sonora-Mono Road corridor.

Camp Dardanelle, built in 1922, just a back room for living quarters and a lean-to added for a store.
Photograph courtesy of the Tuolumne County Historical Society and Museum. (Fred Leighton collection).

John Duane Bucknam was born August 5, 1875 at Curtis Creek near Soulsbyville. His father Ezra Taylor Bucknam repaired farm equipment and worked as a wheelwright and a hoist operator at the Black Oak Mine. He left the area to study law in Oakland and later became a Superior Court Judge in Tulare, California. His mother, Isabelle Adeline Daly Bucknam was thirty-nine when she had John, her last child. John had four sisters and a brother Daly, eight years older. John adored his brother, and they remained close throughout their lives.

Brothers Samuel "Daly" Bucknam, and younger brother John D. Bucknam, standing, in 1885.
Photograph courtesy of Kathlene Baker Clark.

In the summers, the entire Bucknam family would travel from Soulsbyville to the mountains to camp. They especially liked to camp beside the river at Brightman Flat to fish and enjoy the outdoors. J.D. Bucknam, a man with experience as a logger, miner, plumber, and carpenter, discussed with his brother Daly the wisdom of building a resort at Brightman Flat. With Daly's encouragement, J.D. obtained a permit from the Forest Service in 1922 to build a modest summer resort. Bucknam named it Camp Dardanelle after the volcanic rock formations known as Dardanelles Cone, or simply the

Dardanelles. J.D. affectionately named the mountain across from the resort "Mount Delia" after his wife, Cordelia.

The name Dardanelle appears on George H. Goddard's 1853 "Map of Sonora Pass." It was undoubtedly named for its resemblance to the rock formations along The Dardanelles, the strait between the Aegean Sea and the Sea of Marmara separating Asia and European Turkey, known as the Hellespont in ancient times. The Bucknams had heard that the Dardanelle rock formations were named by a party of Russian explorers from Fort Ross passing through the area in the early 1800s.

John D. Bucknam, at twenty-two, married Cordelia "Delia" Margaret Hill on July 4, 1898, in Sonora. She was just a year younger. They had five children, Mildred Irene (Diehl), Adeline Belle (Allen), John William, George Daly, and Mary Ruth (Eproson, Woodbury).

When J.D. consulted with Delia about a hotel venture in the mountains, she was all for it. For two years, when they lived in San Diego, J. D. worked as plumber at the posh Del Coronado Hotel. He knew how a nice hotel should look and how it should be run. Delia had managed the three-story Hotel Salem in San Diego, so she had her own elegant taste and experience in hotel management. The two of them were excited and knew they could create a splendid hotel high in the mountains.

In 1919, John and Delia began to make plans for building a resort. They leased five acres from the Forest Service in 1921 and started building a small structure. By 1923, Camp Dardanelle was open for business, with tent cabins fully equipped for housekeeping.

J.D. had the help of his brother-in-law Orin Ralph. At Cow Creek, Orin operated a business making sugar pine shakes, which could be used for roofing as well as siding. Bucknam obtained lumber from a local mill and hauled supplies on a truck up to the building site.

Work began on the resort in the summer of 1923. J.D.'s two older boys, John W., age twenty, and George D., age sixteen, pitched in to help. With his brother Daly and neighbor James Calder, who was building his own cabin in the adjacent Brightman

Sonora-Mono Wagon Road winds through Brightman Flat.
Photograph courtesy of the Jo Spicer Danicourt collection.

To The Public

Announcing the Opening on July 1st, 1923, of

Camp Dardanelle

At Brightman's Flat

Tuolumne County's Favorite Camp Site, situated on the Sonora-Mono State Highway Fifty-five miles East of Sonora

Tent Cottages Fully Equipped for House-keeping
Store, Oil and Gasoline Station
Truck Hauling of all kinds

For Reservations, Rates, etc., address—

J. D. BUCKNAM, Manager
Camp Dardanelle   Sonora, California

Union Democrat Print, Sonora, Cal.

Poster courtesy of Marty Kellogg.

Flat Summer Home Tract, the resort took shape.

An experienced plumber, J.D. developed a spring at the base of a mountain behind the resort. He ran a pipe from the spring to the building. He engineered a plumbing system that furnished abundant, chilled, fresh spring water.

When the floor was finished, a celebration was called for, as the building had now become a reality.

The Bucknams decided to hold a dance and invited campers and cabin owners to attend. They spread some bar soap on the dance floor to make it smooth and slick. Everyone danced and had a great time. Then it rained, and the floor became a sea of suds!

It took three years to build the resort. When it opened in 1926, it was the most lavish resort on the pass. Delia was an accomplished cook and made sure she had a large kitchen with a huge wood burning cook stove. She hired cooks but always supervised the kitchen. She alone baked the pies, and they were her specialty. The dining room was long and all the tables set with white linens and fresh flowers plucked from Delia's flower garden. Hot meals were served three times a day. Everyone was alerted that a meal was ready by the ringing of a triangle dinner bell. The crisp ring could be heard clearly for miles around.

At the end of the dining room stood a large stone fireplace. Above the fireplace hung a large oil painting of the Dardanelle rock formation. Toward the back room sat their baby grand piano. In later years, the Bucknams learned that their instrument was one of the first three pianos to come

The fall of 1925 with the resort under construction, no windows or doors installed. Two deer hunters' bucks hang in the doorway. *Photograph courtesy of Judy Duncan.*

to California. It was brought to Monterey from Baltimore in 1843. Today, it is displayed in the Murphys Oldtimers Museum.

The store adjoining the dining room was mostly stocked with canned goods. At the back of the building off the kitchen was a bedroom and public restrooms. Outside the back kitchen door was the cold storage building, designed with thick walls to keep the interior cold. In the spring when the resort first opened, it was necessary to drive the truck to higher elevations and load it up with snow. It was brought back and packed tightly into the ice box.

The restaurant in 1926 with a grand piano (now on display at the Murphys Museum in Murphys, Calaveras County), a wind-up phonograph and fresh flowers from Cordelia's flower garden, crisp white tablecloths, and napkins. The painting over the fireplace of the Dardanelles was by local artist, Levi Hough. Note musicians playing in the background. *Photograph courtesy of the Tuolumne County Historical Society and Museum.*

The snow did melt throughout the summer, but it kept the milk and fresh produce reasonably cold.

By June 6, 1924, John D. Bucknam was listed as the Dardanelle Postmaster. The post office was added to the end of the store. Cabin owners and campers could call for their mail over a counter inside the store. Later, post office boxes were installed. Daily newspapers were available too.

A gas station sat adjacent to the end of the resort. Two gas pumps were available and later an oil service was added.

Cars at the filling station.
Photograph courtesy of Dardanelle Resort. (Donated by Sally Wright Bromley).

The rentals needed a lot of fresh linens. They were all washed by hand and hung to dry on a web of clotheslines. On washdays, the white sheets and towels dried quickly, billowing in the mountain zephyrs. The ironing of the sheets was done using flat irons heated on the wood burning range. It was a hot, never-ending job of ironing, folding, and stacking sheets and pillowcases.

In the beginning, the Bucknams had three or four tent cabins for rent. As business kept growing, the need for more overnight accommodations became apparent. With help from his sons and occasional help from his brother Daly, J.D. continued to expand the resort. In 1935, he constructed a six-bedroom annex located in the back by a little spring. The annex burned sometime after the Bucknams sold the resort in 1944. During the time he owned the resort, J.D. was a prolific builder and had constructed fourteen rental cabins.

The resort was built during Prohibition. Knowing that his guests might want to indulge in a libation, J.D. built a hidden basement with stairs leading down under the back porch. Recently revealed during repairs to the porch in 2017, it

J.D. and wife Delia pose in front of their new water fountain. Original Camp Dardanelle building at the right in the background.
Photograph courtesy of Jerry and Ruth Howard.

Samuel Daly Bucknam (left)
Dardanelles, Tuolomne County

In 1932, J.D. Bucknam purchased this Montgomery Ward gasoline powered saw, better known as the "iron horse." It got its name because it was so heavy it practically took a horse to move it even though it had a wheel in the back. This saw served J.D. and Daly for many years in cutting firewood for the lodge. Samuel "Daly" Bucknam is at left, by the gas powered four-in-one single stroke crosscut saw to cut rounds of cedar firewood. Daly and his friends are at the ready with their axes to split the rounds. Daly cut close to 60 cords of wood each year with the "iron horse," plenty of firewood for the kitchen range, massive lodge fireplace, and rental cabins.
Photograph courtesy of Kathlene Baker Clark.

measures six foot high, twenty feet across, and thirty feet long. Lined with stone, it is tall enough to walk around upright. Here he kept the forbidden inventory and served it with discretion. During this time, ladies and gentlemen came to Dardanelle to "let their hair down" away from the authorities and indulge in cocktails in the comfort of the secluded resort.

When Prohibition ended in 1939, J.D. realized that now he could build a saloon. Delia protested, but J.D. knew it could be a money-maker. He built it as a separate building out toward the front of the resort and off to the side a bit. It had a bar, dance floor, billiard table, and juke box. The saloon was all he had hoped for, and never was the cause of any problems.

This building, shown in 1927, was for housing the employees. Ultimately, it burned down and was not replaced.
Photograph courtesy of Tuolumne County Historical Society and Museum.

As the cabins were being built at Brightman Flat during the 1920s, the Bucknams became part of the cabin-owners community. On weekends, the Bucknams hosted card parties in the long dining room with as many as sixteen tables of people

Dardanelle Resort in June 1930.
Photograph courtesy of the Tuolumne County Historical Society and Museum. (Francis Nelson collection).

The hidden basement in 2018. *Photographer Cate Culver.*

playing whist. Prizes were offered and frequently there were hand-crocheted doilies made by Cordelia, or boxes of Hershey bars. On Saturday nights, the dining room was cleared and used as a dance floor. Their young son George played the piano and other musicians would join in to play dance music. By the mid-1930s, they offered skits, live music, wiener roasts and sing-a-longs around the campfire. Mr. Bucknam would often go into the store and come out with Hershey bars for the children. He was skilled at playing horseshoes and would advertise horseshoe tournaments at the resort.

Fourth of July was a time of great celebration. The Bucknams decorated each porch post with an American flag. Patriotic events were planned and people would gather for a day of food and entertainment. Many came to watch the highlight of the day, the popular 'suitcase race'. Two men were each given a suitcase full of women's clothing. Off they ran to a marker where they unpacked their suitcase and had to put on a piece of clothing. Then they packed up and ran to the other end to don another piece of feminine clothing. The one who had all the clothes on first was the winner. Of course, there was a lot of laughter when they put on a piece backwards or met with confusion trying to understand where a garment went.

Sarah Bucknam, granddaughter of J.D. and Cordelia, remembers them well. "He was always called J.D., even by his children. J.D. Bucknam was a handsome man and his hair was kind of sandy, not grey. He was tall and straight and proclaimed that there was still a lot of gold left in the Sierras."

Sarah recalls the time that her grandmother Cordelia rescued two little fawns and brought them into the main lodge to keep them warm. "I think she was trying to hide them from my grandfather. He was a great hunter. The deer eventually were hidden upstairs. From downstairs you could hear the deer running around the upstairs bedrooms jumping from beds to the floor, sounding like a herd of elephants! Many a time my mom and Aunt Adeline had a good laugh recalling the fawns romping upstairs."

Behind the resort and towards Eagle Creek, Bucknam built stables and offered horses for rent. Outdoorsmen could rent horses to take the trail up into the Eagle Meadow area to hunt, or tourists could rent a horse for day rides with their children. The youngest Bucknam son George ran the stables. He was a guide for the fishermen, packing them into the backcountry lakes. He was also kept busy guiding hunters up the mountain during deer hunting season. George would ride over to Nevada to capture some of the wild horses and bring them back. He would break them for riding and they became a part of the stable stock.

In 2013, local cabin owner Glen Duncan shared an incident that happened at the Dardanelle

Entrance to the Dardanelle resort in the 1920s. A Red Crown gasoline sign on the left, in the distance the Dardanelle cone landmark. *Photograph courtesy of Kathlene Baker Clark.*

The McCune sisters, Jeanette and Wilma, in 1948. *Photograph courtesy of Jeanette McCune Barnette.*

Picnic tables to the side of the resort. *Photograph courtesy of Mildred Montgomery. (Wade Coffill collection).*

Delia's Shasta daisy flower garden at the back of the resort. *Photograph courtesy of the Tuolumne County Historical Society and Museum. (Francis Nelson collection).*

stables: "In 1945 at the end of WWII, many of the GIs returned to an Army camp called Stoneman in Pittsburg, California. It was thought that the young black GIs might cause problems in the local white neighborhoods near the Army camp. Full of bravado and perhaps in need of some rest and relaxation to unwind, the Army decided to take them on a holiday to Dardanelle Resort for a week. About twenty or thirty came to enjoy the mountains. The resort offered horseback riding. The young men were to each get a horse but the cowboys were running out of enough horses for everyone. Soon there was only a mule left in the corral." He continues, "The GIs asked about the mule and the cowboys said it was way too high-spirited for them to ride. One cocky GI insisted that he could ride that mule!

"So, they all gathered around the corral to watch. Sure enough, the mule would have none of it and bucked him off. Soon they all lined up, each thinking that he could ride that mule and be the bravest of all and have bragging rights. One by one the mule bucked each one off and each young man lost a bit of pride."

Every fall, the Bucknams closed the resort at the end of deer season. It was a time for saying

Horse stables behind the resort.
Wade Coffill photograph album courtesy of Mildred Montgomery.

Ron Benedix and his sister Janet on a resort pony in 1945. Grandmother Adda Moser holding the reins.
Photograph courtesy of the Ron Benedix.

The Spicer sisters, Shirley at left, and Betty Jo riding at Brightman Flat in 1942. Their father, John Spicer, was the Forest Ranger at the Brightman Flat station.
Photograph courtesy of Jo Spicer Danicourt.

goodbyes and preparing the resort for a Sierra winter. This was a big job. It involved moving the horses to lower pastures, securing the stables and rental cabins, and draining the entire water system. Other chores included emptying out the goods in the store and saloon, as well as bringing in any outdoor furniture to store inside.

After closing, to unwind and give themselves a vacation, the Bucknams went over the pass to Fales' Hot Springs in Mono County. They stayed three weeks, enjoying the hospitality of Mr. Fales and his resort. Fales had tamed the natural hot springs that bubbled to the surface and created a very popular stop for travelers. There was an excellent restaurant at the springs, plus cabins for rent, and hot pools for a healthful soak in the natural waters. Fales, blessed with wit and humor, was himself one of the attractions.

By the end of 1943, J.D. Bucknam was 68 years old and ready to give up the grind of running a mountain resort. Earlier in the year, a cowboy from Stockton, Hobart McCulloch, came by and showed some interest in buying the resort. Hobart was able to come up with the cash by talking his sister Jane and his friend Floyd Sherfrey into becoming partners. On September 15, 1944, J.D. Bucknam sold the resort for $30,000 to McCulloch. The sale included the hotel, store, fourteen cabins, and all the personal property pertaining to the operation of the resort: pack train, stock of goods, and groceries. The Special Use Permit and the right to use the five acres of land in the Stanislaus National Forest were also transferred into Hobart's name.

With the help of his family, J.D. had started with a piece of flat ground by a river and from the ground up built it into a noted luxury mountain resort. He and Cordelia put twenty-two years of their lives into the business. Through the years, they made friends and had many repeat customers, a testament to their enduring passion to deliver high quality service.

After selling the resort, the Bucknams moved back to their home in Sonora. J.D. enjoyed studying history and spent considerable time traveling, but Cordelia's health was failing. It was

Fales Hot Springs in Mono County.
Photograph courtesy of the Tuolumne County Historical Society and Museum. (Fred Leighton collection).

Samuel Fales at his hot springs.
Cate Culver postcard collection.

discovered that she had advanced ovarian cancer. She wouldn't let the doctor tell the family because she did not want anyone to feel sorry for her. So she went through her own private misery until she died on May 5, in 1951, at 73. After Cordelia died, J.D. married a widow named Winnifred Lucille Taylor who lived in Murphys. After six years of marriage, Winnie died in 1957, and J.D. then made his home with his daughter Ruth Eproson in Sonora.

Two years later, while vacationing in Mexico, J.D. was stricken with a cerebral hemorrhage. He was rushed back to the Sonora hospital where he lived for only a few days and died April 4, 1959, at the age of 84.

Sign from the early 1940s.
Wade Coffill photograph album courtesy of Mildred Montgomery.

SOURCES

Appel, James. Personal interview, 2014.

Barnette, Jeanette (McCune). Personal interview, 2013.

Browning, Peter. *Place names of The Sierra Nevada From Abbot to Zumwalt.* Wilderness Press, 1986.

Bucknam, Sarah Nadean. (granddaughter of John D. Bucknam,) Telephone interview.

Clark, Kathlene Baker. "My Research on John Duane Bucknam." Two pages.

Conners, Pamela A. "Historical Overview of Recreational Residences on the Stanislaus National Forest," Apr. 1993.

Nelson, Francis. *The Douglas Station.* Tuolumne County Historical Society. *CHISPA* Quarterly publication Vol. 37, No. 2 Oct.-Dec. 1997.

Danicourt, Betty Jo Spicer. Personal interview, 2014.

Duncan, Glen. Personal interview, 2013.

Gibson, James H. *Plan for Development for the Sonora Pass Road Recreation Area*, Stanislaus National Forest. California. Feb. 1945.

Johnson, Lois Waldrip. "The Dardanelles: *1921-1944."* Dec. 1991 (granddaughter of the John D. Bucknams. 5 page manuscript.

Modesto Bee, Sep. 15, 1944.

"Mrs. J. Bucknam, of the Dardanelles, Dies in Sonora." *Union Democrat.* 10 May 1959, Page 4.

"Pioneer Resident John D. Bucknam Died Saturday." *Union Democrat.* 6 Apr. 1959. *The Pony Express,* Vol. XXVI, Aug. 1959. Tabloid monthly, history-oriented newsprint publication.

Terzich, Irving. Personal interview, 2014.

The Bucknams in 1938. Older brother Daly at left, and wife Cordelia and J.D. Photograph taken at Long Barn.
Photograph courtesy of Kathlene Baker Clark.

J.D. Bucknam stands proudly over a bear he shot in 1925.
Photograph courtesy of Jerry and Ruth Howard.

CHAPTER 16

The Coffills
and the Dardanelle Resort

In August 1947, as a result of a violent knife fight, Wade Coffill became the unexpected owner of the Dardanelle Resort. Three years earlier, a forty-year-old cowboy named Hobart F. McCulloch, purchased the resort from founder J.D. Bucknam. Here is the story of how Hobart lost the resort to Coffill.

McCulloch angrily cornered local forest ranger John Spicer alone at the resort stables and accused him of encouraging tourists to camp and rent cabins from his competitor, Kennedy Meadows. Spicer was enraged at the accusation and they were soon in a heated argument. McCulloch decided to settle the question with a knife fight. He quickly rushed to his bedroom and returned with two hunting knives. He threw the weapons to the ground between them and challenged Spicer to pick up a knife and fight like a man. Spicer refused, and McCullough charged at him, thrusting the big knife at his face. Spicer put his arm up to fend off the strikes from McCulloch as he lashed out and was immediately slashed across his wrist. Next, a kick in the face broke his jaw, and a slash from the knife blade badly cut his eye, which bloodied his face.

Aggravated that Spicer refused to fight, McCulloch forced the knife-point against the ranger's back and marched his victim to the resort lounge, where he tried again to provoke him to fight. Spicer, with blood streaming down his face, and by this time, had an audience of resort visitors, would still not cooperate. Shocked onlookers took the knife away from McCulloch and defused the situation.

The incident was brought to trial and well-known Oakdale attorney, Wade Coffill, defended the resort owner in court but lost the case. McCullough

could not pay Coffill for his legal fees, so, after owning the resort for only three years, he gave him the Dardanelle Resort as payment.

Wade Hampton Coffill had deep roots in the area. His mother, Olive Hampton Coffill, said her ancestor Joe Hampton came during the Gold Rush and settled in Soulsbyville where he operated a stamp mill. Wade's father, Harris Coffill, came from Nova Scotia. Olive married him in Sonora on December 21, 1901. They had four children—Wade, Harris, Bill and Ruth (Lackey) Coffill. Harris was a hard-working, self-made engineer, who helped organize the Tuolumne County Electric Power and Light Company in the mid-1890s. He also was the General Manager of the Columbia Marble Quarry.

Wade Coffill, the attorney, at work setting fence posts.
Photograph from the Wade Coffill photograph album, courtesy of Mildred Montgomery

Eldest son Wade was born January 3, 1903, in Sonora. Wade, a bright scholar, attended Stanford University and graduated from the University of California in 1929. He became a well-respected attorney and noted historian. Wade was widely known as a walking encyclopedia on early history of Sonora and Tuolumne County. With his knowledge of the law, he tried to annex Dardanelle into Alpine County to avoid high taxes, but never succeeded. A complex man, he had numerous interests in mining, farming, and ranching.

When Wade took over the resort in 1948, he was forty-five years old and ran the resort in between court cases on his schedule. He was a tall imposing figure and an intellectual. When he spoke, smoke from his ebony stemmed pipe lingered with his words. He loved the high country and his beloved resort. Wade was by nature one who liked to leisurely putter and tinker. His largest project was to build a duplex cabin located toward the back of the resort. There was always some project he was working on to upgrade the property. He generously gave it some of the best years of his life.

His wife Louise was born in 1906 and was of frail health due to having rheumatic fever as a child. She became a high school teacher in Oakdale where she taught mathematics and algebra. Although she was strict, students praised her as a very good teacher.

The Coffills took in two Chinese men and taught them English, American customs, and helped them attain their citizenship. They worked in the Coffill home, the older man Lee, as a cook, and Jackson, as the houseboy and gardener. Wade and Louise took them to Dardanelle for the summers to help out at the Resort. They both called Louise "Bossman."

Louise was a snob and disdained the campers and cabin owners. She wanted the resort to be a more high-class place and preferred to entertain clientele from San Francisco. She dressed well, frequently in a wool skirt and sweater, or slacks and a blazer. Louise was a quiet type, stern, not very sociable, and abrupt with the public. She ran the restaurant, scheduled the cabin rentals, and supervised the girls who cleaned the fourteen little

Louise Coffill with her pet English bulldog "Britt"
Wade Coffill photograph album courtesy of Mildred Montgomery.

Louise poses with Chinese cook Lee and the restaurant help.
Wade Coffill photograph album courtesy of Mildred Montgomery.

Jackson takes a break from work for a ride at the stables.
Wade Coffill photograph album courtesy of Mildred Montgomery.

cabins. When Wade was gone on court cases, Louise kept a pistol beside her cash register in the store. Everyone knew that she read all the postcards before she put them in the mail slots. Talk among her employees was that Louise worked them hard and paid skimpy wages. Frequently, she hired college boys or local teenagers.

Louise would pamper herself with an occasional trip to San Francisco to the upscale Elizabeth Arden beauty salon for the full treatment. While in San Francisco, she shopped for cut crystal to add to her collection, and bought clothes.

Located some distance from the resort towards the back were the stables, consisting of a corral and a small barn. The one-hour rides were popular with the local tourists, children and campers. The riders could travel anywhere. There were only casual trails. Riders usually explored the large Brightman Flat or rode to the edge of the flat to view the river.

On moonlit summer nights, the Coffills offered horseback rides for couples, which were especially popular. After dark, the cowboys would slowly lead couples on horseback along the edge of Brightman Flat to see the moonlight shining on the river below. In the still night air, the sound of the rushing river water, combined with the view from horseback, was magical. The ride took almost an hour, it was very romantic, and the tourists loved it. The party continued to the Clarks Fork Road then turned back to head for the resort. Sometimes when they returned, they had a steak dinner provided at the lodge, but they usually just gathered for a drink at the bar. Wade disapproved of the moonlight rides and advised, "No one belongs out on a horse at night."

The cowboys packed tourists and hunters on the Eagle Meadow Trail behind Bone Springs Summer Home tract, a well-marked trail to the higher elevations. It climbed about four miles along the Eagle Creek canyon up to an elevation of 7,555 feet to Eagle Meadows. This high county offered much to explore, including Long Valley, Barn Meadow, and the famous Bennett Juniper tree, said to be the oldest living tree, which may be in question now. Lush with meadows full of wildflowers, the scenery has spectacular views of the high peaks in the Emigrant Basin.

Janet (Krogh) Cornell, daughter of a Brightman Flat cabin owner, with little brother Nels in 1949, enjoying a one-hour horseback ride around Dardanelle.
Photograph courtesy of Janet Krogh Cornell.

Wade Coffill relaxes at Dardanelle with his pipe.
Wade Coffill photograph album courtesy of Mildred Montgomery.

The packers at the corral were especially busy during deer season. With a string of a few mules, they packed hunters and their camping gear to hunt the high meadows and forest. Wade would personally help with packing in parties of hunters as he also enjoyed the adventure. By the late 1950s,

This building was originally the saloon. It sustained damage and was again remodeled in 1983 when this photograph was taken. *Photograph by Cate Culver 1983.*

Inside the resort tavern. Betty Miller, left, with friend Louise Coffill and unknown woman in background.
Wade Coffill photograph album courtesy of Mildred Montgomery.

Wade closed the stables, as there was just too much competition from the Kennedy Meadows Pack Station. Additionally a road was built into this same backcountry, and few would rent a horse for the ride when they could drive their car. Soon after taking possession of the resort, Wade moved the saloon, which had been a separate building, into the lodge. He made the building a store. He hired Elbert and Elvira Miller to run the store and provided them with lodging.

Most every evening, Louise liked to entertain her friends with a cocktail at the bar. Wade kept an eye on the saloon customers and was not popular when he told patrons, "That is your last drink, you have had enough." He would not tolerate any foul language and would not hesitate to throw the offender out and even just shut the bar down for the evening.

Interior of resort lobby. Painting over the fireplace by Levi Hough. Fireplace built by John Bucknam.
Photograph from a Dardanelle Resort pamphlet when Wade Coffill owned the resort in the 1950's. *Cate Caldwell Culver collection.*

During their ownership, the resort was well maintained, and the business thrived. They put their whole heart into their beloved historic resort, and no doubt it was hard to pass it on. Wade and Louise sold the Dardanelle Resort to Dennis Dunn in April of 1973.

Wade practiced law on a limited basis and eventually retired from his law practice in 1990. Louise died in 1984. Wade died in 1991 at age eighty-seven after a long illness.

On August 5, 2018, the Donnell Fire destroyed the historic resort, and all that remained standing were the gas pumps. A four-room rental unit and RV Park survived. Plans are in the works to rebuild by new owners, who had acquired the resort in May of 2018 before the fire.

SOURCES
Barnett, Jeanette. Personal interview, 2013.
Coffill, Bill Jr. Personal interview, 8 Jul. 2017.
Duncan, Judy. Personal interview, 2013.
Hamilton, Jack. Personal interview, 15 Jun 2017.
Miller, Elvira. Personal interview. 1 Aug. 2017, and 11 Jan. 2018.
Mitchell, Kenny. Personal interview, 3 Mar. 2017.
Montgomery, Mildred. Telephone interview. 13 Feb. 2018.
Reiterman. Susan Gallison. Personal interview, 2015.
Terzich, Irving. Personal interview, 2013.
Wade Coffill Obituary. *Union Democrat.*

CHAPTER 17

Elbert Miller
and His Vegetable Truck

Elbert and Elvira with the truck at Little Sweden. Behind the cab was the cold storage box for ice, meat, milk and butter. On one side, the boxes held vegetables, and on the other, fruit.
Photograph courtesy of Geraldine Miller and Elvira Miller.

The beloved Elbert Miller and his vegetable truck made a huge difference to the people who spent their summers on Sonora Pass. Having fresh vegetables and fruit delivered on a weekly basis meant they could enjoy the mountains for significantly longer periods of time.

Elbert Miller was born in Oregon, on August 3, 1914. In 1941, while serving in WWII, he married Elvira Ann Ditman, born in Riverbank, February 19, 1922. Elbert was twenty-seven and his bride was a tender nineteen-year-old. During the depression, Elbert bought a house in Long Barn for next to nothing. Upon return from the service, they moved to their Long Barn property. Elbert and his brothers Roy and Sylvester tore down the house and built a grocery store, restaurant, and gas station.

After the war, at the age of thirty-one, and with a wife and daughters to support, Elbert, (known as "EJ,") began a vegetable truck route on Highway 108 over Sonora Pass in 1945. People would go camping along the Sonora Pass corridor to escape the valley heat, frequently for two weeks at a time. There was little refrigeration at the resorts, which sold only canned goods. His weekly delivery of fresh produce was most welcome.

Elbert's truck was a red 1940 flatbed truck, a ton-and-a-half military surplus vehicle. The sides were open with canvas that Elbert rolled up when the truck stopped to sell produce. The truck was stocked with bacon, milk, butter, and 500 lbs. of ice kept in an icebox and sold in 25-lb. blocks. He offered fresh potatoes, corn, beans, watermelon, grapes, tomatoes, squash, avocados, fruit, berries, bread, candy bars, and an assortment of Terzich sodas.

Elbert traveled to Stockton once a week to an all-night farmers market. It was enormous, and it was there that Elbert purchased fruit and vegetables by the lug for the grocery store, restaurant, and Elbert's vegetable truck route. He also bought produce in Oakdale from farmers in the Orange Blossom area, then returned to Long Barn by 4 a.m. and loaded up the truck with fresh produce, grown in the mild climate of the San Joaquin Valley.

Elbert's truck stopped beside the road in 1944 with restless daughters exploring.
Photograph courtesy of Elvira and Geraldine Miller.

Elbert loved the Long Barn neighborhood children and gave them small jobs to do so they could have just a bit of spending money. These local boys, Pete Kerns, Earl Hitch, and Craig Coffee, accompanied him on the vegetable truck route which took two to three days.

At every one of his twenty stops Elbert would yodel to announce his arrival. Customers would look over the selection and ask for what they wanted. The boys accompanying him would climb up into the truck and sort through the big forty-pound lug boxes and complete the orders for the mountain dwellers.

He left Long Barn about 5 a.m. and began the long, road up the mountain. The first stop was the Camp Blue, the University of Berkeley alumni mountain camp and retreat. Then next was the Pinecrest Campground and cabins. Elbert continued on to campgrounds at Bumble Bee, and the cabins at Cow Creek and Cascade Creek. Miles up the road, he turned on the Clarks Fork Road, where they stopped at the Wagner Tract cabins, Clarks Fork Campground, River View Campground,

Sequoia Girl Scout Camp, Peaceful Pines, Liahona Church Camp, Del Real Girl Scout Camp, Arnot Bridge Campground, and Cottonwood Campground. Then back to the main highway on to Boulder Flat Campground, Dardanelle Resort and campgrounds, Jack Hazard YMCA Camp, Douglas Resort, Baker Campground, and Kennedy Meadows Resort.

At Eureka Valley, Elbert would drop his wife Elvira off at a produce stand he had built under two large pine trees. It was made of 1- by 12-foot boards, and poles, with a canvas roof, located across from the Burgson corrals at a bend in the road. The old foundation of Hayes Station was adjacent to their camp. Elvira sold produce to locals, and camped out at the produce stand. This was their base camp for the summer. They were able to obtain water by utilizing a garden hose that was placed in a spring up the cliff, and erected two tents nearby where Elvira slept with her daughters. Elvira kept a rifle close at hand in one of the tents. Earl Foster, the local Highway Patrolman who had a cabin at Brightman Flat, always stopped by and kept a protective eye on the camp.

Elbert and the boys continued on up the Pass, camping for the night above Kennedy Meadows. The next day they continued over Sonora Pass to Leavitt Station to supply the restaurant and campgrounds. Then on to Highway 395 where the truck headed south to supply the restaurant and resort at Fales Hot Springs. From there, Elbert turned back north to Walker, Coleville, and Topaz to supply restaurants and motels.

Near Coleville, he headed east on a dirt road that dead-ended at a small Native American enclave. This was the end of his route, selling the last of his inventory cheap to help out the indigenous people. He patiently waited, sometimes more than an hour for a special customer. A tiny, middle-aged woman, not more than 4 ft. 7 inches tall, appeared from a stand of willows. She bought a slab of bacon and 50 lbs. of potatoes. She used a rucksack to carry her load and needed Elbert's help lifting it onto her back. She paid him with silver coins. If he tried to give her change in paper bills, she would throw them in the dirt, stomp on them, and scold him in her language. She would only accept silver coins.

The grocery store and post office at Dardanelle Resort as depicted by artist L.E. Valentine.
Art from the Cate Culver collection.

In 1949, Wade and Louise Coffill, who owned the Dardanelle Resort, decided to move the saloon inside the resort and use the vacated building for a post office and grocery store. They asked Elbert and Elvira if they would operate the store and offered them accommodations in a rental cabin with the deal. The Millers welcomed the opportunity to avoid sleeping on the ground and have a little dwelling for the summer. Elbert and Elvira kept the store well stocked with meat, produce and sundries. However, Elbert continued his usual route, leaving Elvira at Dardanelle. They managed the store for three years.

One day, a cabin owner came into the store to buy groceries. The lady was impractically dressed for the mountains, decked out in her finery, and caught Elvira's attention. Elvira had just put out a whole lug of beautiful fresh tomatoes. They had paid $20 for the lug in a year when the tomato harvest was slim, so these tomatoes were prized and delicious. The lady carefully fingered each tomato, leaving marks from her long red polished fingernails. Elvira grew angry as each of the tomatoes were damaged. She approached the lady and said, "You have damaged all my fine tomatoes. You must pay for all of them!" The lady replied, "Oh, I have no money, I was just looking." Elvira was furious and demanded that she pay. Wade Coffill happened to be in the adjacent post office sorting the noon mail and overheard the confrontation. He barged into the grocery store and demanded that the lady pay for the damaged

produce. Coffill followed the lady out to her car and came back triumphant with the money.

During the winter, Elbert managed a little ski resort known as Bald Mountain. It went bankrupt in 1945 due to a light winter and little snow. After bankruptcy, Jim Mills asked him to manage Little Sweden, along Highway 108. Elbert and Elvira operated this facility for ten years, living in a small back room. The resort had two tow-ropes, a basic restaurant, and skis and ski boots to rent. Here Elvira set up the earliest First Aid station on the Pass. Little Sweden was demolished in 2012.

In 1947, Elbert and his brother Roy searched for their own place to have a ski resort and started developing Dodge Ridge. They built two tow-ropes and a lodge, but they were ultimately bought out by a developer and didn't make much money from the deal.

Elbert also worked for Sam Kerns between 1955 and 1962, while he was developing Cold Springs. With Sam's son Pete, Elbert helped engineer the water system for the subdivision and laid all the pipe. In 1957 he moved Elvira and his two young daughters, Patsy and Geraldine, to a house in Cold Springs. It was an improvement from the Long Barn home built with salvaged lumber.

Elbert was six feet tall, athletic and quite strong. Known to be kind, caring, smart, and even-tempered, he had many friends. Elbert was legendary as an outdoorsman and was an excellent tracker. He had an uncanny knowledge of the mountains, and navigated through deep snow on skis into the Emigrant Basin backcountry in the dark of night to search for lost hikers and deer hunters. He did this for forty-two years, much of the time as a volunteer. Later in life, he estimated that he probably skied 10,000 miles in the high country and saved over forty lives.

For thirty-one years, Elbert worked for the Department of Water Resources, where his skill as an outdoorsman was valued. He went into the Upper Kern River area on skis to measure snow depth and water content in remote areas of the Sierras. For his own pleasure, he would ski Sonora Pass. Elbert made a point to stop and see Harry Lee at Dardanelle, who stayed all winter caretaking the cabins. Harry and his wife were pleased to have company and catch up on news.

In 1962, Deputy Sheriff Bill Huntley recommended Elbert become a summertime deputy sheriff at Pinecrest. By 1963, at forty-nine, Elbert was working fulltime, eventually becoming the law enforcement officer for Sonora Pass. This began his career in law enforcement, and with a secure job the vegetable truck was retired.

Elbert had little tolerance for hippies and Hell's Angels who came up from the valley to camp at Pinecrest. He would regularly run them out. During his years in law enforcement, his weapon of choice was a large Sportsman flashlight. He never once drew his revolver. He'd shine the flashlight right into the offender's face. If provoked, Elbert gave them a good whack on the forehead! The deputies at the Sheriff's Office would see someone come in with handcuffs and a knot on the forehead and would remark, "Well, that guy met up with Elbert." At his retirement party, they presented him with a bent flashlight. When he retired as a deputy sheriff and turned in his revolver, it was examined, and it was determined that he never once fired his gun.

The teenaged sons of cabin owners enjoyed taunting Elbert. One day the boys decided to play a prank on him. They rode motorcycles amid the trees in such a way that made him mad, and he drove his patrol car through the trees to chase the teenagers. Elbert got out of his car to scold them, and while Deputy Miller was distracted, other boys chained the back bumper of his patrol car to a tree. They gave the chain some slack and when Elbert got back into the patrol car and roared off, the whole rear bumper was ripped off. The day that they got back at Deputy Miller was gleefully retold many times.

Sadly, Elbert Miller was diagnosed with colon cancer in 1982, at age sixty-eight. As he rested at the home of his daughter, he recounted many of his adventures in the Sierra. He remarked, "Sure, I'd do it all over again." He grinned. "I'd just do more of it. Those mountains are my life." The community rallied to raise money for his medical expenses, but unfortunately, Elbert succumbed to cancer in 1983 at sixty-nine.

Elbert and his produce truck were known at every little wide spot on the road in the Sonora Pass region. He became a part of daily life in the mountains. Elbert worked tirelessly at whatever job he could get to support his family, but never behind a desk. He always had to be in the mountains.

His wife Elvira, also known as Ellen, lived another thirty-five years in the town of Tuolumne. She died at age ninety-six on March 26, 2018.

SOURCES
Hitch, Earl. Personal interview, 2015.
Kerns, Pete. Personal interview, 2015.
Miller, Ellen. Personal interview, 2015, and 1 Aug. 2017.
Scruggs, Jim. Personal interview, 26, Aug. 2016.
Fein, Julian. "Medical Bills Mount for Deputy." *Union Democrat*. 22 Jan. 1983.
Bateman, Chris. "Mountaineer Faces New Challenge, and Friends Rally to His Side." *Union Democrat*, 25 Jan. 1983.

Deputy Sheriff Elbert Miller alongside his patrol car in 1972. *Photograph courtesy of Pete Kerns.*

CHAPTER 18

Harry Lee
Wintertime Cabin Caretaker

Harry Lee in front of the Dardanelle store. About 1960.
Wade Coffill photograph album. Courtesy of Mildred Montgomery.

Original painting by Harry Lee.
Photographer Cate Culver. Courtesy of Elvira Miller.

By the 1930s, cabin owners at Brightman Flat felt the need for someone to stay all winter and look after their cabins. They had been experiencing burglaries after closing their cabins in the winter, as well as damage from heavy snow. A caretaker would make the rounds, to check for break-ins, and shovel snow off roofs to prevent damage. Cabin owners could then rest easy.

Harry Lee and his wife Arzalia built cabins in the area, and most cabin owners knew them, so the Lees from Half Moon Bay took on the wintertime job.

Harry Lee's cabin at Dardanelle.
Photographer Cate Culver 2015.

Harry was known to many of the owners because he had built several cabins that overlooked the river at Brightman Flat. In 1938 he built three cabins: No. 55, now the Danicourt cabin, No. 36, owned by Bill and Olga Rodden, and in 1941, the Raggio cabin, No. 35. All were choice cabin sites. He probably worked on the construction during the summer, and in winter he set up housekeeping to do the indoor finishing work. His wife Arzalia, a sturdy lady who always wore men's clothes, worked alongside Harry building these cabins. She frequently did the rockwork on the chimneys. She was friendly and well-liked by the cabin owners.

The Lees brought with them a huge stockpile of food and supplies, thoughtfully planned out for the duration of the road closure from October to April. Much of it was vegetables Arzalia canned from their garden in Half Moon Bay.

To prepare for the long, cold, solitary days, the couple would go up into the higher elevations and gather red fir bark, prying it off downed trees with a crowbar. The bark was thick and full of resin. A huge stack of it was always near his cabin, and the Lees used it for fuel all winter, as it burned hot and slow.

When they made their rounds to check on the cabins, Harry used skis, but his wife preferred snowshoes. It was hard work, regularly making the rounds, and especially shoveling the heavy snow off roofs to prevent damage.

Through the years, the husband and wife team stayed in different cabins during the long winter months. Even though everyone thought well of the couple, eventually there was friction. It seemed best that the Lees have their own cabin. In the 1950s, the cabin owners banded together and supplied him materials to build it. Since Lee was a builder, this arrangement was to everyone's benefit. The cabin had a first floor, mostly used for storage. When the snow was deep, the second floor living quarters could be accessed from outside stairs. Today the cabin is used by State of California game wardens.

Harry, when not building a cabin, kept busy during the winter with his artistic talent. During the 1930s and '40s, the paintings *Blue Boy*, by Thomas

Gainsborough, and *Pinky*, by Thomas Lawrence, were very popular. Prints of the pair decorated many homes. Harry meticulously painted convincing copies of the paintings and sold them for extra income. They were quite realistic and he got a good price. He was an accomplished artist and painted several originals.

Arzalia, a name she despised, collected scraps of clothing, mostly men's suit or coat material, and braided rugs during the winter. She then sold them in the summer.

During the winter in 1958, Elbert Miller, Pete Kerns, and Earl Hitch were passing by Douglas Resort on skis en route to the high country to measure snow depth for the California State Water Resources Board. They stopped at the Douglas Resort, where Harry and his wife were caretaking the resort for the winter. They always stopped to visit, knowing the Lees would enjoy some company, as they had all become old friends over the years. When they knocked on the door, Arzalia was relieved to see the men. Almost in tears, she explained that Harry had suffered a stroke and was unable to speak. She was trapped there, with Harry stricken and needing help. Arzalia had worried for days not knowing what to do. She had realized that going on snowshoes alone for help was foolish, and besides, she couldn't leave Harry alone.

The men immediately skied back to Brightman Ranger Station where Miller had a key. Once inside, they were able to radio a dispatcher, who contacted PG&E employee Johnny Sardella, who operated a snowcat at Pinecrest. Johnny came up the mountain and took Harry and his wife out through deep snow to get medical attention in Sonora.

After Harry's stroke, the couple moved back to Half Moon Bay permanently. They had spent over two decades of cabin caretaking, and now it had come to an end. However, they both missed the mountains and would return in the summer to visit their Brightman Flat cabin.

Harry died on November, 1976, at age 86, and his wife Arzalia Lee died the following year in December, at 78.

SOURCES
Danicourt, Jo Spicer. Personal interview, 2015.
Duncan, Judy. Personal interview, 2015.
Kerns, Pete. Personal interview, 2015.
Miller, Ellen. Personal interviews, 1 Aug. 2017, 26 Nov. 2017, and 11 Jan. 2018.
Remick, Bill. Personal interview, 2004.

Dardanelle Cone
Watercolor by Cate Culver

CHAPTER 19

Douglas Station
and the Nelsons

Newly built Douglas Station in 1921, constructed by William O. Nelson and his wife Bruena.
Photograph courtesy of Tuolumne County Historical Society. (Francis Nelson collection).

The large grassy flat along the Sonora-Mono Wagon Road in Eureka Valley was a casual stopping place for travelers. It was a pleasant place to camp or pause, make automobile repairs, or cool the engine. The river was nearby, so fishermen would park their wagons or vehicles on the flat.

Henry A. Douglass, a rancher from Jamestown, first acquired the Eureka Valley property. The extensive flat took on his name and was called Douglas Flat. After he was killed in a buggy accident, Henry's daughter Frances Rolleri received a patent for 160 acres, for her father's prime land in Eureka Valley on June 29, 1891.

In 1914, William O. Nelson and his wife Bruena of Knights Ferry signed a ten-year lease from Rolleri for the land along the Sonora-Mono Road. They lived in the old Hayes Station building. In spring of the following year, they arrived with their infant son Francis. Bill, thirty-six and a new father, tried his best to make the business thrive. At the historic station, they had lodging, meals, and stables for travelers. The old Hayes Station, used on and off for fifty-five years, was near a state of collapse. After living there and operating a business for six years, the Nelsons decided to move and build their own station.

In 1921, they selected a new site a quarter mile away and built Douglas Station. Hauling supplies by wagon up the mountain made the building construction a huge expense. Douglas Station offered overnight accommodations for both travelers and their stock, much like the previous Hayes Station.

The following winter, heavy snowstorms passed through the mountains. After a snowfall of seventy-two inches, followed by a cold rain and a freeze, the north side of the new roof caved in and collapsed the

Bruena Elizabeth Nelson with her husband William and their infant son Francis in 1915 at Hayes Station.
Photograph courtesy of Tuolumne County Historical Society and Museum. (Francis Nelson collection).

The newly built Douglas Station at Eureka Valley, a buzz of activity in July of 1922.
Photograph courtesy of Tuolumne County Historical Society and Museum. (Francis Nelson collection).

entire wall. Shorty Harris, caretaker at Relief Dam, spotted the damage while passing through Eureka Valley. From Relief Dam he phoned Nelson with the upsetting news. That winter, Bill sent up a crew of men to save what they could. Bill Nelson arrived in the spring to look over the damage. It was not a total loss, and undeterred, he rebuilt it the next summer.

That summer, Bill erected large tent cabins across the road for fishermen and hunters to rent. The river was not visible, but close enough to walk to for fishing or swimming. The tent cabins had sleeping accommodations only. They were very popular, and families would rent them for weeks at a time.

Four years later, the Nelsons realized they had chosen a poor location for the resort, which lacked easy river access. In 1925, Nelson again moved to a

Called Watson Camp, tents were erected for rent across the road and near the river, shown here in July of 1922.
Photograph courtesy of Tuolumne County Historical Society and Museum. (Francis Nelson collection).

new location a mile up the road. The Nelsons built a third time on Forest Service land with a different architectural style for the resort. This building had a bedroom at the east end for the owners' quarters, and one bedroom for their young son, Francis, near the outside entrance. The remainder of the building had a dining room and kitchen. The upstairs was for employees.

Once again, the Nelsons constructed canvas rental tents. At this location, the Middle Fork of the Stanislaus River was just across the road. The tents afforded campers a view of the river, and guests could rent a tent cabin for a dollar a day. Each tent was equipped with a single bed or double for couples and a wash bowl and pitcher. Bruena scrubbed the linens on a washboard by hand, hung the wash out on the clothesline to dry, then ironed the linens as well. A rustic form of bathing was also available.

The newly built Douglas Resort in 1925.
Photograph courtesy of Tuolumne County Historical Society and Museum. (Francis Nelson collection).

Guest cabins at Douglas Station.
Photograph courtesy of Bill Coffill.

Guests willing to pay a dollar were provided with a wash tub, a bucket of hot water and one of cold water, a towel, and a bar of soap. It was just the basics, but a road traveler welcomed the opportunity. Bruena was in charge of the guests' accommodations and did all the cooking. Food was served family style and guests could eat all they wanted. Each meal cost one dollar.

Later, he decided to build rental cabins, so the old Douglas Station building was cut up into sections and moved on rollers to the new location. The sections were rebuilt as guest cabins on both sides of the road.

Bill Nelson built stables and corrals, and he ran a small pack station. He provided guides to take outdoorsmen up the nearby Seven Pines Trail to hunt and view the exceptional scenery. Guests wishing to explore Douglas Flat could rent a horse by the hour.

Not all was paradise in the Nelson family. In the summer of 1926, Bruena, age thirty-three, began an affair with a cowboy from Kennedy Meadows Pack Station. Her husband learned of it, and enraged that his wife would reject him for another man, he confronted her and they argued. He found his wife's lover and killed him with a sidearm.

Sheriff J.H. "Jack" Dambacher arrived at Kennedy Meadows to investigate the murder, and not one cowboy would testify to knowing anything.

Postcard of the third and final Douglas Resort building in 1937.
Cate and Jerry Culver postcard collection.

Sign for the lodge in 1935.
Courtesy Tuolumne County Historical Society and Museum.

Douglas Resort.
Photograph courtesy of Tuolumne County Historical Society and Museum.
(Francis Nelson collection).

Bill Nelson was never charged. Locals joked that you could get away with murder in Tuolumne County. It was a different time and a different code.

Bruena was distraught over the incident. After a fight with her husband, she became hysterical and went to the cabin of guide Fred Hart, wanting his gun. He refused to give it to her, but she knew he kept it under his pillow and grabbed it. He attempted to take it away, but she broke away from him. With the gun in hand, she rushed outside and in despair uttered the words, "I'll end it all," killing herself with a gunshot to the head on August 14. Her boy Francis was only eleven years old. Traumatized by the incident, the memory of his mother lying dead under a sheet became seared in his memory.

Bruena was a native of Stockton and the daughter of Mr. and Mrs. Lewis C. Chase of Big Oak Flat. She was known by many people in the area and her death was a great shock to her friends.

Bill lived in fear of eventually being arrested for the murder of Bruena's lover, and the sudden suicide of his wife left him alone. He would need help to raise young Francis and carry on with running the resort. At a loss of what to do, he advertised for some help. Lottie Pedro answered the ad and was hired to help run his kitchen, take care of laundry and guest cabins, and care for his son. Lottie worked at Kennedy Meadows for many years and was well respected and loved.

Bill Nelson married Frances Wallace after Bruena's death and continued operating the lodge until the mid-1940s. His son Francis was drafted

Bruena Nelson.
Photograph courtesy of Tuolumne County Historical Society and Museum.
(Francis Nelson collection).

in 1942 and served in the Philippines, earning two bronze stars. Bill later moved to Carson City, Nevada, where he owned a fruit orchard. He died at seventy on December 16, 1949.

SOURCES

Atkinson, Rhonda McCarty. Personal interview, 14 Jul. 2018.

Barnette, Jeanette. Personal interview, 2015.

Francis, Nelson. "The Douglas Station." *CHISPA*, Tuolumne County Historical Society Quarterly. Vol. 37, No. 2 Oct.-Dec. 1997.

Nelson, Bruena. Obituary.

"Roof Collapses Under Heavy Snows." *Union Democrat*, 7 Jan. 1922 Front page.

Spicer, Wanda. Interview. 30 Jul 1986. Interviewed by Pam Conners. US Forest Service archives.

Terzich, Irving. Personal interview, 2013.

"Tragedy Ends Woman's Career." *Union Democrat*, 14 Aug. 1926. Front page.

CHAPTER 20

Douglas Station
and the Dentons

In 1956, Jack Denton, forty, and his wife, Virginia, a year younger, purchased the resort from Jack Mattheson of Menlo Park. Virginia was very familiar with the area. Her aunt Lottie Pedro, who raised her from age six, worked for many years at nearby Kennedy Meadows Lodge. Virginia had been to Douglas Lodge numerous times with her aunt.

Right away, the Dentons added a soda fountain. It was a full-service soda fountain with vanilla, chocolate, and strawberry ice cream, malts, milkshakes, and sodas made by hand with syrup and soda water. There were six stools and customers could order a sandwich from the fountain as well. It soon became popular with the teenagers.

The restaurant served breakfast, lunch, and dinner. In the dining room were six round tables and a full bar at one end of the room.

Behind the resort, up on the hill were four duplex cabins for overnight sleeping. Across the highway along the river were eleven housekeeping cabins furnished with kitchens. These cabins were built from the lumber of the older Douglas Station farther down the highway. The resort staff would change the linens and clean the rental cabins.

At the lodge, the staff and Dentons had private quarters upstairs. Jack continued working in Palo Alto during the week as a building inspector, and would return on the weekends to help out.

Three high school girls were hired for the summer season. Virginia had one rule: "You can go anywhere but you cannot go beyond the porch!" The porch wrapped around the entire building. The girls were under strict supervision by Virginia, who

Virginia and Jack Denton in 1958.
Photograph courtesy of the Denton family.

took responsibility for their well-being seriously. Their room and board was provided with the job. She allowed them to take snacks upstairs and relax in their quarters during slow afternoons.

By the end of summer, these girls had good job experience. They waited tables, made change, washed dishes and linens, made beds, and learned to work with the public. It pleased Virginia that she could give them such a good start in joining the work force when they became adults.

On Wednesday nights, they pushed back the restaurant tables to put up a large movie screen and

The horse stable where guests could have an hour ride or be packed in to the backcountry.
Photograph from a postcard. Courtesy of Bill Coffill.

showed movies from a 16mm projector. Popcorn was passed around, and at the end they passed the hat to pay for the movie rental. Campers came from all the campgrounds to watch the movies, along with Kennedy Meadows and Dardanelle resort patrons.

On weekends after the dinner hour, the dining tables were pushed aside to make space for dancing. The jukebox provided the music. Frequently the Marines would come from over the Pass where they were stationed at the Marine Winter Warfare Training Camp. They were welcome guests because they were well behaved and never posed a problem for the locals.

Leonard Reese, a bachelor, operated horse stables in the back. He was in charge of the hour-long rides on trails winding through Douglas Flat. He also packed people in on horseback and mules on the Seven Pines Trail. Leonard liked animals and had a pet fox. He kept it on a chain, and it lived under the barn.

Virginia hired her aunt, Lottie Pedro, to work at the resort. Lottie had raised her, and was known widely as a sweet person and hard worker. It was enjoyable for them to work together.

During the Dentons' ownership of the resort, the Forest Service kept hounding them about the condition of the building, which was thirty-five years old and had withstood some hard winters. Eventually, the Dentons declared parts of the upstairs unsafe and roped it off. In 1960, disenchanted with the demands of the Forest Service, they sold the business to Reno Sardella, who also owned Kennedy Meadows Resort.

As years passed, the resort went through several ownership changes. Few put much money into

The resort staff. Leonard Reese in hat. Owner Virginia Denton at right.
Photograph courtesy of the Denton family.

Perhaps this is the *Gunsmoke* crew that stopped for a photograph before a trip into the high country. Young actor James Arness of the Western television series *Gunsmoke,* at right.
Photograph courtesy of the Tuolumne County Historical Society and Museum.

upkeep of the building. It was a summer resort, and owners had only a few summer months to earn any money.

In 1970, it was owned and operated by Harry and Mary Hughes from England. They came to America believing they were in the 'Land of the Free' so people could do anything. Without proper permits, they put in a trailer park. The Forest Service wanted the resort building moved 250 feet back from the highway, and the riverfront cabins removed. The vegetation by the river was being worn away by the people who rented the cabins. Camping along the river was barred, as was parking vehicles in the meadow next to the resort. The Forest Service gave them two years to make improvements. When the Forest Rangers would arrive, Harry and Mary would throw rocks at them. When their permit expired on December 31,1972, the Forest Service demolished the entire resort and returned the area to its natural state. Only a few landscaping rocks remain, marking the site.

The building materials were salvaged by a local Indian tribe. The lumber was beautiful and clear of

Douglas Lodge interior in 1958. Chick Wright at the bar.
Photograph courtesy of the Denton family.

knots. What was left was burned by the Summit fire crew in a training exercise. The Hughes returned to the burned site and rummaged through the remains in tears, bitter over the whole event.

Douglas Resort, at this site, was in business for forty-seven years. It was always a welcome place for families who camped, fished, or rented horses for a trip up the Seven Pines Tail. When the Dentons put in the soda fountain, teenagers flocked to the place and it became a draw for locals set apart from the competition of Dardanelle or Kennedy Meadows.

Douglas Resort owned by the Dentons in 1958. *Photograph courtesy of the Denton family.*

SOURCES
Denton, Virginia. Personal interview, 2015.
Duncan, Judy. Personal interview, 2015.
Royse, Sid. *Facebook* interview. 30 Mar. 2018.
"Sonora Pass Landmark, Douglas Resort Is Coming Down."
        Union Democrat, 28 Apr. 1972.

Memories of Working
at Douglas Station

Norene Sardella Leonard personal interview in 2015:

"I worked at Douglas Resort as a young girl with my Dardanelle friends Audrey Benedix and Patty Gatzman. My mother Albina Sardella was the cook when I first started at about age thirteen in 1959. We lived in the upstairs where there was a huge, long narrow bedroom. There were three single beds and a large closet with a curtain to hide the clothes, and a fire escape. Parts of the upstairs were off-limits and unsafe. These were very nice large rooms with pretty bathrooms too. The stairway was off the kitchen.

"However, at night we would sneak down the fire escape where we were met by boys from Dardanelle. We would race off to Kennedy Meadows to dance. At Kennedy there was a special building for the teens to have dances, and even the adults joined in the fun.

"Reno's daughter LaVerne paid me $300 in one hundred dollar bills at the end of the season and I thought I was rich!

"Movie stars and crews would rent cabins, when they were filming movies nearby. Milburn Stone of television's *Gunsmoke* fame, stayed and was very nice, so was character actor, Keenan Wynn. The movie crew was supposed to not leave tips, however they did leave money hidden under the restaurant plates. We would fix bag lunches for them when they were out on location.

"Actor Buddy Ebsen preferred to eat in the kitchen with the staff. He was filming the MGM movie *Mail Order Bride* at Kennedy Meadows."

Patty Gatzman Charles personal interview in 2015:

"I worked at Douglas in 1962-3 when Reno Sardella owned it. I was a high school girl. Reno's sister-in-law Bina was the restaurant cook. There were six tables and we served breakfast, lunch, and dinner. My friends Audrey Benedix and Norene Sardella worked there also. We slept upstairs in single beds with a window overlooking the parking lot.

"We were up early to serve breakfast in the restaurant, then off to clean the rental cabins behind the Resort. We changed the linens and did the laundry on an old wringer washer. Sheets, towels, rugs, and bedspreads were hung on the line to dry. And then sometimes we pumped gas. Then back to the restaurant to serve lunch.

"The soda fountain was a busy place serving real soda blended with the machine and carbonation. We served ice cream, the basics vanilla, strawberry and chocolate, ice cream sundaes, banana splits, and of course, soft drinks. After lunch cleanup, we had a break and would relax upstairs. Then time to serve dinner.

"Frequently after dinner, the bar was a busy place. Marines came over for drinks and dancing to the jukebox tunes.

This teapot, part of the tableware of days past at Douglas Resort, is treasured by its owner, Norene Sardella Leonard.
Photographer Cate Culver 2017.

Sonora Pass Landmark
Douglas Resort is Coming Down

Union Democrat article printed in its entirety, April 28, 1972.

The 50-year-old Douglas resort just below Sonora Pass will be demolished next week, owners Mr. and Mrs. Harry Hughes announced yesterday. They blame conflicts with the U.S. Forest Service for their decision to close up and tear down.

Douglas Resort for years included a pack station and riverfront cabins, but in recent years consisted of a bar, restaurant, grocery store, cabins and a small trailer park.

The Forest Service has "done just about everything they could to drive us out," said Mary Hughes.

She cited the Forest Service's refusal to include a pack station in their lease of the resort site, banning of the riverfront cabins and tripling the use fee.

Bill Fredeking of the Forest Service today responded that Mr. and Mrs. Hughes had a two-year temporary permit for the resort and an extension was conditional upon their making improvements.

These, he said, were not accomplished.

Mrs. Hughes argues that the Forest Service barred them from making any major alterations.

Summit District Ranger Tom Hoots today said many of the problems arose from overuse of the area's natural resources.

Because vegetation was being worn away, the camping along the river was barred as were vehicles from the meadow next to the resort.

However, he and Fredeking denied there was any attempt to drive the resort out. There is absolutely no policy of trying to phase out such developments from that section of the Stanislaus National forest, Fredeking insisted. "When issued the permit two years ago, we felt there was a need for a resort there," he said.

Mrs. Hughes noted she and her husband "pioneered" staying in the area all winter a year ago in order to cater to snow mobile tours but could not do so this year.

"The Hughes' permit expired Dec. 31 and this accounts for there being no snowmobile tours into Douglas resort as there were a winter ago," Fredeking said.

The Forest Service's regulations are "so impractical" the Hughes will not sign a new lease, Mrs. Hughes said. In compliance with Forest Service policy, the resort then must be demolished and "restored to forest" she added.

She noted they have offered the building for salvage to the Tuolumne Indians if they will tear it down. They are scheduled to begin next week.

The resort for years was owned by Reno Sardella who later sold it to Lyle Shuey. Two years ago the Hughes bought it.

"It's definitely a shame the building has to come down," said Mrs. Hughes. "It is really an old landmark, a lovely old building."

Douglas Resort in 1970.
Photograph courtesy of Shirley Dahlin.

CHAPTER 21

Peaceful Pines
Church of the Brethren Mountain Camp

The Clarks Fork Road follows the river deep into a granite-lined canyon. On the road are two bridges, the first built in 1937 over the Middle Fork of the Stanislaus, then a second built in 1940, over the Clarks Fork that spans a deep gorge. The road is level as it winds alongside the river. After roughly seven miles, the canyon opens up to Sand Flat, a large, sandy expanse. A few miles farther, the road dead ends at Iceberg Meadow.

In 1946, when a small committee of Church of the Brethren members stepped out of their cars on the pine-needled ground at Sand Flat, they immediately liked the area. It was a yes vote all around. This place would be the site of their mountain retreat.

In the 1920s, the vision of learning in an outdoor setting was becoming a popular idea throughout the country. It was especially important to give young city dwellers a camping experience, with a camp setting that could be a ministry too, in addition to daily vacation Bible school attendance.

The first camp assembly by the Church of the Brethren was held in July of 1923 in Yosemite Valley. Both leaders and participants slept in tents and cooked over campfires. The event was well organized, with outdoor activities, sermons, lectures, and vesper services. It was an astounding success and drew more than two hundred people from all over California.

Other Church of the Brethren assemblies followed in other locations in northern California throughout the 1930s. It was, however, a financial burden to rent private camps for their assemblies. It was soon apparent that they needed to secure

The restrooms under construction. Bags of cement in the foreground.
Photograph courtesy of Church of the Brethren.

a permanent Brethren camp, a retreat in the mountains they could call their own.

An informal committee was organized to search for such a place. The committee agreed that some acreage was needed, preferably in the higher elevations in a central location above the valley. The committee soon found that it was almost impossible to acquire private land in the mountains, so they decided to approach the Forest Service.

After WWII, the Forest Service renewed a drive to open large areas of the Sierras to organized camping. Previously, a few members from the valley churches had camped along Clarks Fork Road and suggested that area as a possibility. The committee arranged to go have a look.

On October 28, 1946, a committee of Brethren members, headed by Paul B. Studebaker, and in the company of forester F.M. Sweeley, traveled to Clarks Fork and were led to Sand Flat. On one side of the road was the Stanislaus River, so the Brethren built on the other side, back from the road near a large granite rock formation. The area was secluded and a small stream cut through the flat, tumbling down from the rocks above. The Brethren agreed to an annual rental fee of $150 for the twenty-two acres and to follow the Forest Service regulations.

After leasing the property, Paul Studebaker, pastor of the Modesto church, and Glen Harmon, pastor of the Live Oak church, who was familiar with the Y.M.C.A. outdoor camps, became a team. Both had experience in leadership and planning.

After a winter of developing building plans, the Brethren group enthusiastically set to work by June of 1947. A bulldozer was brought to the site and the ground leveled for buildings. A cesspool was dug, as well as the campfire pit. The restrooms were to be the first buildings constructed.

The church needed a plan to raise funds. After some brainstorming, the district board devised a presentation to spread the word about the new camp. Photographs were taken showing the beauty of the Clarks Fork and its potential for a mountain retreat. The district board appointed Lawrence Clark to visit churches armed with a slide show and movie presentation promoting the camp. Clark raised nearly $8,000. Ezra and Mary Cool volunteered to be business managers. The funds purchased a generator, dishes, and a kitchen range, and they obtained beds, flatware, and kitchen utensils from the U.S. Army Surplus.

Carpenters purchased rough-sawn white pine lumber from nearby sawmills for the first buildings. Local decomposed granite was used to mix with

The dining hall under construction in 1947. The kitchen was added later.
Photograph courtesy of Church of the Brethren.

The camp cooks in 1950. Left to right: Irene Fike, Martha Heiny, Bertha Shirk, and Hazel Wiemert.
Photograph courtesy of Church of the Brethren.

concrete. All construction was done with hand tools. Many volunteers donated supplies as well as their labor. There was high enthusiasm for the project. The idea of having their own camp propelled them forward. To select a name for the camp, letters were sent to every church for suggested names. The name Peaceful Pines was chosen.

The kitchen and dining hall were completed by the end of 1947. Meals were served family style, seating eight to ten on benches at long tables. A crew of cooks worked diligently to meet the meal schedule and feed great numbers who brought their mountain appetites.

By the end of April 1948, a group arrived to open the camp for the year ahead. But their plans had to be put on hold. As the crew drove onto the compound, they were crest-fallen to observe the winter damage. Their thrift in using pine lumber had been a mistake. Buildings were askew from the heavy snowfall, walls caved and roofs flattened. Many of the buildings would need reinforcement and repairs. Undaunted, members made plans to return with supplies and a team of carpenters. Camp manager James Worthington directed the bracing and reconstruction of all the buildings. Heavy equipment was brought in to pull the dining hall back into alignment. They realized it was necessary to stabilize the building for winter, so cables were attached to the beams to keep it upright. During the first few winters at the camp, the Brethren members were continually surprised by how severe the winters at 6,200 feet were in the Clarks Fork area.

Besides a program for adults under the direction of Paul B. Studebaker in 1948 and S.L. Barnhart in 1949, there was a comprehensive program for children conducted by the District Director of Children's Work. Parents were encouraged to send their children to camp even if they could not be present themselves. Excellent leadership and supervision were provided, and the children loved going away to camp in the mountains.

By the end of the first decade, the camp administration was on solid ground. The District Camp Director turned the major responsibility for operating the camp over to laymen. In addition to church members who volunteered, there were three paid staff members, the camp superintendent, head cook, and cook's helper.

In 1953 and 1954, the dining hall was renovated. The cook's quarters were built above the kitchen. Carpenters constructed an open-air dishwashing area and added a large fireplace to heat the building.

Up until 1950, any food that needed to be kept cold was stored in the cold stream. Finally, a gas-powered walk-in cooler box was purchased for $542.78 and hauled to the camp from Modesto. A few years later, a much-needed washing machine was donated.

The first cabin built was divided into four rooms to house the superintendent, cooks, camp director, and nurse.
Photograph courtesy of Church of the Brethren.

In 1957, when the first Junior Camp was held, the camp committee became acutely aware of the need for more cabins. The boys were housed in tents with dirt floors. There was no place for clothes to be stored and kept clean. As a result, five more cabins were built between 1957 and 1960.

Leaders encouraged outdoor activities. A basketball court was finished in 1948, followed by a volleyball court and a baseball field. Leisure time also included crafts for all ages. Instructors gathered eager students to learn textile stenciling, woodcarving, and leather work. It was always fun to return home with something creative made in camp.

With a focus on young adults and family life, parents brought their children and teenagers. The campfire became a central gathering place in the evenings, often leading to much discussion about spiritual matters well into the night.

The founders of the camp laid a good ground work of meaningful traditions carried on by the future generations. The camp continues to thrive in its setting among the pines.

SOURCES
Ebenhack, Mary Jeanette. *Bless this Camp, The Story of Camp Peaceful Pines*, Oct.1986. Church in-house publication.

Aspens at Iceberg Meadow.
Watercolor painting by Cate Culver.

CHAPTER 22

Camp Jack Hazard
A Mountain "Y" Camp for Young Men and Women

Camp Jack Hazard has long been a presence on Sonora Pass. The "Y" camp has been a summer camp for many of Modesto's youth who have attended for generations.

John Gould "Jack" Hazard was born on July 31, 1876, in Illinois. His father John and his mother Sarah were farmers. Jack married Buena Vista Marshall on October 22, 1901, in Kane, Illinois. Jack was twenty-five and his bride twenty-two. Jack found work in Rock Island, Illinois as a clerk in the post office. In 1920, he moved to Cleburne, Texas, and began his career as a Young Men's Christian Association Secretary. The Hazards adopted two boys, Robert and Richard. The family moved to Modesto, California, a small agricultural town in the San Joaquin Valley.

Jack Hazard worked with the YMCA of Modesto's youth setting up programs for all ages. The group was originally known as the Modesto Christian Association and became the Stanislaus County Young Men's Christian Association in 1921.

A 1923 newspaper article in the *Modesto Morning Herald* stated, "Any boy in Modesto in need of an outing, who cannot afford to enjoy camping life, may do so with the aid of the YMCA committee." This was the work of Jack Hazard.

The YMCA developed a program from youth to adulthood. The core of the program was the motto Mind, Body and Spirit. This was taken seriously as a challenge in life. Camp counselors recommended when each one was ready to move up to another level. Certain colored scarves referred to as "rags" were presented and worn as a badge of honor. Even the younger ones committed to God that they would promise to keep their room clean and be kind to their siblings. The pinnacle, a white scarf, meant you had passed through all the teachings and now dedicated yourself to a Christ-like lifetime of service. Each "Ragger" wore the scarf proudly while at camp.

Hazard began searching the mountains for the right location to transport children from Modesto for annual summer outings in 1924. The location for his camp had to be south-facing, have an adequate spring, and be free of bear activity. Jack explored the Sonora-Mono Road. Just beyond the Dardanelle Resort at 6,000 feet, he found the site he wanted for the camp. It was above the Middle Fork of the Stanislaus River on a south-facing slope with a fine spring. There was good access from the road, huge granite rock formations, and flat areas for buildings. Tucked back into the forest, it was perfect.

By the summer of 1927, he secured permission from the Stanislaus National Forest to erect permanent buildings and recreational features. Forest

"Raggers" Rock where rite of passage ceremonies were held.
Photograph courtesy of the Jack and Buena Hazard Foundation.

Service employee George Miller submitted a survey of the property. Jack named it the Stanislaus-Sierra Y Camp.

Through the 1930s and the Great Depression, the camp was small and primitive, and struggled to come up with enough funds to pay the $25.00 Forest Service fees. Many parents of the camp attendees helped through the lean years. The Lions Club gave support and raised money for new buildings. In the winter, the Lions started planning the design of the buildings and in spring arrived with an efficient team ready to work.

The youngsters who attended the camp were from upper middle class families. Sessions were ten days, and cost $28. The kids were encouraged to earn their way. A small business was set up for boys and girls to go door to door selling bars of Cashmere Bouquet soap. Of course, mom bought some, too.

At first, Jack and his wife Buena packed supplies and a group of Modesto children into a flatbed truck and motored up the mountain to the campsite. They pitched tents, cooked over a campfire, took the children hiking, played baseball in the meadow by the river, and taught them how to enjoy the outdoors.

Once permission was secured from the Forest Service, the permanent camp quickly took shape. By the late 1940s, much of the camp was built and the campers arrived by bus. The bus trip alone was part of the adventure of going to camp. The notorious Patterson Grade was challenging for a bus. To negotiate the turns, the bus had to back up and reposition several times.

The sleeping cabins, which held eight, were rustic and made of wood erected on concrete floors. No doors, no glass windows, no screens, but plenty of fresh mountain air. WWII surplus iron bunkbeds stacked two high were what every camper slept on. The mattresses were thin and the bedsprings squeaked. Although it was not like home, everyone got a sound sleep.

The camp was laid out on several levels on the mountainside. At the lower end was the large granite campfire rock. Next, uphill was a flat area that had the swimming pool, shower house, craft hut, hospital building, and administration building, called the

Typical cabin provided sleeping quarters for ten boys and their leaders.
Photograph courtesy of the Jack and Buena Hazard Foundation.

"Ivory Tower." Up at the next level were the sleeping cabins, mess hall, and farther off into the woods, the chapel rock. Jack and Buena had their own cabin and there was a separate cabin for the camp cook.

The boys' sessions were in June and the girls' sessions were in July. Once the campers arrived, they ate sack lunches and got oriented. Then, up the hill they went to find their assigned cabin and sort out who their cabin mates would be and meet the camp leaders. Most of the leaders were high schoolers who had risen in the ranks. Rules were explained and they were warned about rattlesnakes.

Daily chores were assigned to each cabin of campers. They were expected to keep their cabin neat, with floors swept, beds made, and clothes put away. Some chores were easy, such as raking the trails or gathering firewood. Others were more challenging, such as preparing the campfire for the evening gathering. Some washed dishes, which was needed three times a day, or they cleaned the mess hall, or scrubbed the showers. Then there was the dreaded latrine duty, sloshing the buckets of Pine-Sol, adding fresh rolls of toilet paper, and scrubbing the toilet seats with brushes. All the chores instilled in campers a sense of pride in their camp. They gained confidence in themselves and learned to take on responsibility and work together.

This daily routine kept order in the camp. Promptly at 7 a.m., the bugler played "Reveille" and the youngsters made their way to the communal wash stands, which intermittently had hot water. From the morning wash up, they headed to morning assembly of flag raising and announcements. From there, the

In the foreground is the camp boiler fueled by firewood that heated the water for the swimming pool and showers. In the background are the communal wash stations.
Photograph courtesy of the Jack and Buena Hazard Foundation.

campers gathered at the chapel rock for inspirational words and singing. The camp always had its spiritual underpinnings and emphasized wholesome fellowship. Gospel hymns were sung and soon they all knew the words to "Amazing Grace," "For the Beauty of the Earth," and "Jacob's Ladder." After the hymns, the youngsters sat quietly atop a granite rock. Alan Arnopole, who attended the camp for many summers, describes his experience, "My favorite part of chapel was when we'd sit quietly, like lizards on granite, basking in the morning rays, and meditate on the beauty that surrounded us. A warm glow filled me to the brim and lasted all day right on up through taps." He continued, "Camp is where I really grasped the difference between spirituality and religion. Encircled by the granite giants, their rocky spires reaching to the heavens we lived in the shadow of the Almighty. We embraced nature and learned to exist in its harmony. God's handiwork was spread before us in all its glory. Even a twelve-year old kid got it!"

After chapel, the breakfast bell rang out though the canyon and a herd of hungry children raced to the mess hall. When the meal was over, it was time for cabin duties and then the daily activities began, including hiking, archery, crafts, and swimming.

On Sundays, a church service was held in the "bowl," a land formation that was bowl shaped and offered circular seating on the granite rocks. There was church music and an uplifting sermon.

Each day, a camper was chosen to be mayor for the day. The duties were to lead the Pledge of Allegiance, assist in cabin inspections and hand out the daily mail. Each boy or girl hoped to receive homemade cookies from mom.

Lunch in the mess hall was a rowdy event. The kitchen was run by the iron-fisted Hazel Howenstein, who resembled the sweet Mary See of See's Candy fame. Hazel, a former cafeteria cook, had been in charge for many years and her power was absolute. She presided over a crew of four to five hand-picked older boys, with her foreman, Ted Raleigh. In the Post-WWII days of the camp, the food consisted mainly of army surplus rations. The food was not very good. Much of it was dehydrated vegetables accented with Spam or powdered eggs. Canned pork 'n beans, fruit cocktail, and corned beef hash were included in the menu. Once the army rations were used up, Hazel cooked from scratch and the food became tasty and plentiful. It was served at each table piled high in large bowls and platters. Once a week, Hazel prepared beefsteak, a favorite. She also went out of her way to have some sort of special dessert, even if it was just peanut butter cookies.

Once the food was served, Hazel would appear at the Dutch door of the kitchen in her white apron, holding a large serving spoon. There she stood surveying the eager eaters. Toward the end of the meal, Hazel entered the mess hall. She believed that every child needed to eat at least three prunes daily and patrolled the tables, expecting to find three prune pits beside each plate. The large spoon would rap the table if the proof was not in the pits.

Head cook, Hazel Howenstein.
Photograph courtesy of the Jack and Buena Hazard Foundation.

Rules of etiquette were enforced. No elbows on the table or chewing with your mouth open. Any breach and the hapless camper had to run around the mess hall ten times while their mates repeatedly shouted, "Cabin 12 strong and able, get your elbows off the table."

Campfire program at the end of the day.
Photograph courtesy of the Jack and Buena Hazard Foundation.

After lunch and the mail delivery came a rest period. Each camper was expected to write a letter home to a loved one. Some struggled with this task, and others loved sharing their experiences.

After dinner came the most anticipated game called Capture the Flag. Again, Alan Arnopole describes the event, "It was a wild game of stealth, gamesmanship, and sheer daredevil recklessness. The contest took place in a little valley up behind the mess hall. One side of the valley had a gentle slope with a cluster of trees at the top to secure and protect its flag, which was really just a designated piece of cloth. The other side had steep granite outcroppings where its flag could be easily displayed, yet well-guarded. Both sides had plenty of undergrowth. The two teams were separated by a line gouged down the middle of the valley.

"The object of the game was to penetrate the opposing side, sneak up, snatch the flag, and bring it back through hostile territory to your

Nurses' cabin.
Photograph courtesy of the Jack and Buena Hazard Foundation.

The camp swimming pool.
Photograph courtesy of the Jack and Buena Hazard Foundation.

side, without being caught. The team that did this first, won. If you were ensnared in enemy terrain, you'd be whisked off to 'jail' where you'd have to wait until a teammate crept in and freed you, thus providing safe passage back across the line, where you could once again muster a sortie. It was an awesome sight, a thing of raw beauty as churning feet stomped their way through the Sierra twilight toward victory."

Each day ended at the campfire rock. This was when everyone came together around a roaring fire. Old-fashioned songs were sung in rounds, with both camp leaders and the kids putting on funny skits, and they all reveled in fellowship. Together they sang, "Day is done, gone the sun." As the embers glowed, the details of the day were remembered. Bedtime followed. Lights came on along the trails, guiding everyone to the cabins.

The camp had an infirmary presided over in recent years by "Nurse Nan." The building was large with a fireplace. In the back were the nurses' quarters where Nan Ground had a hot plate to cook on, a bed, and a crib for her baby. The clinic was in the front of the building. Most of the visits to see the nurse consisted of spider bites, sunburn, skinned knees, and a bit of homesickness. For the little ones, it was their first experience away from home and they were a bit overwhelmed with the primitive lifestyle. Nan knew just what to say and off they would run to be with their cabin mates who substituted for family.

In the afternoon when chores were done, the craft hut was open. Making a lanyard was a popular activity, with a whistle or some other ornament attached. Leathercraft was offered, with kits to make coin purses. The campers made things to take home.

Swimming lessons were given by Buena Hazard, who followed the Red Cross manual. Buena was petite, strong, tanned, athletic, and always wore the full-piece black Red Cross instructors' swimsuit. The pool was her domain, and she took her job seriously. The swimming pool water was cold, no matter how hot the summer sun. Despite the cold water, many kids learned how to swim.

Across the highway on a flat, the campers played baseball and other field games. In the spirit of adventure, ropes were tied to trees, which the campers would hold onto and swing across the river. They also hiked the Eagle Meadow Trail or the Eureka Valley Trail for the day's outing.

Buena Hazard drove daily to Dardanelle to get the mail in her 1930s Packard. She would take several children with her, jammed in the back seat. Usually a quiet sort, she broke her demeanor and hit the gas pedal, flying over humps in the highway so the kids hit their heads on the roof. "Whee," she would squeal, delighted with this bit of fun.

During his later years, Jack Hazard spent summers relaxing and filling in with minor duties. He liked to chop firewood and fire up the boiler for hot showers and the swimming pool. Jack, always a good-natured man, wore a hat and rancher clothes

"Y" Camp girls, sisters forever.
Photograph courtesy of the Jack and Buena Hazard Foundation.

The experience that lasts a lifetime.

and was well loved by all the camp members. He was a large man. In his old age his tall frame became stooped and he trembled a bit. He would still come to the camp and spend his days seated outside the mess hall in the sun, facing the Pass. He spoke little.

The Babbingtons, Bob and wife Dorothy, replaced the Hazard team. They had their own cabin. As Camp Director, Bob Babbington was the fiscal agent and had a Board of Directors and a Camp Committee made up of supportive parents. He was fresh out of YMCA training from Estes Park, Colorado. He wore glasses, was husky, muscular, and a no-nonsense leader. Everyone called him "Mister B." He carried a spiritual presence. He was worshiped by the youngsters and they always wanted to please him.

Once each session, the "Pioneer" group of older campers twelve and up left camp for five to six days on a wilderness outing. They were hauled over the summit in a stake-sided flatbed truck, to Leavitt Meadow. At 7,000 feet, the nights were cold even in the summer. Camping gear was minimal—a thin cotton sleeping bag, tennis shoes, tee shirt, hooded sweatshirt, and flimsy flannel-lined jacket. The sleeping bags were rolled up lengthwise with personal items inside and carried on the shoulders.

Off they marched into the pristine backcountry, beyond civilization. A campsite was chosen in a meadow beside the West Walker River. Cooking was done over an open campfire. Each camper had his own gallon tin can with a handle fashioned out of a coat hanger.

Jack Hazard had succeeded in providing the young men and women of Modesto with a well-run, Christian-oriented camp in the mountains. This alpine experience made a lasting impression on the young campers. The friendships they forged lasted into adulthood. It was a time of growing up and self-realization about who they were and the image they wanted to project throughout their life. Those who took seriously the "Raggers" steps of challenges to become a good person benefited from it throughout their lives. It gave young people a foundation of Christian values to guide them to make good decisions.

The camp is currently open under the Jack and Buena Hazard Foundation. The camp continues with much the same structure and values.

SOURCES
Arnopole, Alan. Telephone interview, 12 Jun. 2018, and memoirs of his days at Jack Hazard Y Camp.
Cover, Linda. Telephone interview, 18 Oct. 2018.
Ground, Nan. Telephone interview, 17 Oct. 2018.
Haack, Alan. Personal interview, 7 Jun. 2018.
Marvin, Judith."Historic Structure Report, Camp Jack Hazard." US Forest Service archives.
Miller, Elivra. Personal interview, 26 Nov. 2017.
Norquist, Tom. Personal interview, 8 Oct. 2018
Norquist, Dick. Personal interview, 8 Oct. 2018.
Poisson, Jason. Personal interview, 8 Oct. 2018.
"Y.M.C.A Secures Site in Forest." *Modesto News-Herald,* 27 Jul. 1927. p. 4.

CHAPTER 23

Kennedy Meadows

"Kennedy Meadow"
Watercolor by Cate Culver.

On Highway 108, sixty miles east of Sonora is Kennedy Meadows Resort, and a short walk up the road from the resort a large meadow comes into view, edged by the Stanislaus River. Relief Peak rises like a timeless sentinel in the background, overlooking a well-worn trail that leads to meadow after meadow, where the Kennedy brothers brought their cattle to graze in the late 1800s. This trail is the gateway to the Emigrant Basin, leading to Relief Reservoir and large and small lakes scattered throughout the granite-lined canyons. Wranglers from the pack station have escorted anglers, deer hunters, and tourists into the wilderness for over a hundred years. Although various cattlemen came here for the grazing, it was the breathtaking scenery that drew tourists to the Kennedy Meadows Lodge. The fact that these cattlemen were able to operate a pack station and resort in this secluded mountain setting is a testament to the grit and resilience of these individuals. The following chapters chronicle their legacy.

Owners of Kennedy Meadows

Thomas Kennedy
1886 to 1905

Robert Edwards
1918 to 1927

Charles Ledshaw
1927 to 1929

Frank Kurzi
1929 to 1945

Lou Bittner
1945 to 1947

Cliff Mitchell
1947 to 1957?

Rose Mitchell
1947 to 1960

Reno Sardella
1960 to 1970

Willie Ritts
1970 to 1997

Matt Bloom
1997 to present

CHAPTER 24

Kennedy Meadows
Thomas Kennedy and the Cow Camp

Midway up the Sonora-Mono Wagon Road, much of the contour of the road follows the Middle Fork of the Stanislaus River. Lush, broad flats line the river on the north side. To the south, the river is bound by forested mountainsides. Fifty miles east of Sonora the road meets the start of the imposing Sonora Pass and continues upward. From the base of Sonora Pass, the grassy flats along the river continue for several miles. These meadows and flats are the entryway for the traveler on horseback into the Emigrant Wilderness. It is in these meadows that Tom Kennedy made his mark, and ever since, it has been known as Kennedy Meadows.

In 1830, Andrew Thomas "Tom" Kennedy was born in Stewartstown, County Tyrone, Ireland, a center of the brown linen trade. By 1848, The Great Irish Potato Famine was overwhelming Ireland, and many Irish were emigrating to America. Tom, a young man of eighteen, joined this migration. He arrived in Philadelphia in 1848 and found work as a machinist.

Two years later Tom met the blue-eyed and stylish Jane Murphy, also from the same county in Ireland. In America, the Irish were considered the lowest on the social ladder, and signs in New York bars proclaimed, "No dogs or Irishmen." Being natives of the same area in Ireland, they felt an immediate kinship and developed a bond. The young couple married on November 16, 1855. Thomas was twenty-five and Jane twenty-one. Their first child Elizabeth was born in 1857, followed by a son Charles, who was born ten years later in 1867. Jane also lost two babies who died in infancy before Charles' birth. It was a tragedy that haunted her, and relatives remarked that she was "always sad."

Tom's brother Robert Kennedy, four years his senior, was a successful farmer and cattleman in California. He urged Tom to bring his family west. In the winter of 1868, they crossed via the Isthmus of Panama and sailed into San Francisco harbor.

Robert insisted that Tom join him at his home in Knights Ferry, a farming community along the Stanislaus River in Stanislaus County. Conveniently located between the Port of Stockton and the Sierra

Andrew Thomas Kennedy.
Photograph courtesy of Matt Bloom.

foothills, the locale was a hub of activity on the road to the southern mines during the Gold Rush era.

When the Kennedys arrived at Knights Ferry one week before Christmas, there were no suitable accommodations for the young family. It was winter, and Jane hated it. Cold, wet, and now planted in the midst of a primitive farming community, Jane was miserable. No family or friends were available to console her, and she missed the conveniences of Philadelphia. It was a nearly unbearable challenge to care for her one-year-old son in diapers and a lively ten-year-old daughter.

Cattle at the Kennedy Ranch in Knights Ferry.
Photograph courtesy of Lisa Kennedy Bergantz.

Robert T. Kennedy, member of the Odd Fellows organization, wearing his elaborate costume.
Photograph courtesy of Lisa Kennedy Bergantz.

Robert, a bachelor, welcomed the family into his farmhouse until Tom could build a house for his wife and two children. Jane understood that the stressful situation was a temporary arrangement and made the best of it. Fresh from Philadelphia, the family had to make big adjustments in the rugged environment.

Tom, however, loved it. The green rolling hills and flat rich bottomland offered an opportunity he had not had in the past. He could thrive here and have a successful ranch. The brothers became partners in the cattle business. The 1,500-acre ranch, eight miles north of Knights Ferry, was prime for grazing cattle. Although Tom knew almost nothing of farming or cattle or living in the countryside, he learned quickly and the ambitious Kennedy brothers prospered.

When the summer of 1869 arrived, Robert was eager to take his little brother into the Sierra Nevada mountains. He knew Tom, at age thirty-nine, had never seen such grand mountains in Ireland or on

the east coast of America. Robert packed fishing gear, camping equipment, food staples, supplies for the horses, and rifles onto packhorses, for a trip that would take several days. They traveled the newly-built Sonora-Mono Wagon Road on horseback into the mountains. Tom was smitten with the beauty of the Sierras as he and his brother traveled the primitive wagon road, viewing the Dardanelle volcanic rock formations and the granite-lined canyon of the Stanislaus River drainage. As they rode, climbing higher into the mountains, the sweat of the horses and the aroma of the pines filled the air. At the base of the Pass, Robert left the road and led the way along the Stanislaus River up through one verdant meadow after another. Tom marveled at the snow-capped peaks, granite outcroppings, and quaking aspens along the river's edge. At 6,000-foot elevation, they set up camp along the rushing river, staked out their horses, and Robert caught fresh, pink-fleshed native trout for their meal. The younger brother was in awe. He readily picked up the fishing pole and soon had trout on the line too. Throughout the years, they returned many times to this place of beauty and peacefulness.

This was just the first of many marvels. Robert had plans to amaze his brother even more. They made their way up higher and higher along a small stream into the endless granite terrain of the High Sierra. The horseshoes sparked occasionally against the granite rock with a loud click. The air was clear and silent enough to hear the creaking of the leather saddles and buzz of insects attracted to the horses.

At an elevation of 7,800 feet, Robert led Tom out from the forest and into a basin where a large lake appeared. A breathtaking sight, the lake was ringed with high peaks and edged with meadow grasses. Tom loved what he saw, and the brothers spoke of owning it someday. They built a trail from the lower meadows up to the lake. When Tom realized that the lake had no fish (there was no fish-planting yet in Emigrant Basin), he captured trout from Leavitt Creek some distance away and successfully transported and planted the native fish. It was a great joy to the Kennedys to catch fish in their own lake.

The brothers went to the meadows along the Stanislaus River year after year. Tom soon included his young son Charles, nicknamed "Skipper," on these outings and taught him everything he knew about the mountains. It became the Kennedys' special retreat.

An incident in August of 1882 involving his brother may have caused Tom to take legal action to claim the wilderness land. Robert had come upon

a man fishing in the upper waters of the river and ordered him to leave. The fisherman objected, and Robert drew his pistol. Kennedy felt he had squatter's rights and claimed an unlimited number of miles of the river as his own domain. He objected to anyone trespassing on this land to fish or hunt. He was arrested for drawing his pistol and brought to court where he resolved to plead guilty. Justice Miller fined him $75, a hefty monetary reprimand.

Government Land Office records reveal that Thomas Kennedy acquired 993.66 acres of land by patent via the Swamp and Overflow Lands Act, on August 24, 1886. The property along the Middle Fork of the Stanislaus River included 80 acres with lush meadows on both sides of the river. It soon became known as Kennedy Meadows. The rest of the acreage was located higher in the Sierra, eight miles above the lower meadow. The brothers named the lake in their favorite lush meadow Kennedy Lake.

Robert and Tom were elated that they owned the alpine meadows, and they began to build on the land. They decided that it would be best to have a small cabin at the first meadow, accessed by the wagon road. It was a flat area overlooking the river where they often camped. They brought tools and supplies on their next visit and built a primitive cabin from local timber, which was carefully dovetailed at the

The primitive log cabin built in the late 1880s at what is now Kennedy Meadows Resort. Magdalena Kennedy, wife of Skipper, visits the old Kennedy cabin at Kennedy Meadows Resort in 1958. It was restored in 1988 by Pat Casey, a retired bridge builder.
Photograph courtesy of Lisa Kennedy Bergantz.

Kennedy Lake.
Photograph courtesy of the Tuolumne County Historical Society and Museum.

corners, had a packed-earth floor, and a roof of sugar pine shakes. Here they could stow supplies and spend the nights. It was a beautiful and ideal location by the river, with trout fishing close to their front door.

They could now legally bring their cattle to the property for summer grazing in the meadows. Kennedy Lake, surrounded by a grassy meadow, was the perfect location. They soon referred to it as the Kennedy Cow Camp, and it became their summer home base. Here the brothers built a barn and cabin at the edge of the lake. They fenced an area near the buildings for horse corrals. The primitive windowless cabin was built of local logs with a roof of sugar pine shakes. It measured roughly fourteen by eighteen feet and had no foundation, just a packed-dirt floor.

While Robert and Tom were off in the mountains with the cattle, Jane remained alone at

Barn built by the Kennedy brothers at the edge of Kennedy Lake at their high mountain grazing land. Restored by Willie Ritts and Pat Casey in the 1990s.
Chris Robinson photographer 2015.

Cattle grazing at Kennedy Meadows in 1942. Middle Fork of the Stanislaus River is at the right. This meadow is near the Resort and a tourist favorite.
Photograph from the Cate Culver postcard collection.

Cabin and barn at Kennedy Lake Cow Camp. The cabin no longer exists.
Photograph courtesy of Matt Bloom.

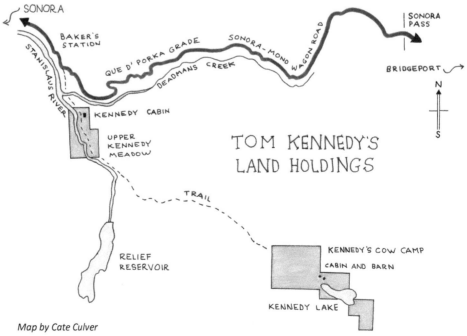

Map by Cate Culver

home. Isolated much of the time on the Kennedy Ranch at Knights Ferry, Jane fought bouts of depression, but managed by herself much of the time. For fifteen years, she had been without the company of her daughter "Bessie," who had married and moved away. That winter Jane became despondent and said she was tired of living. On April 29, 1896, her husband and unmarried son Skipper noticed her strange behavior and suspected she had taken strychnine in her desperation to end her life. They summoned Dr. F.W. Lowe for help, but the doctor arrived too late. Jane, sixty-two, died within minutes at their home in Knights Ferry, and Tom, sixty-six, was left a heart-broken widower. Jane's sudden death shocked the rural community where she had lived for twenty-eight years.

Two years after his mother's death, thirty-one-year-old Charles Thomas "Skipper" Kennedy, married Magdalena Dorathea Jorgensen, age twenty, on February 23, 1898. "Lena" had been born near Oakdale, California, in 1878, and came from a prominent pioneer family engaged in the sheep and cattle industry. Skipper left his father's ranch, and the newlyweds settled in the town of Knights Ferry.

Tom continued with his cattle business, spending summers in the mountains. Kennedy Meadows became a well-known place to picnic and fish, and Tom had to continuously deal with intruders.

At Baker Station, a stage stop just a mile away, patrons frequently fished in the lower meadow area along the river. Often Tom came upon fishermen camped on his property and charged them fifty cents a day to graze their horses, which was his right as the landowner. In the past, the old Irishman had trouble with campers trespassing, and pack trains tearing down fences. His barn had been burned down and his cabin damaged. He was bitter and easily provoked.

In July of 1898, three young men, James Kirkwood, Tony Yancey and Frank Hall, were on the trail to Kennedy Lake to go fishing. Tom Kennedy met them on the trail and warned them not to trespass. When he explained that a fee was charged to pasture animals, they refused to pay. He refused them the right to fish the lake and ordered them to turn around and leave.

A few days later, the three started again for Kennedy Lake, thinking the old gray-bearded man may have returned to the valley, but they encountered him again on the trail, patrolling his property. This time, though, Tom Kennedy was on horseback and carried a rifle cocked in front of him on the saddle. The boys argued with Kennedy, who then fired a shot at the belligerent young Kirkwood. The bullet only grazed his arm, but it passed through Hall's horse, killing it instantly. Stunned by the violent incident, Hall, now without a horse, jumped on behind Kirkwood and the young men made a quick retreat, convinced that Kennedy would shoot again.

Once back in Sonora, James Kirkwood, in retaliation, swore out a complaint before Justice Cooper charging Tom Kennedy with attempted murder. When Kennedy was brought to trial, he testified that the rifle was at the ready because he had seen a deer he planned to shoot. He also claimed Kirkwood had pulled the pistol first. Kennedy must have been convincing because the jury declared him not guilty.

Tom's wife, Jane Murphy Kennedy, in 1868 at age 34. The photograph was probably taken in Philadelphia before they came to California.
Photograph courtesy of Lisa Kennedy Bergantz.

Having been in court, Tom Kennedy looked over his dealings with the government and realized he had failed to pay his taxes on the mountain land. To be on the safe side, he rushed to redeem the land and paid his back taxes of $26.47 on November 17, 1898, to be secure in his ownership.

The old Irishman was aging and in poor health. He had lost his wife two years before and had no one to care for him. It was a hardship to continue his cattle operation alone. On December 8, 1903, he reluctantly deeded his mountain property to son Skipper for $10 in gold coins.

Two years later in 1905, Skipper and Lena were approached by Beach Thompson, a mining promoter who wanted to buy the Kennedy holdings in the mountains. Thompson had the wheels turning to build the Relief Reservoir to supply water and power to his gold mine near Angels Camp. Skipper readily sold the Kennedy Meadows and Kennedy Lake Cow Camp property to Thompson. That same year he also sold the family cattle ranch at Knights Ferry. Everything Tom Kennedy had worked so hard for was now sold off. At forty-six, Skipper shed his father's cattle business and ended up a rich man.

Tom was enraged that his son would have such little interest in his life's work. Despondent over the sale of his land, he went into a decline. By age 73, Tom was in need of some care. There was nowhere to turn but to his daughter Bessie. He moved to San Francisco to live with Bessie and her husband William Lutz, and with his daughter's tender care, he lived another five years. Thomas Kennedy died in San Francisco, September 25, 1908 at the age of 78.

Skipper lived in Knights Ferry with his wife Lena and owned the historic John Dent house where in the past, Dent had occasionally entertained his famous brother-in-law Captain Ulysses S. Grant. Skipper chose not to be a cattleman and worked as a mechanic on school buses, driving a bus route from Knights Ferry to Oakdale High School. Politically liberal and enterprising, he spearheaded community development and became a local historian.

Kennedy Cow Camp has remained in constant use by the multiple owners of the Kennedy Meadows Resort. All the resort owners, with one exception, were cattlemen and still are today.

Thomas Kennedy in 1902.
Photograph courtesy of Lisa Kennedy Bergantz.

SOURCES

Bergantz, Lisa Kennedy. Telephone interview, 26 Sep. 2016.

Conners, Pam and W. Woolfenden, Archaeological Site Record. 11 Aug 1981. US Forest Service archives.

"Dies from Strychnine Poisoning." *Union Democrat,* 9 May 1896. Front page.

1870 Census records for Robert Kennedy.

"History of Stanislaus County," Elliott and Moore, 1881. P. 367.

Kennedy, Andrew Thomas. Obituary. *San Francisco Chronicle*, 17 Sep. 1908, P. 31.

Kennedy Family Bible.

"Narrow Escape." *Tuolumne Independent,* 23 Jul. 1898.

National Register of Historic Places. FS 05-16-53-117/CH-TUO.

1983 Interview with Joan Gorsuch of Jamestown. Interviewed by Bill Shatruck.

"Not Guilty." *Tuolumne Independent,* 19 Nov. 1898.

"R.T. Kennedy Arrested." *Union Democrat*, 12 Feb. 1910. P. 3.

Tuolumne County Recorder's Office. Book 37, P. 543-4, Book 57, P. 572, Book 55, P. 122, Book 23, P. 51.

CHAPTER 25

Birth of Kennedy Meadows Resort
Robert Edwards and Charles Ledshaw
Establish a Pack Station and Store

After Relief Reservoir was completed in 1910, there was a good road into Kennedy Meadows. Subsequently, public access to the delightful vacation area became a reality. It offered a lovely place to picnic, camp, and fish along the Stanislaus River. The nearby Baker Station patrons came by horse or wagon to Kennedy Meadows to ride horseback and explore the backcountry.

Robert "Bob" Edwards was familiar with the primitive backcountry above Kennedy Meadows. In 1917, realizing a demand by hunters and fishermen to be guided into the backcountry beyond the meadows, Bob established a summer horse camp. He made use of the old Kennedy cabin and built a few tent cabins, a barn, and a corral on the flat adjacent to the river. Edwards set up a temporary store, and in his Model T Ford, hauled food staples from Sonora, which he sold to outdoorsmen, tourists and locals. His wife Katherine, or "Kate," joined him at Kennedy Meadows, working beside him for the summer. During hunting season, he expanded his business to Brightman Flat, setting up a small pack station.

Bob Edwards was born in 1870 and spent his entire life in Tuolumne County. Edwards was large in stature and known for his strength and endurance. Bob's big-hearted personality gained him many acquaintances throughout Tuolumne County. Bob was legendary as a fisherman. The story went that Edwards could catch trout from the Stanislaus River, one right after another. On one occasion, an angler across the river could see that Edwards was catching the fish from right under his nose. The mad fisherman threw down his pole and stormed off.

After nine years of operating the pack station, Edwards' business was thriving. While guiding hunters to the high elevations, he noticed his strength failing. Concerned, he went to Stockton for medical help and discovered that he had a heart condition. Within a few weeks, he was unable to continue. Weakened by the condition, he and his wife Kate packed their belongings at Kennedy Meadows and returned to their ranch near Keystone. He knew he would never return to his beloved mountains. Nothing could be done to restore his health and in the spring of 1926, he was gone at the age of fifty-five.

Charles Ledshaw, a skilled mountain lion hunter and wilderness hunting guide, was familiar with Kennedy Meadows and no doubt knew Bob Edwards. In July of 1927, Charles Ledshaw, then forty-seven, and his wife Myrtle, thirty-nine, discussed taking up where Edwards left off. Myrtle loved the mountains, and in the past, she had accompanied her husband on hunting trips. Myrtle threw in her support, and they purchased the lease, which included all the equipment, buildings, tent cabins, and livestock from Kate Edwards. At this outpost, they added a gas station and continued the business called Kennedy Meadows.

Charles William Ledshaw was born on December 5, 1880, in Humboldt County, California. Ledshaw was an exceptional hunter and tracker. Athletic, strong, and relentless in tracking game, his reputation grew and came to the attention of the state. He was hired in 1919 by the State of California to hunt and kill mountain lions. This work took him all over California. However, lion hunting did not support his family, and for many years, he worked as a logger at camps throughout Tuolumne County and was valued as a foreman.

Hunter Ledshaw capitalized on his fame and distributed literature advertising: "I am prepared to take parties into the best fishing grounds in the Sierras such as Kennedy's Lake, five miles and Huckleberry Lake, thirteen miles. Specializing in deer, bear, and lion hunting parties. Bear guaranteed. Rates reasonable saddle and pack horses. Guides and hunting dogs."

The famed lion hunter was particular about his dogs. His redbone coonhound of blooded stock came from the kennels of Berry, Kentucky. Ledshaw and his dogs never gave up and had been known to track a lion forty-five miles.

As he had suspected, his fame as a hunter and guide attracted outdoorsmen, and they were eager to be packed into the high country by the famous lion hunter. Myrtle ran the store and scheduled hunting parties. They were happy and loved their mountain business. Sadly, the enterprise came to an end after only two seasons. Charles Ledshaw suffered a terrible loss when his wife Myrtle was suddenly killed in a car crash on September 1, 1928. It was nighttime and she was coming up the Confidence Grade when she lost control of her car. She and several other employees had gone to Sonora to buy a truckload of provisions for the store. The driver of the truck that was following witnessed the crash. Charles was heartbroken. How could he continue operating the store and pack station outfit without her? Within the next few years, he sold the business to cattleman Frank Kurzi.

At sixty-seven and in failing health, after killing 308 lions, he retired from hunting the supreme predator in 1947. No records have surfaced with dates of his death and burial place.

State Lion Hunter Charles Ledshaw displays a lion he killed in 1930. *Photograph courtesy of the Tuolumne County Historical Society and Museum.* (Fred Leighton collection).

SOURCES

"Auto Crash Kills Mrs. Ledshaw." Myrtle Ledshaw obituary. *Tuolumne Independent*, 6 Sep. 1928.

"A Coon Hound Lion Hunter." *Union Democrat,* 8 Jan. 1921, Front page.

"Death Claims 'Bob' Edwards." Robert Edwards Obituary. *Union Democrat*, 17 Apr. 1926. Front Page.

Dunroamin', a memoir by Rhea McIntyre, Jul. 2000. Unpublished historical account.

Fitzhugh, E. Lee and W. Paul Gorenzel. *Biological Status of Mountain Lions in California,* Wildlife Extension, University of California, Davis, California. 1986.

Ledshaw, Charles William. WWI Draft Registration.

"Lion Hunter and Wife take over Edward's Place." *Union Democrat,* 16 Jul. 1927, P. 6.

"Mrs. Ledshaw in Auto Fatality." Myrtle Ledshaw obituary. *Union Democrat,* 8 Sep. 1928.

Library Oral History series. Oral interview with Walter Booker Interviewed by Annalie Hodge, Columbia College.

US Census records, 1920.

CHAPTER 26

Kennedy Meadows
Frank and Lurene Kurzi Build the Hotel

In the heart of the Great Depression, Frank Kurzi had the foresight to visualize the potential of a summer horse camp at Kennedy Meadows. It already consisted of tent cabins, a small store, gas pumps, and a pack station. Frank and his wife Lurene hoped that owning Kennedy Meadows would be a stepping stone to their dream of a large cattle business. Frank was known to say, "Don't fall in love with anything. If you can double your money, sell it." They discussed the possibility of taking over Kennedy Meadows with the current owner, Charles Ledshaw, who agreed. Thus, in 1929, the Kurzis embarked on their investment in a mountain retreat.

Coincidentally, both Frank and Lurene were born on Bald Mountain, near Sonora. Frank was born on August 30, 1897 and Ida Lurene Shaw was born September 21, 1901, at her grandparents' home. Lurene attended school through eighth grade at the old Phoenix Lake School. It wasn't unusual for girls to not complete their education in the early 1900s. Lurene herself once said this was "because we went to work in those days." She was just sixteen, and Frank only twenty, when the pair were married in 1917.

In the early 1930s, the Kurzis decided to upgrade from tents and build a hotel. Inspired by the architecture of the decade-old Dardanelle Hotel, they built a similar structure, which housed a hotel, store, and

Lurene Kurzi at Kennedy Meadows.
Photographer unknown.

The first Kennedy Meadows Hotel, built around 1931.
Photograph courtesy of Tuolumne County Historical Society and Museum.

Kennedy Meadows Hotel staff 1939
Left to Right: Leonard Reese (butcher, cowboy, handyman), Frank Kurzi (hotel owner), Jim Hawkins (cook), Barbara Kress (housekeeper), Lottie Pedro in bib overalls, (waitress, laundry, housekeeper), Alva Shaw (Lurene's father), Mrs. Johnson (wife of game warden), Zeke Goodwin (logger), Lurene Kurzi (hotel owner).
Photograph courtesy of Donnie Wright.

restaurant. Nine primitive one-room guest cabins for hunters and fishermen lined the road entering the property. All the buildings were constructed with rough-sawn sugar pine, supplied by a sawmill in the upper meadow.

The Kurzis realized that for the cowboy crowd, they needed a saloon and dance hall. The saloon was built as a separate building with a large space for dancing, while the upstairs served to house the wranglers. It was an immediate success, and the cowboys named it the "Last Chance Saloon."

The existing pack station was tucked below the granite cliffs at the back of the hotel. Up to one hundred and fifty horses and mules, many unbroken, were trained on site. Brave buckaroos would halter-break them, climb on their backs in the corral, and ride them on the trail a few times before they were deemed worthy saddle horses for paying customers. Any cowboy asking for work at Kennedy Meadows Pack Station found that it wasn't an easy or glamorous job. Kurzi explained, "I pay by

Frank Kurzi.
Photograph courtesy of Donnie Wright.

The Last Chance Saloon, circa 1955.
Photograph courtesy of the Tuolumne County Historical Society and Museum.

the month; that's thirty days and thirty nights." He expected them to be on call and work all hours.

Frank Kurzi was extremely knowledgeable about the terrain in the backcountry above the resort. He participated in extending the trail system into the Emigrant Basin. The new trails opened routes to lakes for anglers and fresh destinations for eager deer hunters.

When Frank was not leading pack trains into the wilderness, he paid close attention to his repeat customers and treated them well. He would frequently buy them a free drink at the saloon and make them feel welcome. He preferred leisurely socializing over drinks and talking politics. Frank had a strong dislike for communists and his hot temper flared over the subject. He could be found in the bar most afternoons with an audience of like-minded chums, gesturing with a cigarette to emphasize his political opinions.

The Kurzi's personal quarters were located upstairs in the hotel. Frank was frequently up at 2 am. For slippers, he cut the tops off old boots and stomped around in the middle of the night, keeping Lurene and the staff awake.

Also upstairs were rooms for the staff and the hotel office. Lurene, a chatterbox, with a glass of whisky by her side, managed the office and was the heartbeat of the business. In contrast to her husband Frank, Lurene was a hard worker. She kept the books, scheduled the rental cabins, ran the

restaurant, cooked, waited tables, tended bar, took pack trip reservations, and saddled horses. When she barked, employees jumped.

Her right hand was Lottie Pedro, affectionately called "Aunt Lottie." She was tireless, managing the laundry and housekeeping, and pitching in on any work that was needed. Frank Kurzi knew what a jewel he had in Lottie and always treated her with respect.

Through the Prohibition years, 1920 to 1933, while shrewdly protecting his illegal activities, Frank took the local Bureau of Alcohol, Tobacco, and Firearms boys on private deer hunting trips to his cattle range at Clavey Meadows, out of Long Barn. He guided them to the best locations for bagging big bucks. In exchange, the officials turned a blind eye to the sale of alcohol at Kennedy Meadows

During Prohibition, the saloon had a row of four or five illegal slot machines. These were all dime machines, which were set on the bar counter. They were the property of Al DeVoto, who operated a pool hall and later the Wagon Wheel restaurant and saloon in Sonora. DeVoto, a small-time mobster, drove a big, expensive Packard convertible. He became known as the wheeler-dealer of the Sonora underworld. He installed slot machines at the outer edges of civilization at Kennedy Meadows, Dardanelle, and Douglas, and collected a percentage of the take.

On Saturday nights the saloon was packed with wranglers, campers, tourists, and outdoorsmen. With stogies in hand, they told tall tales of their hunting and fishing adventures, punctuated with the raucous laughter of disbelief. It was a manly place, filled with male voices full of bravado.

With Tex Ritter jukebox tunes permeating the smoky air, coins and whisky glasses clinking, Frank held court at his usual perch at the smoke-filled bar. Along with the prohibited alcohol, the illegal slot machines boosted his profits. He'd slap each new customer on the back, inviting him to a drink, delighting in the comradery and the clatter of money filling his till—the place was a real moneymaker.

Frank Kurzi took full advantage of the movie business. As a result of so many films being made in the area, the Sonora Motion Picture Association

The new Kennedy Meadows Resort, built in the spring of 1941. *Photographer unknown.*

was established in 1936. From the beginning, Kurzi offered livestock for the movies, and supplied movie extras and wranglers from his pack station. This provided a nice income for Frank and Lurene through the Depression years.

In 1940, Paramount Pictures approached the Kurzis about renting their establishment as headquarters for the filming of *For Whom The Bell Tolls*. Elated over the good news, the Kurzis looked forward to the arrival of the film company. Unfortunately, a disaster interrupted these plans.

On December 23, 1940, two young men were en route to Reno over Sonora Pass. It was a foolish escapade to travel the high pass in the winter, but Hugh Calloway, a 22-year-old Air Corps private from Hamilton Field, and 23-year-old Lowell Swinford, a Southern Pacific employee, embarked on the dangerous journey. The two pals encountered a snowstorm and were forced to turned back. Near Chipmunk Flat, the car skidded on the narrow icy road and plunged over the bank. The two were uninjured and abandoned their car. They headed down the mountain to Kennedy Meadows Resort, trudging on foot in twenty inches of soft snow. The young men had struggled for a distance of seven miles to reach the resort, which was closed for the winter. To use the phone, they broke into the hotel.

One man located the phone while the other started a fire, since they were cold and wet. He poured kerosene into the wood stove to start the fire, not knowing that there was a can over the chimney. The fire flamed up quickly and blew out the front of the stove! Soon the entire hotel was ablaze. The fire completely destroyed the structure, and spread to a small storehouse thirty feet away. No water was available to fight the flames, which leveled the buildings in about twenty minutes.

The two were shaken and still cold and wet. They broke into a rental cabin containing firewood and food where they warmed up and spent the night. The next morning the hapless men walked another seven miles through the snow down to Dardanelle, in hopes of using a phone or getting a ride off the mountain. As they approached Brightman Flat, which had numerous cabins, they caught a whiff of smoke through the sleet. Their spirits rose as they soon saw a cabin with smoke curling from its chimney. Answering the door was Harry Lee and his wife, caretakers who were paid to stay all winter and look after cabins. With much excitement, the two young men explained that they had accidentally burned down the Kennedy Meadows Hotel!

With the mules packed, a party poses for a photograph on departure for the high country in the 1940s. In the background is the resort and at the right the saloon. *Photographer is not known.*

Mrs. Lee prepared a hot breakfast as they discussed what to do. The storm had increased in intensity, and there was nothing for the men to do but wait it out as guests of the Lees. Calloway and Swinford stayed with the Lees for three days, helping with chores and catching the Lees up on news of the day.

Stranded, the young men were concerned about missing work. Would their families be concerned when they did not return as scheduled? In two days it would be Christmas. The Lees were pleased not to spend Christmas alone and went all out to make it a special day, with a fine meal and Mrs. Lee's famous chocolate fudge for dessert. That day the storm subsided.

The day after Christmas, everyone geared up with snowshoes for a trip down the mountain. The Lees escorted the men to Niagara, where the group spent the night at a cabin. In the morning, Calloway and Swinford continued to descend the mountain in their search for a telephone. On December 28th they were picked up near Strawberry by Tony Freitas, a local PG&E employee, who brought them

to Pinecrest. From there, they were able to call the sheriff's office. The sheriff arrived, and Calloway and Swinford were taken into custody, but charges were not filed against them.

Sheriff J.H. Dambacher released the men shortly after their arrival. After their ordeal that included sliding off an icy mountain road, hiking through deep snow, burning down a resort, and trudging through a snowstorm to find help, they felt a huge burden lifted when the sheriff determined there would be no charges. They were free to go.

The Kurzis were devastated to hear of their loss. The damages were estimated at $12,000. Fortunately, the buildings and all their contents were partially covered by insurance. The entire stock of linens, kitchen equipment, and office furnishings was destroyed.

In the spring of 1941, the Kurzis quickly rushed to rebuild, in hopes of regaining business with Paramount Pictures. Bill Belcher, an architect and contractor from Sonora, was hired to rebuild the resort on the same site. The rush job took only about three months and cost the Kurzis $8,000.

The new building consisted of twin gables and was unlike any other structure along Highway 108. No longer referred to as a hotel, it evolved into a summer resort where families were welcomed. The main floor hosted a general store with a walk-in refrigerator and a restaurant. At the back was a large kitchen with a big commercial gas range, and an island in the center to prepare food. Off the kitchen was the "cowboy room," where meals were served through a "pass through" to the cowboys seated at a large oak dining table that seated twelve. Also at the back was a small laundry room. It contained many shelves for the folded linens, a large mangle for ironing, and a gas-powered wringer washer. All the clothes were dried on a clothesline outside. Upstairs over the lobby were the Kurzis' private quarters that included an office. Both spaces were attached to a large hallway with rooms for guests and employees. The Kurzis painted it green and proudly opened their resort on July 4, 1941.

Although they were able to rebuild quickly, the Kurzis lost a lot of business to the Dardanelle Resort six miles down the highway. The main building was not finished in time for Paramount Pictures to occupy it as their main headquarters. The buildings untouched by the fire, however, were rented to the cast and crew members. To quickly accommodate more employees of the film crew, Kurzi built tent cabins at the back of the resort property. They were simply a wooden structure, built off the ground with a floor and frame for a canvas roof, and were used primarily for sleeping.

Losing the full occupancy of the film company was a huge blow to the Kurzis, although the film crew kept it a busy place, and the Kurzis made a good profit. Working late into the winter months, their last day of shooting was December 7, 1941. Everyone was shocked to learn that the United States had been attacked at Pearl Harbor.

By 1942, WWII had overwhelmed the country. Employees were hard to find, since many men had been drafted into the service. Gas rationing limited travel for vacationers heading to the mountains. These factors impacted the business. Frank and Lurene struggled to keep the resort and pack station going enough to make

Winter of 1942 Lurene poses in the snow at the resort. *Photograph courtesy of Pat Wright Day.*

a profit. Although discouraged by the lack of customers, they remained open.

Frank, a cattleman at heart, longed to be released from the financial burdens of the resort and go into the cattle business full time.

In July of 1945, Lou Bittner, owner of an amateur basketball team in Oakland, offered Kurzi $35,000 for the business. Selling the resort included the hotel, bar and dance hall, plus ten rental cabins, the power house, shower and bath house, tool house, outside toilet, and three redwood water tanks. Also included were eight permits for parcels of land to pasture horses. At the pack station with all their tack, Kurzi sold his twenty-seven mules and forty-eight horses. The saloon came with wine and beer, and the distilled spirits license. Most importantly, the Pacific Gas and Electric Company lease for the resort grounds was in the deal. It was perfect timing. Kurzi was done with it all. They bought a little cabin at Dardanelle on Brightman Flat. Mostly it was Lurene's, as Frank was elsewhere. She loved it and stayed many summers.

At age forty-nine, Kurzi was eager to start his cattle business, and had dreamed of this moment. With his newly acquired $35,000 stuffed in the glove box of his 1939 Buick coupe, Frank immediately drove to the Clover Ranch, located between Valley Home and Oakdale, and bought two hundred acres of irrigated cattle range. His newly acquired ranch did not require taking stock to the mountains to graze the meadows in the summer, so he gave up the Clavey allotment.

From Tom Hughes he later leased a huge winter range for his cattle at Marshes Flat near Moccasin. The Kurzis now owned about four hundred head of cattle. Frank and Lurene moved from their home at the end of Stewart Street in Sonora and settled into a house at Marshes Flat.

Frank, isolated on the ranch, missed the attention of his bar buddies, and began to frequent the Louvre Saloon in Sonora, operated by Al and Millie Lyons. There he fell in love with Millie, and the Kurzi's marriage fell apart. He divorced Lurene, and Millie divorced Al.

Millie and Frank moved to Fallon, Nevada, to be near her son from the former marriage. There they operated the Corral Saloon. Frank became very sick with pneumonia and died at age seventy-four, on January 8, 1972.

A year before Lurene Kurzi died, she was the Grand Marshall of the Motherlode Round-up Parade. She was one of Tuolumne County's most famous female ranchers. Lurene Shaw Kurzi died of emphysema on June 7, 1978 in Sonora, at the age of seventy-six.

SOURCES
Agreement. Tuolumne County Recorder's Office. Vol. 17, p. 427.
Barnette, Jeanette. Telephone interview, 26 Jan. 2018.
Day, Pat Wright. Personal interview, 2016, and telephone interview, 23 Jan. 2018.
Krause, Kenneth H.; Letter, Matt Bloom collection, Jun 1998.
Kurzi, Frank Obituary. *Union Democrat*, 10 Jan. 1972, p. 6.
Kurzi, Lurene Shaw obituary; *Union Democrat*, 8 Jun. 1978.
"Lost Men Return Safely; Resort Accidentally Burned" *Union Democrat*, 27 Dec. 1940. Front page.
The Pony Express; "Stories of Pioneers and Old Trails." Apr. 1963 issue, p. 7.
Ralph, Bob. "Along the Upper Stanislaus." Union Democrat, 4 Jul. 1941, p. 3.
Rosacso, Jean. Personal interview, 12 Mar. 2016.
Wright, Donnie. *Union Democrat* interview, 2008.
Wright, Donnie personal interviews, 6 Apr. 2017, 13 Dec. 2017, 19 Jan. 2018.

Frank Kurzi built this lodge in the early 1930s. It burned down December 23, 1940, when two young men who were stranded in the snow broke in and accidentally set it afire. *Courtesy of Bill Coffill.*

CHAPTER 27

Lou Bittner
Basketball Comes to Kennedy Meadows

In July of 1945, an ill wind in the form of Louis Bittner came to Kennedy Meadows. The lovely mountain resort was purchased by Bittner, a sports enthusiast from Oakland, and for the first time, the resort was not owned by a cattleman. At thirty-eight, dark-haired, and sporting a thin mustache, Bittner was a businessman with a checkered past, lacking in both the moral fiber and skills to manage a place like Kennedy Meadows.

Bittner took an interest in the resort when he joined his friends Johnny Vergez, a baseball talent scout, and Harry Borba, a San Francisco sports writer, at Kennedy Meadows for a fishing trip. Enthralled with the place, Bittner bragged to his friends that he could buy the resort.

Louis Bittner, born December 6, 1907, in California, opened a tax consulting insurance business in 1944 in Oakland. Bittner was also a sports promoter who sponsored a variety of amateur teams and athletes in the Oakland area. A wily businessman and one-time Internal Revenue agent, he made a fortune employing twenty tax experts and selling insurance in the Bay Area.

Lou Bittner owned a basketball team named the "Oakland Bittners" that he had recently organized. It occurred to him that Kennedy Meadows would make an excellent summer training camp for his new team. The players would be isolated and able to focus without the distractions of girlfriends, wives, and family. Plus, the altitude and fresh air would build their lung capacity and endurance.

Bittner considered himself a keen bargain driver. He approached owner Frank Kurzi, who had built Kennedy Meadows from the ground up, with an offer of $35,000. Kurzi agreed, as he was anxious to revive his cattle business and unload the resort. The transaction did not include the cattle business held by Cliff Mitchell at Kennedy Lake, which in the past was part of the deal. Kurzi and Bittner made plans to sign the necessary papers.

When Lou Bittner arrived in August, he handed Kurzi $35,000 in cash. A flat area in front of the saloon was paved with asphalt, and hoops were attached to trees for a basketball court. He brought his team up to the mountains for practice sessions in the fresh mountain air. Bittner, uncomfortable with cowboys and deer hunters, decided to make Kennedy Meadows a private club, catering to his friends in the Bay Area sports world.

The team arrived with their coaches and gear. They took over the upstairs quarters of the lodge. At first, the basketball players, an oddity in this cowboy enclave, attracted a lot of attention. No doubt their interaction with the wranglers created some awkward moments. Paul Napolitano, one of the star players, set himself up as the bartender, talking basketball with the patrons. The tall athletes were an amusing curiosity, but most mountain tourists were not interested in watching a basketball practice session. The players soon looked foolish and were ignored.

When Kurzi's repeat customers returned, they were surprised to find a new owner, and were told they had to be club members to rent a cabin. The new rules seemed ridiculous, and they left in a huff. Bittner, dressed in a short-sleeved dress shirt and slacks, looked like he was in the wrong place. Locals did not warm up to this outsider.

The Kurzi employees that Bittner retained found him to be a cocky 'know it all,' and had no respect for the man. The business became mismanaged, and the former employees soon were fed up with this city boy and left. Bittner clearly was not cut out for running a remote mountain resort.

Apparently, he thought the pack station would just run itself. He had a condescending opinion of the cowboys, and considered them a rowdy, uneducated bunch, and paid them low wages. To him they were expendable, a dime a dozen. Word soon got around, and few wranglers wanted to work for Bittner. Business was slow and the cowboys sat idle.

On the other hand, his Oakland basketball team was doing well. In the summer of 1946, the team's credibility shot up when Bittner announced that he had persuaded Jim Pollard to join the team. That year the team entered the American Basketball League, where they played for two seasons. For a short time, they were a winning basketball team and one of the best in the country, but Oakland's sports enthusiasts took little notice.

However, basketball and the mountain resort did not mix well. Nothing went right, and the resort was not making money. In 1947, after a heated argument with his mountain neighbor, cattleman Cliff Mitchell, Bittner unexpectedly sold out to Mitchell for $50,000 and returned to the Bay Area, where his shady business dealings eventually caught up with him.

His trouble started when his name got into the newspapers. *The Oakland Tribune* reported in July of 1949, "It is no secret that many of the young men who have played for Bittner were displeased with the manner in which the team's business affairs were operated." In July of 1949, he was expelled from the Amateur Athletic Union and fled to Manila, where he had dreams of making a fast dollar and settling in the Philippines.

In 1950, he was charged with failure to pay his publicity man and business agent their wages, and neglected to show up in court. In 1956, his tax consultant license was revoked after a hearing in

Old postcard from 1946 during the Bittner days.
Photograph courtesy of Roger and Evelyn Ericksen.

which he was accused of "acts of gross negligence" in handling a trustee account. In 1958, Bittner was arrested on a battery charge when his son Kenneth was served papers for a civil matter. Bittner got upset and punched the process server in the jaw. No other information has surfaced about Bittner in his later years, as to his successes or failures, or where he is buried. Louis Bittner died at age seventy-three on May 29, 1980.

SOURCES
"Add Predictions." *Oakland Tribune*, 30 Aug. 1945. p. 24
Barnette, Jeanette. Telephone interview, 26 Jan. 2018.
"Bittner Buys Kennedy Meadows." *Oakland Tribune*, August 1945 p. 15.
"Bittner Departs Basketball." *Oakland Tribune*, 28 Jul. 1949 p. 32.
Grundman, Adolph H. "Golden Age of Amateur Basketball." The AAU Tournament,
"Louis Bittner Arrested for Row Over Son." *Oakland Tribune*, 2 Jul. 1958 p. 25.
"Louis J. Bittner Misses His Trial." *Oakland Tribune*, 24 May 1950. p.4.
Mitchell, Kenney. Personal interview, 3 Mar. 2017.
1921-1968 University of Nebraska Press, Lincoln and London, p. 101.
"Plentiful Deer at Kennedy Meadows." *Oakland Tribune*, 20 Sep. 1945. p. 27.
United States Social Security Death Index.
"Vergez Back at Work." *Oakland Tribune*, 18 Jul. 1945, P. 11.
Wright, Donnie. Personal interview, 13 Dec. 2017.

CHAPTER 28

Kennedy Meadows
A Cattleman Takes the Reins

After Tom Kennedy left the high mountain meadows, the Mitchells were the first cattlemen to take over his cow camp at Kennedy Lake. The Mitchells were an early pioneer family that made a lasting impact on Kennedy Meadows and the cattle industry.

Addison "Mills" Mitchell, Jr., was born in 1879 in Vallecito, California. Mills met a local girl, Millie Sletten, who was twenty-three when the two married on September 14, 1904. The twenty-four-year-old Mills was an ambitious rancher and good businessman like his father. The young couple had two children: Kathleen, born on October 24, 1905, and son Clifton, born on September 23, 1909. Mitchell's father came from a family of buggy manufacturers in England and was a merchant in San Francisco for a short time before he moved to the small gold mining community of Vallecito in Calaveras County, where he operated a livery stable and store. He married neighbor girl Sarah Batten and started a family. Addison Mills Mitchell, Jr. was their only son.

In 1905, Mills Mitchell observed the construction of a large camp being erected in Vallecito, for the huge Relief Dam project and its Camp Nine Powerhouse. The Union Construction Company headed up the massive project. The dam would be in the high mountains above Kennedy Meadows. The camp was a source of labor for the massive project, and had a cafeteria to feed the workers. Mitchell saw a business opportunity right in his own backyard. He negotiated a contract, providing food supplies and beef to the kitchen. This became the start of Mitchell's cattle business. Supplying Camp Nine soon led to his contract for

supplying goods and meat for the Relief Dam project.

During this time, Mitchell obtained summer grazing rights from the Union Construction Company at Kennedy Lake, not far from the Relief Dam project. The Mitchell cattle were now in close proximity to the dam, and were easily slaughtered on site for fresh beef to feed the workers. Mitchell hired a crew of men to look after the cattle, and help with the delivery of the fresh meat. A Chilean, Bensie Morales, was the butcher. Bensie brought his family with him and they camped near the old Kennedy cabin at the lake.

It was a successful business, bringing the Mitchell cattle from Vallecito to the high mountains for summer grazing. The Mitchell grazing allotment remained in the family for many years. During the Great Depression, Mills was also able to buy up ranches that were in foreclosure. Thus, he owned ranches in the lowland towns of Milton, Farmington, and Vallecito, and built his cattle empire.

By the 1930s, Mitchell was in failing health, worn out from managing his large cattle empire. He died on June 16, 1936 in San Francisco, at age fifty-seven. The cattle legacy he built passed to his son Clifton and daughter-in-law Rose, both in their mid-twenties.

On their way to the Kennedy Lake cattle range, the young couple lodged at the primitive old Tom Kennedy cabin, with a floor primarily of dirt. Mostly they stayed at Kennedy Lake, where Cliff and Rose built a new cabin and used the old one as a barn. Rose's cousin, a carpenter, designed a fourteen- by-twenty-foot cabin for the couple. He designed the cabin to be assembled at the building site, so all the pieces were pre-cut. They hauled them to Kennedy

Mitchell's snug new cabin at their Kennedy Lake cow camp.
Photograph courtesy of Matt Bloom.

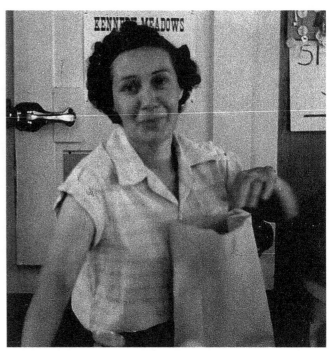

Rose Mitchell bagging groceries at the store.
Photograph courtesy of Matt Bloom.

Lake by pack train, and assembled the little cabin right at the lake. Unfortunately, the carpenter never traveled there to see it completed.

In the fall of 1947, at age thirty-eight, Cliff Mitchell was bringing his cattle down from the mountains to be trucked to his winter range in Vallecito. Cliff herded the cattle into a meadow adjacent to the Kennedy Meadows lodge, holding them there until the cattle trucks arrived. Lou Bittner, who operated the resort and pack station at the same time, brought hunting parties down from the mountains to the pack station. The respective groups encountered each other in the meadow. Bittner, no horseman, lost control of the pack animals, and soon they were loose in the meadow, mixing with the cattle and causing havoc. Upset with Bittner's incompetence, Cliff had sharp words with the man.

Soon the situation escalated. Cliff picked up a shovel and chased Bittner, who ran into the store and bolted the door against Mitchell. Cliff started banging on the door with his shovel. Bittner, frightened and frustrated, shouted, "I'm done with this place. I'll sell it to you for $50,000." Cliff agreed, and they arranged to meet up the following Tuesday with money and legal papers to sign. Bittner then cautiously emerged from the store and went to the saloon, where he cleaned out the cash register. He next went to the store and took all the money from that register and proceeded upstairs to his office, where he cleaned out all the drawers. He nervously packed his car and left.

The news of Bittner's hasty flight spread like wildfire. The pack station was going full tilt with hunters packing in to the back country to hunt deer. Cowboys who disliked him quickly walked off the job, and the pack station emptied out. It could not have happened at a worse time.

Bittner had taken all the office reservation books and logs. Therefore, the Mitchells had no records of what hunting parties were still up in the mountains waiting for a cowboy to come pack them out. It was a huge mess. Loyal staff members were stunned. Lottie Pedro stayed and helped in the restaurant. Leonard Reese, the all-round handyman, and kitchen helper, and Mrs. Johnson, remained to be of help.

Meanwhile, disgruntled deer hunters returned by walking out of the mountains because no packers came to get them and their gear. Mitchell's cowboys, who had just brought the cattle down from the high country, were now sent back into the mountains to search for the hunters and bring them back, leading them in the dark.

At the bar there was no money to make change, so every drink was rounded off to the dollar. As darkness approached, lights were left on all night, so the deer hunters could find their way to the stables, saloon, and restaurant. And so began the Mitchells' ownership of Kennedy Meadows Resort and Pack Station.

Cliff and Rose put Kennedy Meadows back in business and established good customer relations. The saloon was a roaring success with popular Western music, dancing, and DeVoto's slot machines. The Mitchell family had a widespread affection for the area. Now, all the land once held by Tom Kennedy was held by the Mitchells.

They put long-time Kennedy Meadows employee Leonard Reese in charge of the store. The store mainly had staples for campers like bread, milk, and canned goods, but lacked fresh vegetables. The well-stocked shelves also supplied beer, whisky, cigarettes, and fishing supplies.

Cliff Mitchell would have wranglers bring down a few head of cattle from Kennedy Lake to the pack station. Leonard Reese would butcher them for the restaurant, and hang meat to cool in the old Kennedy cabin in front of the resort. The cabin's floorboards could swing out and allow the cold air under the cabin to cool the meat. The restaurant hired skilled cooks, and served prime rib dinners, which became their signature Saturday night menu. Campers, tourists, and cabin owners came faithfully from miles around for the fine meal served high in the mountains.

Kenny Mitchell, Cliff and Rose's son, remembers, "Business at Dardanelle resort was slow compared with Kennedy Meadows. Dardanelle owner Louise Coffill, who was also the postmaster, was notorious for reading all the postcards and examining everyone's mail. If she saw people making reservations for Kennedy Meadows she would hold the mail back." Thus, the reservation was not made in time, and when the tourist arrived at Kennedy Meadows the cabin was already taken, causing an unpleasant situation. The Mitchells suspected that Louise notified the IRS, thinking the Mitchells were not taxing the customers for one-hour rides at the stables.

Frequently, Cliff would tend bar at his Last Chance Saloon, a separate building adjacent to the pack station and hotel. The watering hole was a busy place, with wranglers and outdoorsmen who came to relax and socialize after a day on horseback or a day at the river. It was a lucrative part of his business.

Inside the Kennedy Meadows resort store in 1957, with Leonard Reese, who worked there for many years, behind the counter. *Courtesy of the Tuolumne County Historical Society and Museum.*

However, if Cliff thought the clients had too much to drink, he would close down the bar and escort them over to the restaurant.

Mitchell recalls, "Louise Coffill tipped off the Bureau of Alcohol and Firearms that there was under-age drinking at the saloon. Actually her efforts had little effect, and we ran an honest business and had many loyal customers through the years."

In addition to the Kennedy Meadows Resort, Cliff built and managed a resort on Lake Tulloch, known as Black Creek. The two resorts plus the cattle business put a great deal of stress on the Mitchell's marriage. Cliff and Rose divorced in 1959. In the settlement, Rose got Kennedy Meadows, and Cliff ran Black Creek Resort and his cattle business.

Rose, although a petite lady only about five feet tall, was hard-working and well-liked. An efficient business woman, she did her best to make the resort thrive. Rose managed to stay on top of all the employees' comings and goings, as if she had her own underground informants. Not much got by her. She leaned on long-time Kennedy employee Leonard Reese for help running the business, but took poor advice from others. There was always friction with the cowboys who did not like a female boss. Despite obstacles, Rose continued working to make the resort a successful enterprise. She even came up with a clever advertising scheme. She had an arrangement with a Sonora Cadillac dealer, John Kelley. She had him install a big billboard advertising Cadillacs and the dealership at the entrance to Kennedy Meadows. She drove Cadillacs exclusively, and could often be seen with her Cadillac trunk full of hay for the pack station.

At fifty-two, after owning the resort for fourteen years, Rose decided to sell. It was hard work managing it all on her own, trusting only family and a few friends. On July 30, 1960, she signed the bill of sale and sold to Reno Sardella for $70,000. The deal included the hotel, cabins, café, bar, grocery, and pack station. Complete furnishings, equipment, sixty head of stock, buildings and fixtures were also part of the transaction.

Cliff continued running his cattle at Kennedy Lake for the summer and bringing them down the mountain to the resort to be trucked to the winter grazing range. On October 2, 1966, with help from family and friends, they gathered the cattle and ordered the trucks. To celebrate the end of a season, Cliff rented a cabin at Kennedy Meadows and planned a big dinner to celebrate. Everyone arrived at the cabin that evening for a delicious meal prepared by the family women.

When the meal was finished, Cliff lit a cigarette, pushed his chair back from the table and enjoyed the satisfaction of the summer season coming to an end. He looked toward a less hectic winter at home. Suddenly, his cigarette dropped to the floor and a loud crash echoed throughout the room. Cliff fell over backwards in his chair and lay unconscious. Immediately family member, Ron Adams, an off duty Deputy Sheriff, rushed to his side and performed CPR, but Cliff could not be revived. Later, it was determined that Cliff had suffered a massive heart attack. The family remained to sort out what do next and begin the funeral arrangements. The grieving cowboys who had faithfully helped over the years, stayed to load the cows on the cattle trucks and drive them down the mountain.

It was a day of great loss. Cliff was only fifty-seven, precisely the age of his father when he had passed away. Cliff's untimely death came as a total shock. His sons Kenny and Mills continued to run the family cattle business.

Cliff Mitchell on the porch of the saloon in 1964.
Photograph courtesy of Tuolumne County Historical Society and Museum.

After selling the resort to Reno Sardella in 1960, Rose continued to live in Vallecito at the Mitchell family residence. Friendly and a good sales person, she went into the real estate business. She was a member of the local garden club and the Cowbelles, a women's cattle owners organization. Rose died August 8, 2008, at the ripe old age of 100.

SOURCES
California Birth Index, 1905-1995 database.
California Marriages, 1852-1952 database.
Haigh, Gary. Personal interview, 3 Aug. 2016.
Krause, Millie. Personal interview, 8 Jun. 2017.
Miller, Elvira. Personal interview, 1 Aug. 2017.
Mitchell, Kenny. Personal interview, 3 Mar. 2017.
Record of the sale of the Kennedy Meadows to Reno Sardella, Jul. 30, 1960.
Rose Lucille (Gurney) Mitchell Obituary.
Whittle, Donnie. Personal interview, 10 Feb. 2017.
United States Census 1930.

CHAPTER 29

Reno Sardella
Patriarch of the Pack Stations

Reno Sardella—even the sound of his name is memorable and evokes the romance of the Old West. He was a horseman, known far and wide on the Sonora Pass corridor. Idolized by younger men, and movie star handsome, he played hard, worked hard, and drank hard. For breakfast, he was known to down two raw eggs, followed by an "Early Times" bourbon chaser, mount his horse, and go to work.

Reno's father Giovanni, born into a large Italian family, emigrated from Pontremoli in northern Italy. In 1910, he left home and came with a wave of Italians to America. He followed his brother Joe, who had come two years earlier, and made his way to California to secure a job at the U.S. Lime Products Corporation's quarry on Lime Kiln Road near Sonora. Giovanni was welcomed by his brother, and the two young men boarded on Henry Sanguinetti's ranch. After two years of working at the lime quarry with Joe, he had saved enough money and sent for his wife Maria and four children.

Reno was born July 1, 1913, at the Sanguinetti family ranch house, and was the first Sardella child born in America. Eventually the Sardellas bought their own ranch, just east of the lime quarry, where four more siblings were born.

Through the Great Depression, the Sardellas made wine and cheese, and tended a large vegetable garden. They primarily sold wine, but also produced and sold cheese to Sonora merchants, and bartered for staples. Frequently the boys also worked at the lime quarry to bring in extra income.

In 1923, at age ten, Reno was helping with the cattle and horses at the Sanguinetti Ranch. All the ranchers knew each other and many were from Italian families. Reno was a quick learner around animals. He had a natural talent and an eye for stock, and even as a youngster enjoyed the challenge of taming a horse so difficult the owner was inclined shoot it. Through his teenage years, he spent his time with his brothers developing horseback riding skills, and became an excellent horseman.

When Reno was sixteen, he set himself up with a small pack station at Boulder Creek, near the Dardanelle Resort. It was just a small-time summer business, and Reno loved it. He knew that owning pack stations was what he wanted to do with his life.

Reno married Geraldine "Gerry" Bristol on October 18, 1935, at a Catholic church in Reno, Nevada. She was eighteen and he was twenty-two. Gerry had been born in a tent on June 25, 1917, near Copperopolis in Calaveras County. Her parents were James and Elsie Burnam Bristol. Her paternal grandmother's family, the Bogans, owned a lot

The Sardella family in 1944. Reno, daughter LaVerne, and wife Geraldine.
Photograph courtesy of the Sardella family.

of land near Stent, which was known in the early days as "Poverty Hill." Gerry grew up in Stent and Jamestown, and attended Sonora High School. Her family raised cattle. She was fun-loving, and liked to dance, sing, and yodel. As newlyweds, they moved in with Reno's parents at the Sardella Ranch. Reno and Gerry had one child, a daughter named LaVerne, who was born in Sonora in 1936. Baby LaVerne was the first Sardella grandchild.

To support his family, Reno worked many years as a lineman for PG&E. However, his reputation with horses led him to jobs with the local cattlemen. He worked for Louis Price, George Gorham, Tony Pedro, Del Adams, the Rosascos, and Joe Martin.

Frank Kurzi, the owner of Kennedy Meadows on Sonora Pass, was the livestock contractor for the Sonora Motion Picture Association, which attracted filmmakers to Tuolumne County. In 1935, Kurzi's stock was used for filming *Robin Hood of the El Dorado,* a movie about the bandit Joaquin Murrieta. Much of the movie was filmed on Sonora Pass near Douglas Station. The film had a lot of action and scenes of lawmen on horseback chasing after

Reno's work truck for the stables.
Photograph courtesy of the Ray Sardella family.

Murrieta's outlaw gang. Reno was already known in the area for his skill with horses, and Kurzi recommended Reno, twenty-two, and his brother Curly, to work as stuntmen for the dangerous, fast-paced horse scenes. Both able horsemen, they eagerly arrived at the movie set ready to work. It was a new, exciting experience, and Reno's introduction to working with Western filmmakers in Tuolumne County.

In 1942, when *For Whom The Bell Tolls* was being filmed on Sonora Pass, Frank Kurzi hired Reno to be responsible for the livestock for the film. This was a big job, because it was a high-end movie, run by the big Hollywood professionals. Reno was just twenty-nine, but Frank had confidence in Reno's abilities with the stock, and how he would handle himself with the film company. Frank was not disappointed, and hired Reno again for other movies. They built a trusting relationship, and the two men became lifelong friends. In 1949, at Pinecrest, Reno and Gerry operated a small horse stable where they rented out horses for hour-long rides to the public. During the winter, they offered sleigh rides, which were extremely popular.

Outdoorsmen were eager to pack into the backcountry of the Emigrant Basin to hunt and fish. Here was a business opportunity beyond hourly horseback rides. Reno had a good eye for horses, and in 1957 he set up a pack station at Bell Meadows, and hired Alec Anderson to manage it. It was a

At age 17, Reno playfully atop a horse in 1930.
Photograph courtesy of Renalda Salyers.

Reno at work at the pack station in 1964.
Bob Forrest photographer. Photograph courtesy of the Cassinetto family.

Reno Sardella in the 1940s.
Photograph courtesy of Renalda Salyers.

Reno opened pack stations in Mi-Wuk and Long Barn. He continued the business and expanded to include pack stations at Douglas on Sonora Pass, and Cherry Valley, in the backcountry, some distance from Highway 120. Reno knew the backcountry like few others, and was familiar with the high mountain trails, lakes and terrain. He was an avid fly fisherman who fished the surrounding lakes. He was happiest in the high mountains, riding a horse with a pack train of mules in tow. This is what he knew, and this is what he was passionate about.

The business required 600 to 700 horses and mules, plus saddles, tack, and other equipment. His wife Gerry was always at his side, cooking for patrons and the hired cowboys. Running the pack stations required long hours. Reno frequently drew on younger family members for help, and gave them their first job, knowing they could be trusted employees. He hired help to keep track of all the reservations for pack trips, and later his daughter LaVerne took over this task.

A tale about Reno has followed him after his death, and has frequently been embellished. Jack Reveal, the Stanislaus National Forest District Ranger recalls, "In 1952, the local packers contracted with someone whose name I can't recall, to make a promotional film. They invited some of the local big shots to go along as guests, in order to make up a party of ten to fifteen people. I got to go along,

profitable business, packing hunters and fishermen into the back country on established trails. Soon he moved the stables to Kerrick Corrals, an old sheep camp. He fenced the land and moved two railroad cars on the property for buildings.

Reno, in 1962, returning from the Emigrant Basin with a string of pack mules. *Photograph courtesy of the Sardella family.*

too. With the cameraman and his equipment, we rode out of Kennedy Meadows Resort with Cliff Mitchell and Reno Sardella leading the parade. We stopped here and there for the film to be shot in appropriate settings. The weather was perfect, the food outstanding, and the booze plentiful. We rode into Pinecrest on the third day, or maybe the fourth, after a number of short stops to pass the bottle along the line of jolly riders. When we reached the lodge, Reno, who was in the lead, rode his horse up the lodge steps and would have ridden on into the bar, but the doorway wasn't high enough for both him and the horse. The 30-minute film that resulted from the escapade was very good, and widely shown in the area. Obviously, the filmmaker had stayed sober, which couldn't be said of the actors."

In 1958, Reno and Gerry built their own home on some acreage in Stent, a one-time Gold Rush settlement outside Jamestown. The ranch was just over the hill from the old Sardella Ranch, where Reno was raised. It was also near the land Gerry's ancestors had owned, and where Gerry was raised. Both Reno and Gerry, close to kin and childhood memories, felt right at home in Stent. In the past, economic necessity had required the couple to rent various houses or cabins as their place of residence. Years of hard work with his pack stations and the

Reno and his wife Gerry in the 1950s. *Photograph courtesy of Renalda Salyers.*

movie industry now gave them the means to finally purchase a ranch of their own.

Chuck Knowles, who worked for Reno, remembers, "Reno's wife Gerry was the boss. Even though Reno was loud, bullheaded, impulsive, boisterous, and hollered, what Gerry said went. She laid down the law and was Reno's rock."

Reno Sardella.
Photograph courtesy of the Bashford York family.

Reno had taken over the livestock contact for the Sonora Motion Picture Association from his longtime friend, Frank Kurzi. He provided horses, mules, and rolling stock, such as stage coaches, wagons, buggies for the local film companies. Many television Westerns were shot on his ranch at Stent and at Kennedy Meadows. Reno was well known, well liked, and had a large network of friends to call on for special props and skills. Reno could count as friends many of the popular Western stars, including Warren Oates, Buddy Ebsen in *Mail Order Bride* and Lee Majors in *The Big Valley*, plus the cast of *Little House on the Prairie, Tales of Wells Fargo,* and *Bonanza*. They all knew each other, were in the same business, and worked well together.

Reno continued with his contracting for the film industry, gaining a respected reputation. He trusted everyone, and finalized many a business deal

with a handshake. Generous to a fault, he often would accept livestock in trade for a debt owed him. Being an old horse trader at heart, he was not always the best businessman. However, he was one of those stubborn individuals who did everything the hard way, and got it done his way.

Joanne Knowles recalls, "Reno was a storyteller and a showman. He liked to be the center of attention. When he was telling a story or on a rant, he walked backward, waved his arms above his head, and threw his hat into the air! A natural performer. Yet he also had a quiet, thoughtful side that ran deeper than his public persona allowed.

"His wife Gerry was just the opposite. Quiet, calm and supportive. Gerry was a great believer in the phases of the moon, and how astrology affected people's lives. She consulted her 'moon book' before making any decisions."

In 1960, Reno purchased Douglas Resort from the Dentons, where he already ran a pack station. It included rental cabins, a restaurant, soda fountain, bar, dance hall, pack station, and gas pumps. He hired friends to manage the daily operations.

On July 30, 1960 at age forty-seven, Reno purchased Kennedy Meadows Resort from Rose Mitchell for $70,000. The transaction included 240 acres and a spring, plus all the inventory and sixty head of stock. This place was dear to his heart. It had been something he had always secretly aspired to obtain. Kennedy Meadows was the jewel of Sierra pack stations. Reno was overjoyed to own the exceptionally beautiful mountain real estate that was widely known as the place to go for relaxation, fishing, hunting, and packing into Emigrant Basin and Yosemite National Park.

The Sardellas operated Kennedy Meadows for ten years. Shortly after purchasing the resort, Reno discovered he had bladder cancer. Alarmed, he went to Stanford University Medical Center for treatment. He had surgery, and left the hospital with a cystectomy bag that collected his urine outside his body. This was an entirely new procedure. He was forty-eight, and the doctors gave him two years to live. The news spread, and friends were concerned.

The Big Valley, a Western television series that ran from 1965 to 1969, included many scenes in

Reno tending bar at the saloon.
Photograph courtesy of Renalda Salyers.

Tuolumne County and the Sonora Pass area. Reno met the young actor Lee Majors during filming near Kennedy Meadows, and they struck up an immediate friendship. Lee enjoyed tending bar at the saloon and the whole Kennedy Meadow environment. The young actor so admired Reno that he offered to buy Kennedy Meadows and operate it until Reno recovered, and then sell it back. This generous offer was never realized, although it was a testament to how Reno was loved by those who knew him.

Knowing he was limited by health problems, Reno and Gerry decided it was best to sell off the pack stations in preparation for their future. First to be sold was Long Barn, followed by Mi-Wuk, Douglas and finally, the distant Cherry Valley. He kept Kennedy Meadows, and daughter LaVerne managed Kerrick Corral.

When Gerry came to the resort for the summer season, she worked tirelessly in the background, cleaning rental cabins, waiting tables, doing laundry, and fixing many a meal for a hungry cowboy. She had a reputation as an excellent cook, with a mix of Italian and Irish dishes. Gerry, although she was friendly and greeted everyone warmly, could hold her own, keeping the rough cowboys in line.

It was a busy place full of tourists, fishermen, deer hunters, backpackers, and heavy-drinking cowboys. It was hard work for both of them, with problems to solve day and night. It was a business with supplies to order, books to keep, reservations to be scheduled and loyal employees who could fix plumbing, unpack a mule, pump gas, or step in to wait tables. Even long-standing customers and extended family stepped in to help keep the business running smoothly. Reno was known to say, "The pay may not be much but the hours make up for it."

The hired wranglers were expected to be busy all the time. The resort grounds were immaculate. The stables were spotless with no flies, the stock were groomed and fed on schedule, and the tack cleaned and ready for the next rider. The wranglers also kept the pine needles raked around rental cabins, stocked firewood at the campfire pits, and kept the road in good repair. The employees had a sense of pride in the place and the family they worked for. Reno's stature as a pack station owner, resort owner, and his work with the Sonora Motion Picture Association brought him great respect. Even people who had never met him still remembered his name and knew he was a larger-than-life personality. By the 1960s, along the Sonora Pass corridor, almost everyone had heard of Reno Sardella.

In the late 1960s, Reno hired two retired railroad cooks, Cooper and Frank Baust, who worked in shifts. One got up at 3 a.m., fired up the propane oven, and put in a large beef roast. That was the meat for all day. Although they were experienced cooks, they served up a simple menu of meat and potatoes. Once in a great while, they would bake a pie.

Reno spent much of his life in the saddle in the backcountry of the Emigrant Basin. He loved the pristine alpine lakes, granite monoliths, the wind in the pines, and the serenity and beauty of it all. It pained him to see the trash visitors left behind. He and his employees hauled out tons of litter from mountain campsites. The Stanislaus National Forest also had concerns, and put into effect Wilderness permits with regulations to further manage the backcountry. Reno helped enforce the wilderness permit system, and would educate the public about the new rules for their safety, and how to be respectful of the wilderness they came to enjoy. Conditions improved.

High school friends relax and chat on the porch of their cabin at Kennedy Meadows resort.
Photograph courtesy of Norene Sardella Leonard.

Kennedy Meadows pack Station.
Photograph courtesy of Renalda Salyers.

The Sardella family was always close, and Reno was thoughtful concerning his extended family. Reno's niece, Norene, fondly remembers, "In 1962, I graduated from high school. My uncle Reno, as a graduation gift, arranged for me to bring five of my friends for a week at his Kennedy Meadows Resort. He explained that we would have our own cabin, could eat all our meals at the restaurant, and could ride the horses at the stable. He especially mentioned that we were only to ride the horses as far as the upper meadow. All free of charge. Oh, we were thrilled!

"So we explored the area and rode the horses. We hung around the stables looking over the cowboys, but found none to give a second look. Bored, we knew some boys at Dardanelle and decided to ride the horses six miles to Dardanelle and look for the boys we knew. So against Reno's wishes off we went, enjoying a scenic ride through grassy flats and alongside the Stanislaus River, arriving at Dardanelle. Louise Coffill, owner of the Dardanelle Resort, noticed us on horseback and knew we probably were not where we belonged. She phoned Kennedy Meadows and reported us.

"Soon a cowboy drove up with a horse trailer. He asked us to dismount, and loaded the horses in the trailer and drove away. Embarrassed at being caught, we were left to walk the six miles back to Kennedy Meadows. I dreaded an encounter with my uncle. However, when we met next he never said a word about the horse incident!"

Reno was honored by the Stanislaus National Forest personnel for his conservation and for furthering good management and proper use of the Emigrant Primitive Area. Reno received a Certificate of Appreciation and plaque, presented by Forest Service supervisor Gary Cargill at an annual meeting of the livestock advisory board for the Stanislaus National Forest. It was unusual for the Forest Service to recognize cattlemen for their conservation efforts, so this was a great honor.

Reno's knowledge of the terrain saved many lives. His older brother Miller worked in law enforcement, and in 1962 was elected Tuolumne County Sheriff. He was a well-known and popular lawman. The two brothers were close and had great love for each other. Reno had intimate knowledge of the backcountry, and many times Miller called upon him to help rescue injured or lost persons.

By 1970, Reno was suffering from arthritis, and was weary from the hard work, many hours in the saddle, and the grueling schedule of running Kennedy Meadows Resort and Pack Station. When Reno was only fifty-seven he decided it was time to give up his beloved mountain resort. He and Gerry sold it to their capable friend, Willie Ritts, a packer who had worked there for years.

Reno was honored in May of 1971 as Grand Marshall of the Mother Lode Round-Up parade, held each year in Sonora. He was selected by the Tuolumne County Sheriff's Posse, of which he was a charter member. Reno had willingly served his community through the years, by supplying wagons and horses for community events.

In May of 1986, Reno was again honored by the High Sierra Packer's Association, to be the "Packer of the Year" for Bishop's Mule Days parade. This was a popular event, with hundreds of people in attendance. Reno was presented with a silver belt buckle. He commented, "I'm kind of demoting myself, riding a mule, I've been a horseman all my life."

Aspen Meadows Pack Station was operated by his daughter LaVerne. Reno, in his seventies, still helped with the livestock. From his home in Stent he herded a few cows to his beloved High Sierra. In the winter, from his easy chair Reno would recount stories of the horses he broke and the movie stars and cattlemen he knew.

On May 5, 1995, after watching Johnny Carson's *Tonight Show* on television, he bent over to take off his socks, gently slid onto the floor, and peacefully died. Although he was bent from hard work and arthritis, death transformed his body to be straight once again. His grieving relatives were stunned by the miraculous change. Reno was eighty-two years old.

Reno Sardella in later years.
Photograph courtesy of the Ben Cassinetto family.

SOURCES
Authorization to Sell and Owner's Statement, 30 Jul. 1960 (Rose Mitchell sells Kennedy Meadows).
Cassinetto, Ben. Personal interview, 30 May 2016.
Haigh, Gary. Personal interview, 4 Aug. 2016.
Knowles, Chuck. Personal interview, 27 Oct. 2016.
Knowles, Joanne. Personal interview, 6 Jun. 2016.
Leonard, Norene Sardella. Personal interview, 18 Jan. 2017.
Mc Hugh, Mike. Personal interview, 10 Sep. 2016.
Modesto Bee, 4 Feb. 1954.
"Posse Selects a Parade Marshal – Reno Sardella." *Union Democrat,* 5 May 1971.
Reno Sardella's Obituary, *Union Democrat*, 6 May 1995, Front page.
Reveal, Jack. "A History of the Summit District, Recollections of the Years 1948-1960."
"The Sardellas: An American Story" by Suzy Hopkins. 15 Mar. 2009. *Friends and Neighbors* magazine.
Saylers, Renalda. Personal interview, 6 Jul. 2015 and 17 Nov. 2018. (granddaughter).
Waterbury, Kathe. "Family, Friends Mourn Rancher Reno Sardella." *Union Democrat*, 20 May 1986.

CHAPTER 30

Lottie Pedro
The Mountain Queen

Her death in 1989 made the front page of Sonora's *Union Democrat* newspaper: "Aunt Lottie" Pedro dies at 98." Her fame came from working many years at Kennedy Meadows, and caring for others.

In addition to the various owners of Kennedy Meadows, there were also a number of noteworthy employees who made significant contributions to the operation of the resort. Lottie Pedro was one of these.

In a 1976 *Union Democrat* interview, Lottie explained, "I've worked at all of them up the line. At Dardanelle, Douglas and Kennedy. Guess I'm like a piece of furniture." Indeed, various owners of Kennedy Meadows appreciated that for nearly four decades Lottie showed up yearly to open the resort.

Her grandparents came to Tuolumne County from Mexico and Peru, and settled there during the Gold Rush. Lottie's mother was born in Chinese Camp, her father at Tar Flat. The families moved to Oakdale, where Lottie's parents met and married. The young couple then moved to Fresno and welcomed their first girl Lottie on November 4, 1890.

Edward was the oldest of six children in the family. Then came Lottie, Delphina, Isabel who married Chick Wright, Trina who married Charles Gore, and the youngest, Adolph Vergara, who went by "Dolf" and married Idamae Whittle of Angels Camp. The Vergaras were a hard-working fun loving family that played music and liked to dance and have a good time together.

Lottie moved to Tuolumne County in 1905, after the family of an elderly woman she knew in Fresno urged her to come to work at El Congreso Tamale House, a restaurant on North Washington Street in Sonora. Owner Julia Ralston also owned the profitable Hope Gold Mine. Lottie, a confident fifteen year-old, was anxious to leave home and earn her own money. It was a new world for her. She learned to cook in a restaurant, follow recipes, and wait tables. She gained a reputation for her good cooking. Enchiladas became her specialty, which she often prepared for guests.

It was at the restaurant that Lottie met Manuel E. Pedro, a frequent patron who lived at the Pedro ranch on Union Hill outside Columbia. Manuel Pedro was born at Browns Flat, outside Sonora on Union Hill Road, on March 30, 1881. The family of Portuguese descent lived on the Pedro Ranch. The large family with seven children operated a small dairy

Restaurant advertisement February 1, 1906, in the *Union Democrat*.

Lottie Pedro in 1908.
Photograph courtesy of Patricia "Pat" Wright Day.

ranch, and the Pedro boys ranched and mined for gold. Manuel was known to be ornery, disagreeable, and frequently in fights with his brothers.

Unfortunately, when restaurant owner Julia Ralston became ill, she had to close the business for two months. Lottie was without a job and moved back home to Fresno. Manuel pursued her there, and they married December 2, 1906, in Fresno. Lottie was just sixteen years old, eleven years younger than her husband. It would be a difficult marriage for her.

Manuel, who had a good eye for horses, raised them on the Pedro property and then sold them. Lottie worked beside him breaking colts. She was an excellent rider. She loved horses, and skillfully raced them at the popular track near the present day Race Track Road in Sonora.

To make some money during the summers, the newlyweds traveled to Kennedy Meadows on Sonora Pass. It was busy with the building of the Relief Dam, just six miles above Kennedy Meadows. Teamsters were constantly hauling equipment,

workers, and supplies to the dam site. Lottie was overjoyed to be in the mountains, and returned to the high country at every chance. Manuel brought his "dude" horses for guests to ride.

When Lottie was eight-five, Lynne Jerome interviewed her for the *Union Democrat* in 1976 and wrote: "Lottie crossed the Sierras in 1909, on horseback with her husband, who hauled fresh vegetables and fruit into the mining town of Bodie. She also accompanied him on numerous cattle drives into Yosemite. Lottie says, 'It used to make me mad. Those men would always send me ahead to ride and try to hold those horses back while they rode in the back and smoked cigarettes and talked,' she laughed."

In 1916, the young couple decided to operate a pack string of Manuel's horses and mules at the popular Yosemite Valley, which had more visitors than Kennedy Meadows. Tourists were anxious to see more of the valley than what was visible by wagon or on foot. The fame of Yosemite had spread, and people flocked to see it. The Pedros packed parties into the extraordinarily scenic backcountry for fishing and hunting during the summer season. Lottie loved it all; she was friendly with tourists, and easily drummed up business. Before long, they had a nest egg to get through the winter months.

In 1915, Manuel and his brother Tony had a falling out. It was decided that Manuel should have

Lottie and Manuel in Yosemite in 1916.
Photograph courtesy of Patricia "Pat" Wright Day.

his own property. The brothers struck a deal for $250, giving Manuel six acres with a house and barn. Manuel and Lottie set up housekeeping on their own property at Browns Flat, where the road from Angels Camp and the road from Columbia converge. The area had been heavily mined for gold, leaving huge rock formations of limestone jutting up from the ground and not much topsoil. But the Pedro property was on a rise and included some pasture land. From the house were views of the surrounding foothills. A few trees offered shade, and the property was mainly open. Lottie, twenty-five, had a house of her own and set to work making it comfortable. They built a new fence and made repairs, and she landscaped trails lined with small limestone rocks.

The marriage to Manuel was a mistake from the beginning. He was a womanizer, and it soon turned into a strained, unhappy relationship. Manuel was a gloomy person who carried a dark cloud throughout his life. Mean-spirited, cold, and stubborn, he was not good husband material. As a young woman, Lottie may have seen these qualities but figured she could change him. After all, they both loved horses, and he was so good with them. Both were Catholic, so a divorce was out of the question.

Lottie was known to be a happy person with a quick smile that made others happy. A small woman, she was a bundle of energy, eager to please, and she loved children. Bright and loving, she was also skilled at nursing, and worked as a practical nurse during the winter. She frequently cared for the elderly, working in people's homes and at local hospitals. From her restaurant experience, she was also hired as a cook.

Her little sister Trina had married Charles Gore. They had a little girl they named Virginia. The marriage was unhappy, and he walked out leaving her with nothing. Trina, desperate, moved in with Lottie and Manuel, bringing the toddler Virginia, too. Amazingly, Manuel was fond of Virginia and had few complaints about the arrangement.

The two sisters loved being together, and it was a happy family, but the joy of their companionship did not last. Trina developed a nagging cough with chest pains. She began to lose weight, was tired all the time, and developed a fever. Lottie, with her experience in caring for the elderly, recognized the symptoms of tuberculosis and was concerned. With Lottie's loving care, Trina lingered on, but it seemed best to send her to the Weimar Sanitarium in Placer County. On September 27, 1924, Lottie's little sister Trina Gore succumbed at age twenty-six. The Vergaras family was devastated, and they turned to Lottie, who gladly took in and raised Trina's daughter Virginia, who was just six at the time of her mother's death. Now, unexpectedly, Lottie became a mother. She was overjoyed to have this little girl in her life.

Unfortunately, the Pedro house burned down in the early 1920s. Undaunted, they moved into the barn and started remodeling. It was a large barn, and only half of it was made into living quarters. It was primitive, with a hand pump for water at the edge of the kitchen sink, and no electricity. The upstairs loft was curtained off for sleeping quarters. Next to the barn they built an outdoor barbecue of stone and bricks, which was a favorite place to cook during the hot weather. Lottie lived there with her dog Cindy until she was ninety-one. Later the barn was burned down as training practice for the Fire Department.

Manuel developed devious ways to add to the family income. During the winter, when the road was deep in mud, he would purposely dig the pot holes deeper on the main road near his house. When a wagon became mired, he would offer to pull it out with his horse team, for a small charge. If a car became stuck and they refused his services, seeking help elsewhere, Manuel would drain their gas tank.

The large, two story primitive barn that Lottie and Manuel lived in after their house burned. Photographed about 1940.
Photograph courtesy of Patricia "Pat" Wright Day.

Lottie needed to separate herself from Manuel. In 1927, when Bill Nelson, owner of Douglas Station on the Sonora-Mono Road, advertised for help, she took the job. He had lost his wife and was looking for a woman to take charge of cooking in the resort restaurant, wait tables, and clean the rental cabins. He also had an eleven-year old boy, Francis, who needed care. The job meant that she would be in her beloved mountains again.

When the job at Douglas ended, Lottie knew she could get work at Kennedy Meadows. Known to be hard-working, cheerful and industrious, she was hired at Kennedy Meadows Lodge by Frank Kurzi in the 1930s. She stayed on into the 1980s, working for fifty years through the string of owners, including the Mitchells, Reno Sardella, and Willie Ritts.

She thrived in this environment. Lottie was a fireball of energy and "the one to see if you wanted something done." Her room was at the top of the stairs over the lobby. In her room, she kept her personal items, a bed, clothes, and her sewing

Lottie at rest on the stairs of a primitive "tent cabin" used at Kennedy Meadows. This cabin Lottie has just cleaned before the canvas roof would be installed for the season.
Photographer not known.

machine. She was an accomplished seamstress. During the time Reno Sardella owned the resort, she made clothes for Reno's granddaughter, Renalda. Lottie also worked at several other mountain resorts, including one summer at Fales Hot Springs, over the pass in Mono County. When her niece Virginia Denton owned Douglas Resort from 1956 to 1960, Lottie worked for her, too.

During the mountain summers, Lottie had a loving companion who adored her, Leonard Reese. Leonard was hired at the resorts and was skilled at many jobs. He worked as a handyman, butcher, maintenance man, and pack station manager. Leonard was good with animals, and trained a little white dog named Nipper to sit and smoke a pipe, walk on its hind legs and jump rope. This was a big hit with the children. Leonard followed Lottie wherever she worked. Through the years, they kept their relationship private at the resorts where they both were employed. Seen in photographs of the staff at Kennedy Meadows and Douglas, they would stand some distance from each other. Lottie's family accepted Leonard, and he was welcome at their family gatherings.

Among her other duties, Lottie was in charge of the laundry room. The linens were cleaned in a gas-powered wringer washing machine, and the sheets and pillowcases were fed through the rollers on a hot laundry mangle to smoothly iron the linens. Her clothesline stretched one hundred feet, from the back of the laundry room to the saddle barn. Lottie also managed the young ladies, hired to clean cabins and help in the laundry. She was known to be fair with the girls.

In 1937, during the Great Depression, Lottie's sister Isabel's husband Chick Wright lost his job. Over Manuel's complaints, she took them in with their four children, and they all managed in the barn. By then it had electricity. The children played with the goats and tended the chickens and raised rabbits to sell. Half of the building still functioned as a barn where they stored saddles, chicken feed, hay, and tools. All this was new for the Wright children, who had moved from a house in Oakdale. Lottie was very fond of her sister and could not ignore her sister's situation. Isabel took over the landscaping

Lottie in 1942 at age 52.
Photograph courtesy of Patricia "Pat" Wright Day.

old and staying with her at Kennedy for the summer. I had a side job selling worms to the fishermen, and especially enjoyed hanging out with the wranglers at the stables. A six-foot-two, nineteen-year-old cowboy, Toots Warren, thought it was funny to teach me dirty songs and have me perform for the resort guests. Lottie got wind of it, and with her laundry stick in hand, marched to the stables, found Toots, and gave him a good whack on the side of his head." After that, Donnie didn't sing for guests anymore.

Judy Duncan, longtime Dardanelle resident recalls, "Lottie cooked, washed dishes, waited tables, helped in the store, managed the laundry, cleaned the rental cabins, and supervised the young workers. She could outwork any man well into her 80s. She was thoughtful, witty, and well loved. She would stop and make a sandwich for a tired hungry cowboy. Without Lottie, the place would fall apart."

In 1942, during the filming of *For Whom The Bell Tolls,* lead actor Gary Cooper frequented the Kennedy Meadows saloon after a long day of filming. Almost everyone knew the witty and outspoken Lottie, including Gary Cooper. Lottie

and planted a vegetable garden and flowers. Eventually Chick found employment and they moved out, but Isabel was always extremely grateful to her sister for the help in hard times.

During the winters Lottie sometimes worked for Frank Kurzi, owner of Kennedy Meadows, on his 8,000-acre ranch at Marshes Flat near Moccasin. She mostly cooked for the round-up crew, and worked beside his wife Lurene.

Although she and her husband did not have their own children, Lottie mothered many youngsters while working at the resorts. Her nieces and nephews frequently joined her during the summers. It was a big adventure for them to leave home for the summer and be with Aunt Lottie in the mountains.

Donnie Wright, whose mother Isabel was Lottie's sister, recalls from 1940, "Lottie was a tiny lady only about five foot one inches. I was eight years

Lottie Pedro in 1957 at Douglas Resort.
Photograph courtesy of Virginia Denton.

loved to dance, and Gary asked her to dance with him at the saloon. They made quite a pair, Cooper at six-foot three, and Lottie at just over five feet, as they spun around the dance floor.

Manuel had become badly crippled with arthritis, and died in 1959. Lottie was left to manage as a widow at sixty-nine. Lottie asked Isabel and Chick to move into the barn and live with her again as they had done years ago during the Depression. The Wrights were now in their sixties and gladly accepted the offer. Chick added indoor plumbing, with a bathroom in the barn, and one in the house. The three lived there comfortably for several years.

In 1976, Lottie was honored as the first female Grand Marshall for the Mother Lode Round-Up parade. At eighty-five, she insisted on riding a horse, and refused to ride in a carriage. Smiling and waving in her parade outfit, she proudly wore her gold and silver belt buckle, engraved "Mountain Queen." It was presented to her by her family, and designed by her nephew Donnie Wright, in recognition of her service in the High Sierra resorts. Through the years, she rode in the parade many times, claiming she only missed one year when she was in Yosemite.

In her old age, Lottie became senile and could not live alone. Her niece, Virginia Denton, who Lottie had raised, moved Lottie into a nearby care facility at Browns Flat. She passed away January 18, 1989, at the age of ninety-eight.

After Lottie's death, a plaque in her honor was placed on display in the Kennedy Meadows bar.

AUTHOR'S NOTE:

I had never heard of Lottie Pedro until I walked into the bar at Kennedy Meadows and saw the plaque. I was dumbstruck that a tribute to a woman in this cowboy enclave existed. I like to celebrate the women, so this got my attention. She was widely known and obviously well loved.

As I started my research, there was no shortage of people to interview. Someone suggested that I interview her adopted daughter, Virginia. I was shocked, figuring she was long gone. Nope, I found her in an assisted living facility in Angels Camp. Still spry at ninety-seven, she recalled her days owning Douglas resort in the 1950s, and shared some old photographs from her album. Overall, I interviewed eight people who shared their memories of Lottie.

In January of 2018, I took the photo of the barn with me, and went looking for the property on Union Hill Road, where Lottie and Manuel had lived. The barn was gone of course, but remnants of the old barbecue still remain. Looking closely, I saw the iris that Isabel had planted, and a circle of rocks for a flower garden were still evident. After doing so much research about Lottie, it was a pleasure to walk the ground where she had once lived.

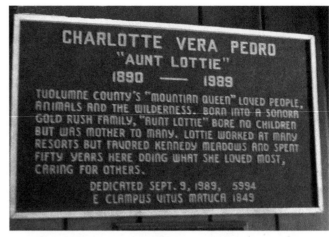

This plaque displayed in remembrance of this great lady is mounted in the Kennedy Meadows saloon.
Photographed by Cate Culver 2015.

SOURCES

"Aunt Lottie" Pedro dies at 98." Lottie's obituary. *Union Democrat,* 19 Jan. 1989.

Barnette, Jeanette. Telephone interview, 26 Jan. 2018.

Day, Patricia "Pat" Wright. Personal interview. 23 Jan. 2016. Telephone interview. 22 Jan. 2018. (Her mother Isabel Wright was Lottie's sister).

Denton, Virginia. Personal interview, 2015 (Virginia was raised by Lottie, and was her niece).

Duncan, Judy. Personal interview, 2015.

Fiscus, Marilyn Vergara. Personal interview, 2015. Niece (Her father Adolph Vergara was Lottie's brother).

Garner, Betty Whittle. Personal interview, 2015. (Niece by marriage).

Mitchell, Kenny. Personal interview, 3 Mar. 2017.

Sayler, Renalda. Personal interview, Reno Sardella's granddaughter.

Trina Gore Obituary. *Union Democrat,* 4 Oct. 1924, Front page.

Interviewed. by Lynne Jerome for the *Union Democrat* newspaper issue 4 May 1976.

United States Census 1900.

Wright, Donnie. Personal interview, 2015 Nephew (His mother Isabel Wright was Lottie's sister).

CHAPTER 31

Artie Scruggs
The Cowboy's Cowboy

Another employee who played a significant role in the operation of Kennedy Meadows was Artie Scruggs. He brought his wife, stayed year after year, and made a difference at the pack station. Interviewed by the *Union Democrat* for the upcoming Mother Lode Round-Up he said, "Once you get it in your blood, you're not satisfied with anything else." Scruggs worked with cattle and horses all his life.

Artie was born June 26, 1911, in Indian Territory at Duncan, Stephens County, Oklahoma. His father James Columbus Scruggs was a farmer, and his mother, Sarah Burch Scruggs, tended their twelve children. The family was dirt poor, and lived a hardscrabble life. Artie went to work at a young age, and never graduated from high school. As a teenager, to make extra money for the family, he entered the amateur rodeo circuit in the bull riding and roping events.

The family left Oklahoma in search of work, and moved to a one-room adobe in Las Vegas, New Mexico, a stop on the old Santa Fe Trail. Later they settled in Watrous, New Mexico, then just a wide spot in the road. It was as a young man in New Mexico that Artie first became aware of his talent for working with horses.

In 1934, during the Great Depression, he hopped a freight train and made his way to California. Young, strong, and gifted with horses, at twenty-four he soon made a name for himself in rodeo events as a roper and bull rider in California.

Locals who attended the rodeo noticed how well Artie handled horses. He soon found work on the Louis Price ranch on Rock River Road. This ranch was at Keystone, below Jamestown. Artie managed the ranch for Louis Price, who lived in Sonora with his wife Melba. In the summer, Artie took the cattle to the Prices' grazing allotment at Hull's Meadow, near Long Barn.

Artie made his way to Kennedy Meadows and saw the busy pack station. He was impressed, and figured he could get a job at the corrals, and with some training, pack outdoorsmen into the backcountry.

Artie was quickly hired at Kennedy Meadows Resort, first working for Frank Kurzi, and then the

Artie Scruggs, legendary packer at Kennedy Meadows.
Photograph courtesy of Matt Bloom.

Mitchells. During the Frank Kurzi years, young Artie packed tungsten ore out on mules for L.W. Osborn, who was developing tungsten mines deep in the backcountry of Emigrant Basin.

Artie was also a great dancer, and in his bachelor days attended many of the local dances. Handsome, athletic, and graceful, he was in wide demand as a partner. Patricia Wright Day, "Pat," a petite lady who attended the dances remembers, "We would dance the jitterbug and he could throw me in the air and swing me around."

Then the bachelor met Janice Marie Kimball, a petite dark-haired beauty with snapping brown eyes. Born February 12, 1925, in Columbia, she was fourteen years younger than Artie and stole his heart. When she was just twenty, she married him on April 2, 1945, in Columbia.

Artie brought his bride to the Louis Price ranch, where they moved into a large stone house with three bedrooms, hardwood floors, and a nice living room. Here they raised their two children. Their first child, Sarah, was born June 30, 1947 followed by son Jim, born June 28, 1948.

Just out of high school, Janice worked for Pacific Telephone as a long distance operator, a career that lasted twenty-six years. Her steady income sustained the family. Artie's jobs were not paid by a salary, and many times he did not know where the next paycheck was coming from, yet he worked hard to support his family.

In 1955, when the children were of school age, Artie and Janice bought a house in Columbia on North Airport Road. The house came with seventeen acres and a chestnut orchard. He raised hogs, a milk cow, and kept a few beef cows for the family meat supply. The ranch had several small corrals used to train horses.

After moving to Columbia, Artie's reputation as a horse trainer grew, and he was always in demand. Training horses was an instinctive process for him, and he could easily manage a horse that proved too difficult for other trainers.

His wife Janice would sometimes watch Artie with a new colt. She explains, "The colt would come into the corral and put its head in a corner with its back to Artie. He would just stand there calmly and

Horseman Ed Burgson at left, on his ranch at Keystone, with Artie kneeling by the horse.
Photograph courtesy of Chris Robinson.

start talking to the horse until it would turn around and face him. He would observe the horse and think about his approach, knowing each horse is different. Artie never rushed the colts and was very patient. The next morning he would put on the same clothes so the horse would recognize his scent."

After training a horse, he tested it on his own children. Jim recalls his dad saying, "Legs on either side, mind in the middle, heels down and toes out."

Ranchers from as far away as the San Joaquin Valley would seek him out. Artie was widely known for using a hackamore when training young horses. A hackamore is a bridle without a bit and not so rough on a young horse's developing mouth. Ranchers who wanted their horses to be trained with special consideration came to Artie. Sometimes horse owners just needed their horses to have a tune-up for better behavior, get ready for the rodeo, or just break some bad habits.

Artie liked the challenge of working with a difficult mount, and it wasn't unusual for cowboys to challenge him to ride a rogue horse. Eagerly, they gathered around the corral in anticipation of seeing Artie dethroned. A man modest about his talent, he stayed firmly in the saddle, dismounted, and walked away—much to their disappointment. He quickly earned their respect.

Artie worked many years for Ed Burgson, a well-known local horseman who sold two-year old quarter horses. Ed frequently hired Artie to break and train his prized horses. The two men were great friends who would often ride newly trained colts together to the Winkin' Lantern, below Jamestown, to get lunch and then head back to Ed's ranch.

At Kennedy Meadows he was valued by every owner through the years. He was kept on and given responsibility, partly because he was not much of a drinker, and could be depended on to show up and give his best every day. Artie worked hard, and was easygoing and generous to a fault. People often saw him with a pack of cigarettes and a cup of coffee on cold mountain mornings. He was the quiet type, lingering in the background, listening to a conversation. He didn't speak up much, but when he did, everyone listened.

After Janice retired from the telephone company, she worked the lobby desk at Kennedy Meadows, taking reservations. Artie finished out his career with Reno Sardella, who had appointed him his corral boss. At the pack station, Artie ushered in a new era. Horses no longer were broken with a heavy hand and forced to submit under fear. Artie taught the wranglers to be more sensitive to the horses, and engage with them in a gentler way. Even details of how to handle the horse when putting

Artie's belt buckle awarded to him as the Grand Marshall in 1981 with his name engraved at the bottom.
Photograph by Cate Culver.

on a saddle were explained. He was a good teacher, patient and knowledgeable. The wranglers looked up to him.

He also worked during the winter for Reno Sardella at his ranch in Stent. Reno had an excellent reputation as a horseman and respected Artie's exceptional skill at training and breaking horses. Through Reno, Artie frequently got side jobs working in the movies.

Chuck Knowles, a neighbor, recalls, "Artie was self-educated as a horse trainer and breaker. A great guy that would do anything for you. He worked in the local movies as a stunt man with the horses and joined the union."

Breaking horses is a dangerous occupation. At six feet tall and a fit 180 pounds, Artie's body took a beating. When he was a young man, the insteps of both feet were broken from a bad fall, so he would take a knife and cut his new boots to fit more comfortably. Later, he broke a leg and walked with a limp, but he never was intimidated by the hazards of horse training.

Artie was so admired by the local cattlemen and horsemen that he was selected as the Grand Marshall for the Mother Lode Round-Up parade in 1981. It was a great honor, and locals were happy to see such a quiet man get recognition. He was pleased with the accolades, but uncomfortable with the attention.

Artie developed lung cancer, and while resting in bed enjoyed watching soap operas on television. His daughter-in-law Karen recalled, "Artie, this big tough cowboy, would be watching the soaps and call me to hash over all the intrigue. We both enjoyed the episodes, and got caught up in the drama. It was fun to share that with Artie in his last days."

Artie's death made the front page of the *Union Democrat* newspaper. "The Cowboy's Cowboy is dead at 77." Artie Scruggs died of lung cancer on October 10, 1988. Janice, widowed at sixty-three, continued on working summers at Kennedy Meadows, long after her husband's death.

RELEIF PEAK AND STANISLAUS RIVER   A632

Postcard of the Middle Fork of the Stanislaus River as it flows through Kennedy Meadows in 1942.
Jerry and Cate Culver postcard collection.

SOURCES
"Artie Scruggs Cowboy's Cowboy, Dead at 77." *Union Democrat*, 10 Oct. 1988. Obituary, Front page.
Krause, Millie. Personal interview, 8 Jun. 2017.
Robinson, Chris. Personal interview, 30 Aug. 2016
Scruggs, Janice. Personal interview, 14 Feb. 2017.
Scruggs, Jim. Personal interview, 28 Aug. 2016.
Scruggs, Karen, 29 Aug. 2016.

CHAPTER 32

The Making of a Wrangler
Coming of Age at the Pack Station

High Country oil painting by Chuck Knowles, nationally known artist.
Photograph by Cate Culver.

It was during the summer of 2003 that Colin Peterson, just out of high school, had his life suddenly change. He was hanging around the stables when he was noticed by Matt Bloom, who owned the Kennedy Meadows Resort. Matt, broad-shouldered, tall, and handsome, approached Colin and said, "I see that you are tall and walk fast. Would you like a job as a packer?" Colin, much surprised replied, "Yes, I can start Monday." He then called his father and asked to borrow money to buy the necessary equipment: a saddle, snaffle bit, Levis, a sharp knife, rain gear, long-sleeve cotton button-up shirts, cowboy boots, and a cowboy hat. He told his dad he'd be home sometime in October.

The life of a cowboy has always been romanticized in dime novels, Western movies, and song. How would you learn to be a cowboy? Where does a city kid find his dream job? His best hope would be getting hired on as a wrangler at the remote Kennedy Meadows pack station. Packing tourists on horseback with a string of mules into the high country, even if only for one season, would forever shape a young man.

The life of a wrangler has changed little over the last hundred years. The attraction is the independence of being in charge of a string of pack mules and a party of campers and fishermen, with no boss to tell you what to do. Still, nature can take control when a rainstorm approaches, or a rockslide blocks the trail. Horses or mules can suddenly act up and cause havoc. But your day is filled with views of mountains and meadows untarnished by mankind, and your charges are thrilled with their ride, taking in all the wonders of the pristine Sierra Nevada mountains.

On Monday, Colin, 18, thin and angular, arrived eager to start his new job. Board and room were provided. He must do his own laundry, and look neat and clean at all times. The boss led him to his quarters where he and the other high school age boys slept in the attic of the barn. The room is large and open with six single beds. He stowed his clothes, and was shown his bed and where to find clean linens. Once a young cowboy is assigned a bed, he keeps it year after year until he is too old to lodge with the high schoolers.

Next, kitchen privileges were explained. He could order anything from the restaurant. Some chose to rummage through the kitchen and fix their own food. They all ate in the cowboy dining room, which was a large table with a side table for condiments and flatware.

Colin explains, "I knew the first week on the job that this was what I wanted to do for the rest of my life. Right away, it was important for me to become the very best packer. If there was a difficult job to do, I wanted the challenge. I wanted the boss to give me the job, confident that I could do it."

As a new wrangler, Colin had a lot to learn. There were no breaks; a cowboy must work hard and stay busy at all times. He must be up at 4 a.m. in the dark, to feed the horses and mules. While the stock was occupied with eating, the young wranglers got them saddled. Not just any saddle and tack would do, but the gear must match the right animal. In the tack shed, all the saddles were neatly placed on racks with the horse's or mule's name labeled below. After cleaning up the corrals and sweeping the area, the cowboy then headed to the restaurant for his own hearty breakfast.

There were about one hundred and fifty horses and mules, and twenty wranglers. Mules are the backbone of any pack station; a hardy, strong animal, with sturdy feet, they can carry a heavy load farther than a horse. A mule never overeats, and is less prone to injuries. Mules like to bond with the horses and be near them, although they are separated in the corrals.

The new wrangler learned the names of all the

Wrangler Colin Peterson in 2016.
Photograph by Cate Culver.

Upper Kennedy Meadow, the destination of the one-hour horseback rides.
Cate Culver photographer, taken in 1970.

stock. When he was told to get Spade ready, he knew which horse to single out. Some of the names were Mojo, Bullet, Jackpot, Tombstone, Chubs, Rooster, and Blue Duck. Several are named from their brands such as DD and CC. Two sets of mules that liked to be together were Molly and Polly, and also Bonnie and Clyde. Colin says, "I was overwhelmed at trying to learn all the names. Matt Bloom told me to just look at each one, as I would a person. It took about three years before I was confident with the names." By 6 a.m. it was time to be at the loading docks when the customers arrive with their gear for the trip. The mules' bags were carefully packed and weighed, so they were seventy-five pounds on each side. To pack the mule, there were special knots to learn, and a procedure to be followed. Only the experienced packers took the pack mules and public on the trails into the Emigrant Basin.

During the day, young Colin was busy cleaning the corrals and unloading huge ninety-pound hay bales twice a day off the hay truck into the barn. Dust and debris flew everywhere, with the smell of manure and flies in his face. It was hard, dirty work, and a cowboy builds muscle and endurance.

Wranglers knew their corral stock, and rode the more spirited horses to calm them down and train them to be gentle for the public to ride. The lively colts needed to be trained regularly, for their lifetime of being a good saddle horse. A cowboy with free time took these colts for short rides to get them comfortable with the reins, a saddle, and verbal commands from a wrangler. Once the horse was ready for the inexperienced rider, he was labeled a "dude" horse.

Kennedy Meadows Pack Station offered "One Hour" rides. When the boss felt the cowboy was ready, the young cowboy accompanied the horseback riders up the trail to Upper Kennedy Meadow. Here the Stanislaus River flowed at the meadow's edge, accented with cottonwoods and sand bars. High granite rock formations surround the meadow, with views of the Emigrant Basin in the distance. This was what the Bay Area tourists came to see and experience on horseback. It was exciting to be chaperoned by a real cowboy, if only for an hour.

As with the young colts, the high school boy needed careful training, too. When the boss felt the young wranglers were reliable and competent with horses and mules, they were allowed to join them on the trail, to pack in a party of outdoorsmen and women into the high county. The packer takes only five head of stock (horses and mules) at a time. He needed to be able to see the pack train at all times. If there were more, he could not see all of them going around sharp turns.

Emigrant Basin has a network of back trails. A wrangler needed to learn the best campsites and know which trail leads to which camp. Much of the terrain was difficult to navigate, and it took some

practice to be confident, managing the stock across steep slopes and expanses of slippery granite.

Colin commented, "A packer has a dangerous job, right up there with firefighters, ocean fishermen, and loggers. If you are not vigilant, you can get hurt."

To achieve excellence as a packer it was necessary to be very observant. Colin explained, "I learned to read the animals. I can predict what is going to happen by listening carefully. I hear everything before I see it. Most incidents happen when I'm not watching. There are always warning signs, and they are hard to learn."

Accidents sometimes innocently happened when a hiker moved to stand by the side of the trail to let the pack train pass. If a mule, tied to other mules, got spooked by the sight of the hiker, pulled back, and the next mule lost its footing and fell, then suddenly the scene could become a huge wreck. It takes courage to keep calm in the midst of panicked animals thrashing about. The packer would quickly jump from his horse and cut ropes to free each mule.

Wreck a Makin' oil painting by Chuck Knowles, nationally known artist.
Photograph by Cate Culver.

Then he needed to get each mule back on the trail, make sure the frightened animals were safe, unhurt, and the packs were secure. Then he roped the mules all together again.

A tired horse or mule can, while half asleep and tied up in camp, get itself entangled in rope and suddenly panic and thrash about. The wrangler would need to be quick with his sharp knife and cut the rope to free the frightened animal.

Colin Peterson at the horse corral.
Photograph by Cate Culver 2016.

In his overnight bag, Colin took a bedroll, with a canvas cover to protect him from wet weather, and his personal food: most likely a sandwich, a candy bar, and beef jerky. He carried some lighter fluid to start a campfire if the wood was damp, and a large, sharp knife. Also included was a bag of grain to feed the stock.

After they arrived at the campsite, he unloaded the packs from the mules. He assisted the party in setting up camp, and built them a campfire if needed. Excited to have reached their destination, the campers got acquainted with their new surroundings before dark. To get the stock cared for, Colin attached a "high line" or rope between two trees and tied the horses to the rope for the night. The mules were set free to graze, with bells around the necks of dominant mares. Because the mules bond with the horses, they do not stray far. The packer bedded down close to his stock during the night to keep a watchful eye. At daybreak, Colin was up with his bag of grain to lure the mules to be caught and fed with the horses. The wrangler usually returned to the pack station, leaving the party to enjoy the high country and go back again to pack them out.

The wrangler's day was done by 5:30 p.m. He showered, ate dinner, and sometimes shared an evening around the campfire, reliving the day's adventure with the people he packed into the high country that day. Then he would go off to bed by 8:30 p.m.

After four years, Colin's quarters were moved from the barn attic with the high school boys to a two-room bungalow, which was nicer, and located near the stables. With years of experience, Colin was expected to be on call through the night should an emergency occur with the stock. He was also a first responder when needed to break up fistfights in the bar, fix a backed-up septic system, or repair the generator when it wheezes to a stop. He found every day to be different. Nothing was routine, and there was always something new to learn. Colin worked at Kennedy Meadows for well over a decade, and declared he has no intentions of changing careers.

At the end of August, the high school cowboys returned to school. Many had a passion for the high country and returned to work for another season, while others, having experienced the gritty reality of the job, never return. During the winter, some went on to attend college or chose to work on cattle ranches. Some make a career of packing people into the high country, and go to work for the National Park Service in Yosemite.

The more experienced wranglers stayed on until mid-October. Deer season was a busy time, packing hunters into the backcountry, and then picking them up to pack out the deer they have killed. After deer season the resort closes. A caretaker stays through the winter, shoveling heavy snow off roofs and making repairs. When the roads are plowed in the spring around the end of April, the loyal resort crew returns for another season.

The lure of packing into the high mountains of granite and pristine lakes continues much the same as it did a century ago. Horses, mules, saddlebags, cowboy hats, boots, and a bedroll. Not much has changed. For some young men it is a lifestyle they cherish, and choose as a lifetime career. Others return to the city, but both have come of age, learning confidence in themselves and responsibility they carry forth to any job they seek.

SOURCES
Inwood, Tyler. Personal interview, 2015.
Peterson, Colin. Personal interview, 2016.

CHAPTER 33

The Cattlemen

Don Whittle at left, and Clenn Whittle, in 1945, herding their cattle up toward
Pinecrest to their cattle allotment at Crabtree.
Photograph courtesy of the Whittle family. Angie Whittle photographer.

Cattle herd grazing at Kennedy Lake in 2018.
Photographer Chris Robinson.

Cattlemen are an independent sort, self-reliant and knowledgeable outdoorsmen. Raising cattle is labor intensive. It includes branding calves, giving shots, dehorning, castrating, ear marking, maintaining fences, growing feed, gathering herds for the mountains, then gathering them up again in the fall to bring them back to the home range, and hauling the cattle to market.

Many California ranches are family owned and inherited from early homesteaders, and many remain in the same family, passed down through the generations. Children grow up on the ranches and learn the business first hand. The daughters make good cattle ranchers as well, much to the surprise of their brothers and fathers. The cattleman builds his herd by buying up the best rangeland, which gets passed down through the family. The beef market fluctuates and income is uncertain. During hard times, they may sell off acreage to keep out of bankruptcy.

When a stockman is on horseback, patrolling his range in the mountains, it brings him great joy to watch over his herd in the meadows and see the little calves grow and romp about. Time spent in the Emigrant Basin is treasured, a time to be free of the problems on the home ranch and reflect on nature and its bounty.

In the early days, a cattleman in the valley or foothills took their livestock to the mountains each summer. In the heat, the grasses at their ranches dried up, so the herd was moved to the mountain meadows for fresh feed. Cattle drives started in late June. Every family member who could ride a horse became a cowboy. It was a time of hard, dusty work, combined with the adventure of leaving the home base. Cattle drives frequently took three to five days to reach the mountains. Sometimes neighbors' herds joined in the drive. They had designated places to stop each night, preferably with a corral. The cowboys slept under the stars, cooked and ate around campfires, and tended

A cattleman driving his cattle from the winter grazing range up to the summer range in the mountains.
Photograph courtesy of the Joe Martin, Sr. family.

the horses and cattle. Once in the mountains, they sorted out their cattle and each went to his own summer range.

There were no government regulations in the nineteenth century, and no boundaries set. Cattlemen were free to select their own range. Ideally, each wanted land with a stream and a meadow. The area needed to have some natural barriers of granite rock formations to mark each grazing range. Simple, temporary drift fences were put up during the summer to keep cattle contained, and taken down as they left in the fall. Salt licks were placed at strategic areas to keep the cattle attracted to their own range.

Several cowboys would stay through the summer moving the herd, so the cattle would not overgraze. Cattlemen built primitive cabins at their mountain ranges. Usually they selected a site overlooking the meadow, where breezes would blow off the mosquitoes. The cabins had bunkbeds and a wood cook stove, hauled in on a mule. They were

a shelter from summer storms and chilly mornings. New supplies were brought in by mule or horse, as there were few roads.

Cattlemen knew their neighbors, and would socialize when they came and went from their range. Some became lifelong friends, and knew each other and their ranches in the San Joaquin Valley and foothills.

Once they were in the mountains, the cattle knew what not to eat, and avoided the poisonous larkspur, and taught their calves not to eat it. Cows taught their calves how to forage in the brush and rock outcroppings. They grazed up rocky embankments, carving trails used year after year.

In 1923, the U.S. Forest Service started designating allotments to each cattleman. Maps of the allotments were drawn up, records kept, and permits issued. The cattle were allowed in the mountains from July 1 to October 1. A cow and calf counted as one.

If a cattleman wished to give up his allotment, the Forest Service required that the new permit owner buy up some of the herd from that allotment in the fall. The new permit holder would drive these cattle back to his ranch for the winter.

The following July, when the stockman drove his cattle to his new allotment, the "mountain" cattle knew the way, guiding the new cattle, raised on flat ground in the valley. This prevented cattle unfamiliar with the mountains from getting lost. The mountain cattle also taught the new livestock how to forage and climb through dense forest and rocks.

Cattle grazing was not without problems. In 1924, Babe Airola, a cattleman at Cow Creek, discovered the first cow in his herd sick with hoof-and-mouth disease. The animals became sick with a fever and developed blisters on their feet and in their mouths that easily ruptured, spreading the infection. A viral disease, it is highly contagious and can spread overnight, even to the deer populations. Airola immediately reported it to the authorities. Federal officers arrived and put a strict quarantine in place. All stock, even entire herds within the vicinity of the infection, were shot and buried on the spot in deep trenches. Once the disease was eradicated, cattlemen traveled to Nevada to buy new cattle to restock their herds.

By the mid-1960s, the cattle drives came to an end. The adventure of a cowboy herding cattle from the valley to his mountain range was over. Cattle were now trucked to the mountains and back again, in the fall to winter grazing ranges. The highways had become filled with cars, and the once-open land was fenced. The adventure and romance of herding cattle to the mountains had ended, replaced by cattle trucks rattling down the highways. However, the cattle industry thrives throughout the state, and continues to be an attribute of the Old West.

SOURCES

Airola, Bill. Personal interview, 1 Mar. 2017.

Hooper, George. "Cattle Drives Fading Into the Past." *Quarterly Bulletin* of the Calaveras County Historical Society, Jan. 1994.

"Killing Many Cattle in the Infected Area." *Union Democrat*, 12 Jul. 1924. p. 4.

Krause, Millie. Personal interview, 8 Jun. 2017.

Whittle, Donnie. Personal interview, 5 Feb. 2017.

CHAPTER 34

William F. Cooper
Establishes Cooper's Meadow

Ed Burgson stands at the door in 1928 at Cooper's cow camp.
Photograph courtesy of Chris Robinson from the Ed Burgson collection.

William F. Cooper arrived in California in the days of 1849 and liked what he saw. Ambitious and smart, this handsome blue-eyed man bought up grazing land. Cooper was one of the earliest pioneers to bring his cattle to the High Sierra, then known as the Emigrant Primitive Area.

Born in New Harmony, Indiana on June 10, 1825, he grew up on a farm. A patriotic young man, he served in the Mexican War as a lieutenant in the Sixteenth United States Infantry. He was discharged in April 1849, while acting as adjutant of a battalion. During the war, many of his comrades spoke of traveling to see the West, and coming home as rich gold miners.

Single, and twenty-five years old, William soon caught gold fever, and arrived in the Sacramento Valley on October 10, 1849. He first located at Long's Bar on the Feather River, then mined on the Yuba River, Stanislaus, and Tuolumne Rivers until 1852.

With all the hard work and little gold, Cooper became disenchanted with mining and moved to Sonora, where he operated a livery business. By August of 1858, he started buying land and engaged in farming and stock raising. He built a two-thousand acre ranch in Stanislaus County, and he raised seventy head of cattle, one hundred and forty hogs, three thousand sheep, and twelve hundred lambs, plus one hundred and twenty head of horses and mules. Four hundred acres of farm were suitable for crops, and he grew wheat, barley, and hay. The huge ranch, known as the Rock River Ranch, later became Cooperstown, located twenty-two miles from Sonora.

Cooper met and married Miss Levinia Hall in 1860, the daughter of a local merchant and a native of Brooklyn, New York. Cooper was prosperous and ready to marry and start a family. They had two sons, William and Thomas.

Again entering military duty, William became a sergeant in the Sigel Guards of Sonora. This unit was active from 1862 through 1866. When they mustered in during 1863, he was a First Lieutenant in the Third Brigade of the California Militia in Company B.

Cooper needed a mountain grazing area for his stock. After four years of searching the high mountain watershed, he selected this meadow below the prominent Castle Rock landmark. In 1861, he inscribed his name and date in a nearby tree and established it as his own. He was thirty-six and in his prime.

William F. Cooper, September 13, 1890.
Photograph courtesy of the Tuolumne County Historical Society and Museum.

Cooper's cabin built 1865. Photograph taken in 1960.
Courtesy of the Stanislaus National Forest.

Cooper's second cabin built about 1875. *Photograph taken in September of 1960. Courtesy of the Stanislaus National Forest Service.*

In 1865, he had the need for a permanent structure at his mountain cow camp. According to Joe Sanguinetti, the cabin was built using mortise and tendon construction by the skilled Irishman, Ed Jenness. A second cabin was built ten years later, in 1875, by an employee of Cooper, Captain John Smith.

The second building is made from hand-hewn squared timbers, connected at square jointed corners. The logs are so precise that neither chinking nor mudding were necessary to keep out the winter

cold. The cabins are situated on a slight rise at the meadow's edge where a breeze constantly blows, which kept the mosquitoes away. The snow melts early on this exposed slope, giving him the advantage of arriving early in the spring with his stock.

Fred McMillan recalls, "Old man Cooper raised mules and horses, and he had a mountain range. He milked cows up there in the summer, about fifteen

Unknown horsemen in Cooper Meadow in 1985.
Photograph courtesy of the Ray Sardella family.

or twenty cows. In 1894, there were about twelve of us that got saddle horses and went up to Cooper's Camp. We stayed there for four days. I, and Henry Geary were riding for Cooper, and for George Bunson, too. "He had three pens built. They had about seventy-five milk pans set out all around, and let the cream rise. They would take the cream off the pan and put it into a big churn about three feet high with a dasher. He packed it out on horses. He would peddle that butter as far as Stockton in the fall."

Donnie Wright, of Sonora, remembers, "Cooper would put the milk in cans and pack it down the mountain on mules. When they arrived in Strawberry, the milk had become butter. At Strawberry it was loaded on a wagon and sold in Oakdale."

Sometime during the summer of 1867, William

Cooper had been thrown from his buggy and his head was badly injured. His friends perceived that he was not the same after the accident. Soon after the accident, an unexpectedly strange and peculiar incident happened in Cooper's life. On November 27, 1867, Cooper became deranged and shot his wife while in the bedroom. She ran to the porch where he stabbed her four times as she lay dying, and then he fled.

The *Union Democrat* newspaper reported on December 7, 1867, "Last Sunday, about 11 o'clock a.m., W.F. Cooper was arrested in La Grange, Stanislaus County. He came into town of his own accord, and seemed to be unconscious of the fearful tragedy he had enacted. He enquired how his wife was, and appeared to have a vague idea that he had done something wrong, but did not know what. He was put into a wagon and taken to Knights Ferry. When crossing the Tuolumne in the ferry boat, he jumped overboard; and was with great difficulty rescued from being drowned."

On December 9th, Cooper was committed to the San Joaquin County Lunatic Asylum. After a year, he was discharged. There were no more reported incidents of unusual behavior, and Cooper went on to be a very successful farmer and stockman.

The Sierra Railway purchased land from Cooper in 1897 and established a railroad depot. It grew into Cooperstown, and the little place had a grocery store, a two-story house used as a hotel, with four rooms, and a restaurant that served mostly mutton. The town became a busy transfer point, with stagecoaches leaving for Jamestown, Sonora, Coulterville, and La Grange. Cooper himself set up business and ran a dry goods store and a saloon.

Cooper grazed his cattle at Cooper Cow Camp until 1900, but at seventy-five he no longer made the trip to his mountain cow camp. He sold it to Henry Stockel, a German who later sold to Father Guerin, in 1909. Guerin operated the camp until 1912.

Cooper was one of the prominent pioneer stockmen of his time. He stands among the men that built the West and prospered in California. William F. Cooper died September 9, 1908 at 83.

SOURCES

Beard, Franklin. *Grain Fields to Green Fields,* La Grange, CA: Southern Mines Press, 1987, p. 11, Fred McMillan interview.

Conners, Pam. "A Century or So of Land Use on the Central Stanislaus Watershed Analysis Area, 1848-1958." 1993 Summit District, Stanislaus National Forest. Apr. 1993.

"Cooper's Arrest." *Union Democrat,* 7 Dec. 1867, Notation: p. 4.

Elliott and Moore, *History of Stanislaus County*: *Sketches of the Prominent Citizens.* 1881. p. 208.

French, Gerald. *When Steam Was King*, p. 44. Eureka Publishing LLC. N.d.

Gorsuch, Joan. "David Henry Sanguinetti." *CHISPA* Tuolumne County Historical Society publication, Jan. Mar. 1977.

Historic California Militia and National Guard Units.

Information from the Tuolumne County Museum.

"Terrible Tragedy at the Rock River Ranch." *Union Democrat,* 30 Nov. 1867. p. 2s

Wright, Donnie. Personal interview, 2015.

CHAPTER 35

Henry Sanguinetti
Cattleman at Cooper's Meadow

Cabins at Cooper Meadow in 1960.
Photograph courtesy Tuolumne County Historical Society and Museum.

The Sanguinetti family has unquestionably left its mark on the Tuolumne County landscape. Brothers Henry and Joe both became renowned stockmen. When the Forest Service gave Henry the opportunity to choose his cattle grazing allotment in the national forest, he selected Cooper Meadow, also known as Cooper's Meadow, as his choice.

Their father David came to America from northern Italy in 1860 with his first wife, who died in childbirth, as did their baby. He settled in Sonora, where he first was a teamster, and then raised vegetables.

When David was thirty-five, he met Maria Peirano of Douglas Flat in Calaveras County, who was nine years younger. They courted for a while, and their families wondered if they would ever marry. They wed August 18, 1877, at St. Patrick's Church in Sonora, followed by a large celebration.

David and Maria raised a large family of four boys and four girls. The family ranch, consisting of one hundred and sixty acres, was located a mile and a half east of Sonora on a slight rolling hill. Gardening was David's passion. He cultivated vegetables and sold them locally, three times a week. During the summer, he hauled his vegetable wagon with fresh produce to Tuolumne, Soulsbyville, Confidence, and Sugar Pine. He also transported vegetables over Sonora Pass to Bodie, where he sold the produce for a good price and came home with cash in his pocket.

Henry David, the fourth son, was born May 2, 1889, on the Sanguinetti Ranch. The boys, at age ten or twelve, each had a cow and calf to raise for the family meat. They learned from oldest brother Joe how to raise stock, and started in the cattle business. Both Joe and Henry became prominent cattlemen.

The family attended church regularly and knew their priest, Father Patrick Guerin, well. The priest ran cattle at Cooper's Meadow from 1909 to 1912. Father Guerin loved the mountains and asked Henry, age twenty-three, to work for him at Cooper's Meadow, and look after his cattle herd. That same year, Father Guerin mysteriously left. In 1913, the Sanguinettis obtained a Forest Service grazing permit in the Emigrant Primitive Area and took over the Guerin allotment. They set up at William Cooper's cabin and barn at Cooper's Meadow. Brothers Joe and Henry stayed most of the summer, returning to Sonora for supplies about once a month.

The cabin had windows on the north and south walls, an iron-framed double bed, a small sheepherder wood burning stove, and a few cabinets on the wall. Inside the cabin are names carved into the walls of people who came by in the early days. The stairs to a sleeping loft in the cabin were built by Chinese men, who carved their names on the stairs. Of interest is the fact that the stairs have very short steps to accommodate the builders.

Henry considered himself a horseman. He wore chaps, gloves, a denim jacket, cowboy hat, and boots. He always smoked cigars.

Henry married Rose Margaret Copeland in San Francisco on April 22, 1919. They had three sons— Ray, Marion, Henry David Jr., and a daughter, Lee.

Rose had an elder care business in her home. She also was the radio dispatcher for the City of Sonora Police Department, and she operated in the living room. The children and elderly roomers were not allowed to touch the radio equipment.

During the Depression, Henry, a good businessman, bought up land, paying with cash in

Henry Sanguinetti in his barn in 1978.
Photograph courtesy of the Sanguinetti family.

silver dollars. He raised cattle and horses on a ranch on the west side of the area, where Lake Tulloch is located. Henry also had grazing rights at Upper Relief Meadow and Whitesides.

Henry's brother Joe knew that with the outbreak of hoof and mouth disease his herd would be slaughtered. So, he drove the herd from Cooper's Meadow a back way to his ranch at Chinese Camp to avoid the authorities.

Henry had a dude ranch in Twain Harte. He would tell the customers, "Sit up straight, and be proud to be on a horse." A rodeo became a popular attraction. The dude ranch venture lasted about thirty years, and later became a golf course.

Every morning before he got out of bed, Henry had three sips of brandy. A short fellow at five foot eight, he was quiet and reserved. When he did have something to say, it was generally true, and "You

Hentry Sanguinetti.
Photograph courtesy of Tuolumne County Historical Society and Museum.

could take it to the bank." Henry trusted everyone. His friends in Sonora called him Grandpa, even if they were not related. A generous man, he gave each of his grandchildren a horse. When they visited the ranch, he would lead the horses into the corral and let each child pick out the one they wanted. If the horse wasn't broken for a child to ride, he would take care of that, too. His wife Rose looked after the ranch hands as though they were her own sons. W.C. Koch of Oakdale remembers his impression of the Sanguinettis when he was a young man, "They were the traditional old Italian family. When you came to the ranch for any reason, you were expected to accept a glass of the homemade red wine, served with salami and cheese on homemade bread. It tasted so good. Henry pressed you to have more than one drink, and out of politeness you accepted. The wine kept coming, there was no limit."

After twenty-eight years of marriage and three children, Henry and Rose divorced in 1947. Rose moved to Twain Harte.

Henry took a supply of his homemade red wine to Cooper's Meadow every summer. He hid a jug of wine in a hollowed-out tree stump near his cabin. A wire on the stump was attached to the jug handle to pull the wine up out of its hiding place. From horseback, Henry could reach the wire, pull up the jug, and have a sip.

During World War II, the cattle business thrived. After the war years, the county taxes made it hard to make a good profit. All the cattlemen struggled. The last Sanguinetti cattle drive was in 1964. After that, they were hauled by truck.

Henry rode a paint horse he named Moneybags. When he became elderly, Henry had trouble mounting a full-sized horse. But, being knowledgeable about horses, he knew how to solve the problem. He bought a Shetland stud and bred him with a quarter horse, so he would have a smaller horse to mount.

His ex-wife Rose died before Henry on July 9, 1975. He lived to be 92 and died on a cold winter day. On January 9, 1982, news of his death was on the front page of the *Union Democrat*. He was known throughout the county as a cattle rancher and a top authority on horse breeding. His capable sons

Henry Sanguinetti at Cooper Meadow barn on his half Shetland, half quarter horse mount. *Photograph courtesy of Matt Bloom.*

took over the ranch and carried on the family cattle empire built by the pioneer brothers.

The Sanguinetti Ranch house still exists. It is known by subsequent family members as the "Home Place." The Home Place became the name of a restaurant operated by some of the Sanguinetti descendants.

SOURCES

Gorsuch, Joan. "David Henry Sanguinetti." *CHISPA* Vol. 16, No. 3, Tuolumne County Historical Society publication, Jan.-Mar. 1977. P. 558.

"Henry Sanguinetti Dies at Age 92." *Union Democrat,* 11 Jan. 1982, Front page.

Knowles, Chuck. Personal interview, 27 Oct. 2016.

Koch, W.C. Personal interview, 5 Jul. 2017.

"Oral interview with Henry Sanguinetti." Neil Mill. Columbia Collage Oral History Series. 8 Mar. 1978.

Sanguinetti, Lynn. Personal interview, 21 Mar. 2018.

Sardella, Dan. Personal interview, 1 Jul. 2016.

Whittle, Donnie. Personal interview, 10 Feb. 2017.

CHAPTER 36

Ed Burgson
The Cattleman with a Passion for Cars

Ed Burgson, called "Burgie" by his close friends, may be remembered as one of the most accomplished outdoorsmen on Sonora Pass. Ed became a businessman, had a wide range of friends, and built a cabin on Sonora Pass. He knew every creek, meadow, lake, road, and most of the people who owned cabins and businesses in the area. His legacy is part of Tuolumne County's history.

His father had a great influence on his oldest son who, like his dad, raised horses. Ed's father Frank was born April 14, 1874, in Sweden. At 16, he immigrated to America and settled in Wisconsin. There he married Anna, a young Swedish girl who had come to Wisconsin a year earlier, in 1894. Frank and his wife Anna had four children, Edward V., Pearl E., Ethel V., and Roy P., all born in Wisconsin. Anna's brother, Charles John Anderson, came from Sweden in 1898 and lived with them.

They came to California and settled in Sonora in 1902. Frank raised and sold Thoroughbred horses from his stables off Lyon Street. By 1910, the census shows Frank was employed as a cook at the Gem Café in Sonora, owned by Thomas F. McGovern. Frank Burgson eventually bought out McGovern, remodeled the restaurant, and ran a very successful business.

Ed was born June 16, 1896, in Ashland, Wisconsin. He helped in his father's stables and learned the art of breeding horses. He graduated from Sonora High School in the class of 1914. Unlike many of his classmates, he went on for higher education and attended Heald Business College in Stockton.

Ed Burgson in 1930 on a trip to the mountains.
Photograph from the Chris Robinson collection.

Fresh out of the service, Ed was an ambitious young man, and he started working for First National Bank of Sonora, which later became the Bank of America. He stayed in the business for eighteen years. From his experience in banking, he had the opportunity to buy up ranches that were in foreclosure. Ed bought the 1400-acre Keystone Ranch, and the Flood Ranch, both out of Jamestown.

In 1922, Ed's father built a primitive cabin in the mountains on Sonora Pass, near Dardanelle Resort. In summer, the family would retreat to the mountain cabin, escaping the hot Sonora summers. Ed was twenty-eight when his dad built the cabin, and he loved the High Sierras. With his best friend John Balestra, a local pharmacist who married Ed's sister Pearl, the two men explored the mountains on horseback. They both became capable deer hunters and fishermen.

Ed Burgson stands in front of his father's cabin at Bone Springs in 1922.
Photograph courtesy of Chris Robinson.

Ed met and married Eileen May Shine, born May 16, 1896. She was a member of a local pioneer family from Chinese Camp. The Burgsons were a handsome couple and well liked in the community. They owned a two-story Queen Anne-style house on Bradford Street in Sonora. Ed commuted to his Keystone horse ranch. They had one daughter named Betty, born August 24, 1924, in Sonora.

Eileen taught ballet and ballroom dance classes and worked as an assistant county librarian. When she was thirty-five, Eileen purchased the "Orchid Shoppe," which was an upscale dress shop in downtown Sonora. She was successful, and the business flourished. Eileen operated the shop until

Ed Burgson, passenger, travels with friends through the Que de Porka. License plate reads 1927. Vehicle is a 1926 Chrysler G70 with wire wheel option.
Photograph courtesy of Chris Robinson collection.

1946, when she sold it to Catherine Livermore of Taft.

Ed's father Frank was very familiar with the Sonora Pass area. In 1932, it was Frank Burgson who led naturalist Clarence Bennett to the largest juniper tree in the world, on Joe Martin's cattle ranch on Eagle Meadow Road. It is now known as the Bennett Juniper.

Fisherman Ed Burgson in 1945.
Photograph courtesy of Chris Robinson.

During the Great Depression, with his eye on property for sale, Ed bought one hundred and sixty acres on Douglas Flat in Eureka Valley. It was a choice, rare piece of private property. The acreage fronted the Middle Fork of the Stanislaus River, with trout fishing and lush meadows. He quit banking in 1939 at forty-two and devoted more time to his ranch. Ed went into the cattle business with his partner, Joe Ghiorso of Shaw's Flat. They grazed their cattle on the Piute Range out of Pinecrest, in the Emigrant Basin. He remained in the cattle business for nearly thirty years, driving the last cattle out of the mountains in 1968.

Ed's good friend and fellow cattleman, Cliff Mitchell, owner of Kennedy Meadows, asked Ed if he could build a corral on his property, along the road by the old Hayes Station. In 1956, Mitchell built corrals for his own cattle and horses. The good friends agreed that Cliff would be allowed to use the corrals for a dollar per year.

Influenced by his father, Ed had a trained eye for horses. Naturally, he went into business breeding and selling registered Quarter Horses. His prized stallion, Colonel Cat, was the heart of his operation. Ed was well known for his fine horses, and took top prizes at the county fair. His right-hand man was Artie Scruggs, who was exceptional at breaking horses, and worked with Burgson's colts for many years. The two men were lifelong friends. Burgson was primarily a horseman, but his pleasure came from driving the finest cars. He upgraded whenever he could, and took great joy in his automobiles.

In 1954, Ed's mother Anna died at seventy-seven. His father was at a loss without her, and became unsettled and depressed. On impulse, a year later he sold the little mountain cabin at Bone Springs. The sale of the cabin led to a chain of events that influenced Ed and his family. The buyer was Eleanor Gallison, who purchased it for $2,000, sight unseen.

When Eleanor first arrived to see what she had actually bought and opened the door, she was surprised to see all the furniture and household goods still in place. Dishes were still in the cupboards and blankets on the beds, family photographs still in a drawer. Frank had just walked away from his cabin

Ed Burgson's cabin at edge of Eureka Valley.
Cate Culver photographer 2015.

of over thirty years. His children and grandchildren, and even his great-grandson, Chris Robinson, had all treasured the little cabin. The family was shocked at the sale of the cabin, and hurt that they were not consulted. Three years later, Frank died.

At sixty-two, Ed no longer had a home base in the mountains. In 1958, he decided to build a small cabin on the private land he had purchased along the Middle Fork of the Stanislaus River at Douglas Flat in Eureka Valley. The property was flat, and encompassed both sides of the Stanislaus River. Lush meadows edged with wildflowers were perfect for grazing his fine horses.

Ed chose a secluded site to build his cabin away from the road, overlooking a bend in the river. The cabin was primitive, with just one large room for a bedroom, living room and kitchen. The only plumbing was a hand pump, that brought water indoors to the kitchen sink. A small wood burning stove served for heat and cooking. A deck overlooked the river with a stunning view of the mountains. It was some of the most beautiful, prime land on the Pass. The cabin was a place to enjoy his beloved mountains. He added a deck overlooking the river, and as he aged enjoyed watching the water currents roaring by, destined for the valley.

Ed's daughter Betty and her husband Ben Robinson came to the cabin when they could get away from their busy schedules in Sonora. They brought their thirteen-year-old son Chris, who had spent many summers with his great-grandfather at the Bone Springs cabin. Chris was happy to be in the mountains again.

In his later years, Ed came down with shingles, and the rash of blisters spread to his face. He was a rather vain man who always dressed fashionably, but disfigured, he isolated himself from friends and family. The blisters spread to his eyes and alarmed the doctor who did what he could, but Ed lost sight in one eye. Afterward, Ed also lost his confidence in driving, and made fewer and fewer trips out to his Keystone ranch. It was a hard blow for the automobile enthusiast to give up driving.

Through hard work, Ed Burgson had become a successful cattleman and horse breeder. His love of the mountains, his father's cabin, and then his own cabin at the river's edge gave him great joy throughout his lifetime. Ed died from a heart attack on March 28, 1978, at eighty-two.

His daughter Betty and her husband Ben Robinson enjoyed the family cabin, spending as much time there as they could. In 1971, they upgraded the water system to bring water to the kitchen sink, and added an indoor toilet and shower, a pantry, and an upstairs bedroom. The cabin is still in the family and is owned by Ed's descendents.

Chris Robinson at five with his great-grandfather Frank Burgson, at Dardanelle near the Burgson cabin in 1950.
Photograph courtesy of Mildred Montgomery. (Wade Coffill collection).

SOURCES

Anderson, Bob. Personal interview, 12 Nov. 2016.
Cassinetto, Ben. Personal interview, 26 Jun. 2016.
Mitchell, Kenny. Personal interview, 3 Mar. 2017.
Research by Pat Perry, Sonora City Historian. 8 Jun. 2108.
Robinson, Chris. Personal interview, 2015.
Terzich, Irving. Personal interview, 2013.
United States Census records.

CHAPTER 37

Joe Ghiorso
His Cows and His Money

Joe Ghiorso was one of the early cattlemen who led the way for stockmen through the 1900s. Joe ran cattle for sixty years in the Piute region near Pinecrest, where the grazing rights were first offered in 1909. That year, Joe made his first cattle drive at 16, with Dolph Ratto and his herd of two hundred and fifty Durham cows. As a teenager, he loved it.

Born to Italian parents on November 27, 1892, Joe was raised on the family ranch where Sonora High School stands now. His father, Giovanni, peddled vegetables and fruit that he delivered to the local gold mines. He had a good business with few employees.

Joe's mother, Maria, died while giving birth to him. The death affected Giovanni severely. He went crazy and abandoned the family of five boys and one girl. Giovanni did eventually marry again. Joe and his brother Peter went to live with their older sister Kate, who had married nearby rancher, Adolph Ratto. Kate and Dolph took in Joe and his brother Peter and raised the Ghiorso boys. Joe remained on the Ratto ranch his entire life.

In 1977, Joe was interviewed by historian Richard L. Dyer. When asked about his education, Joe replied, "Oh hell, I walked to the Browns Flat one-room school. I went about five years. I didn't like school much and quit. I was needed on the Ratto Ranch. My brother Pete continued on with school and became a barber. I became a cattleman." He also worked as a plasterer, cement finisher, and bricklayer. Joe learned to be a stonemason from "Swiss" Foletti, a well-known Sonora businessman and stonemason. Joe built many rock walls

Joe Ghiorso, Mayor of Piute, in 1960.
Photograph courtesy of Ben Cassinetto. Photographer Mike Ghiorso.

Joe Ghoirso's cabin at Piute. In 1924 Joe built this cookhouse with a cement floor and shingle siding. However, it was so cold during the fall that in 1961 he put stucco on the outside to keep it warm inside.
Photograph courtesy of Chris Robinson.

throughout Sonora. He would walk four miles to Sonora, carrying all his tools, and never felt the need to ride a horse. After a full day of work, he returned to the ranch to finish chores. Joe Ghiorso served in the army infantry during WWI, but he devoted the majority of his years to cattle ranching.

Donnie Whittle remembers, "Joe was known to be a straight talker and could size up people pretty fast. You knew right away if he liked you or not. It was best to not get on his wrong side or you could be sprayed with four letter words."

Joe was careful with his money, and hid paper bills in cans on his back porch and under his house. One time his house flooded and much of the money floated out into the meadow. The money was $100 bills, always with the serial numbers in order. Joe had a stack of Social Security checks that he never cashed, because he distrusted the banks.

At one time, he hired a housekeeper. He returned home one afternoon to find his back porch all cleaned up. He frantically looked for the housekeeper and found her about to take a match to the pile of debris and old cans full of money.

Ben Cassinetto recalls, "He distrusted banks and hid all his money. Inside his house you could pull out a drawer and find $30,000."

On the Piute summer range, in 1924, he built a small cabin. Not the usual log cabin, but one built of stucco to secure against the cold, rain, and snow, with a cement floor to withstand the harsh winters at the 7,560 foot elevation.

Joe ran about one hundred and twenty-five head of cattle on his own. His fellow cattlemen affectionately called him the Mayor of Piute, where he presided over his cattle and two dogs for many summers. One summer in the mountains his cow dog Brownie went missing. Joe was very fond of the dog and concerned about what might have happened. Fortunately, the dog found its way down the mountain and back to the Ratto Ranch. Joe was much relieved to see his favorite dog back home again.

partnership with Ed Burgson in 1959, a horseman who owned a cattle ranch at Keystone, near Jamestown. Together they operated the B and G Cattle Company, which operated until October 20, 1968, when they drove the cattle out of the mountains for the last time.

At age seventy-seven, in 1969, Ghiorso reluctantly gave up cattle ranching. His partner, Ed Burgson, was in poor health and died the next year. Joe maintained his interest in ranching, breaking in a few horses, and managing the two-hundred-and-sixty-acre Ratto Ranch off Jamestown-Shaws Flat Road, himself.

Joe had a green thumb and planted a large vegetable garden on the Ratto ranch every year. He was well known for his huge Beefsteak tomatoes, but also grew squash and beans. He frequently shared his produce with the other cattlemen he visited, on the way to his Piute cattle range in the mountains.

Traditionally during the holidays, Joe would make his famous raviolis from an old family recipe. On long tables he rolled out the raviolis with great care. They were all to be given away. Friends and family arrived with pans to take raviolis home for their holiday meal. This was his gift to them.

Joe had a summer cookhouse, where during the heat of summer meals were cooked outdoors. Sometimes on Sunday, his brothers Frank and Pete would bring their families for Sunday dinner. They all spoke Italian at these Sunday gatherings, keeping old traditions alive.

In his later years, Joe had a longtime girlfriend named Madeline McBride. They had plans to marry, but sadly, Madeline became ill. Joe would bring her food and keep her company, but in 1952 she passed away at fifty-two.

Joe owned the old Johnny Gerber ranch by Tuttletown. He used this ranch to keep his cattle in the winter. When the New Melones Dam was going to be built in the mid-1960s, Joe sold this property to the Army Corps of Engineers for a good sum of money. This land is now submerged under New Melones Reservoir.

Joe lived out his life at the Ratto Ranch on Jamestown-Shaws Flat Road. The ranch was self-sustaining, and they grew everything they needed.

Joe Ghiorso in 1974 inside his gold mine.
Photograph courtesy of Ben Cassinetto, photographer.

In the mountains, Joe would often be seen leading his horse. He rarely rode it, preferring to walk. On the cattle range, he looked out of place, as he always dressed in his familiar farmer clothes, bib overalls and work boots instead of Levis and cowboy boots.

To make the best use of his grazing allotment, he would tuck his cattle into every little meadow and make the rounds, to know where they all were grazing. Joe herded cattle with two dogs, one as a good tracker and one as a heeler to keep the cattle moving.

Through the summer season, the stockmen worked hard cutting back the willows and young tamarack pines that, left unchecked, would consume the meadows needed for grazing their stock. In the fall, when Joe left the mountains, he and other cattlemen would set fires to burn out all the undergrowth, and open the forest to more sunlight.

Joe ranched with Adolph Ratto for many years. Adolph died in 1935. Later, Joe went into

Joe Ghiorso at the Ratto ranch.
Photograph courtesy of the Tuolumne County Historical Society and Museum.

He valued the land and the place where he grew up. Although Joe was wealthy, he never saw a reason move or live anywhere else. He drove a 1943 Willys pick-up all this life, and never bought a newer automobile. Throughout his life, Joe liked to mine gold and had a mine near Columbia named the Hidden Treasure. He mined with his partner Bill Moyle. Joe didn't need the money. If they hit any gold it was never mentioned. It was a hobby and a passion that gave him great pleasure.

A frugal man, Joe invested in land and died a wealthy man at 92, at the Ratto Ranch on January 11, 1984. A man of Italian tradition and hard work, Joe added color and texture to the fabric of the Central Sierras.

SOURCES
Cassinetto, Ben. Personal interview, 26 Jun. 2016.
Dyer, Richard L. Columbia College Library Oral History Series interview in 1977.
Fuller, Patty. "Joe Ghiorso- 60 Years of Cattle Drives." Obituary, *Union Democrat*, 12 Jan. 1984, Front page.
Ghiorso, Mike. Personal interview, 13 Nov. 2018.
Knowles, Chuck. Personal interview, 25 Oct. 2016.
Robinson, Chris. Personal interview, Jun. 2016.
Whittle, Donnie. Personal interview, 15 Sep. 2016.

CHAPTER 38

Joe Martin, Sr.
Eagle Meadow Cattleman

Joe William Martin was one of Sonora's leading citizens during most of the twentieth century. A prominent cattleman and an astute businessman, he was known widely and belonged to many organizations. He was born in Soulsbyville on March 9, 1895. His parents, Joe and Elizabeth, were pleased on that spring day to welcome the first son to a family that eventually had nine children. His father was a gold miner.

By eight he was learning how to butcher. When he was a young man he worked in a livery stable, cleaning harnesses, the barn, and stables. He learned quickly and was good with livestock.

Joe owned the Palace Meat Market with his partner J.C. Garaventa in Sonora. Martin ran a slaughterhouse on Sanguinetti Road, just out of Sonora, which provided the fresh meat. It had three corrals and a sturdy barn. Here he butchered lambs and steers, and slaughtered hogs. About eighty-five animals per week passed through Martin's slaughterhouse. It was a thriving business for twenty-five years.

Joe's skill with the carving knife was astounding. He was very particular about his knives and sharpened them himself. To test their sharpness, he wiped the blade across his arm to watch how well it cut. Joe smoked unfiltered Camel cigarettes and was rarely seen without his cowboy hat, blue jeans, and a nicely pressed Western shirt.

A good businessman, Martin bought the Eagle Meadows cow camp from Frank McCormick. It had 1,600 acres, including the land where the famous Bennett Juniper was located. McCormick had built a cabin and barn overlooking Eagle

Meadow as it spreads out below the landmark Eagle Peak, at an elevation of 9,385 feet. Eagle Creek runs through the meadow, and plunges down to meet the Middle Fork of the Stanislaus River at Dardanelle. The cow camp is a choice piece of mountain property. It is a scenic place with timber and lush meadows for cattle to graze, and there was no road into the camp until 1948.

The log cabin had a lot of holes, and Joe insulated the inside with knotty pine to keep it warm. He added a toilet, shower, wood stove, hot

Joe Martin, Sr. in 1962.
Photograph courtesy of Joe Martin Sr. family.

Early photograph of McCormick's cow camp at Eagle Meadow. *Photograph courtesy of Bob Brennan.*

water tank, and enough bunk beds to sleep eight. He added a sleeping loft with hinged stairs by the fireplace.

Martin would drive six hundred head of cattle to Eagle Meadows from his winter grazing land, which was the old McCormick Ranch on O'Byrnes Ferry Road near Jamestown. It took five days to move the cattle, accompanied by his hard working

Jesse Martin in 1917 at age nineteen.
Photograph courtesy of the Joe Martin Sr. family.

border shepherd dogs. He hired about five local cowboys who knew the country well.

Joe married Jesse Reynolds, a tall blonde from Farmington, on August 20, 1917. They raised three children: Joe Jr., Melvin, called "Meb," and daughter Aloha, who married Neil Sinclair. In the 1950s, after the children were grown, Joe and Jesse divorced. Both were stubborn and clashed throughout the marriage. They decided that no attorney was needed, and asked their oldest son Joe Jr. to make the decisions about how the estate should be divided. Both felt this was the best way, and he would be fair.

After the divorce, Jesse moved to Sonora and lived in a house on Shepherd Street where she opened Dee's Candy Shop. Jesse made and sold an assortment of candy, specializing in pine nut rolls and caramel turtles. She also raised and sold canaries and African violets. A very independent sort, if she wanted something she created it herself. If she wanted some art on the walls, she painted a picture. If she wanted more room in her house, she dug herself a new basement. Her backyard flower garden was her pride and joy. She never remarried. Jesse died of a heart attack in the fall of 1983.

Martin had extensive land holdings in the mountains. Many privately owned cabins on Eagle

Meadow Road were originally Joe Martin's property. He also had property in Long Valley and several other isolated parcels within the boundaries of the Stanislaus National Forest.

He owned a pack station adjacent to Leland Meadows, which came to cause him grief. Originally owned by Bert Reed, it was a popular stop for travelers to Cooper's Meadow and the Eagle Meadow area. In 1943, Joe Sanguinetti, with Joe Martin and J.C. Garaventa, purchased Reed's Pack Station with all the improvements. It was a good location, and they used the place as a headquarters for grazing operations in the Herring Creek Range Allotment, and as an overnight stop en route to their allotments. The two cattlemen agreed to share the building.

It has been rumored that one day an argument took place between Joe Martin and Joe Sanguinetti. As it became more heated, they came to blows, and to the amazement of the cowboys standing by, it became an all-out fistfight. After the fight, the two

Bert Reed's pack station near Leland Meadow.
Photograph courtesy of the Tuolumne County Historical Society and Museum.

men never spoke again. In order to continue sharing the building, a wall was built down the center. Each side had its own quarters and each had a front door, wood stove, and water system. The cowboys from the two camps were not allowed to speak with one another. This arrangement with its grievances continued throughout their lifetimes.

As Joe aged, he came to realize that he must delegate the division of his land holdings. Joe sold half his land and gave the other half to his children, Joe, Jr., Meb, and Aloha. Joe, Jr. purchased the cattle ranch from his father and was prominently known

Corrals at Joe Martin's Cow Camp, with Eagle Peak in the background. Corrals and framed gates built by Bob Brennan.
Photographer Cate Culver.

for the cattle ranch, plus his logging and trucking companies. Meb dabbled in logging, worked with horses, and was a Jack-of-all-trades sort of guy.

After the divorce, Joe continued to live in the family home alone. He tended a large vegetable garden where he grew string beans, tomatoes, squash and corn, and numerous other vegetables. The front of his home had large windows where he displayed his photograph collection of the family, including historic photographs of the area. He enjoyed his many friends who would visit and bring food. Punny Dambacher and former sheriff Miller Sardella were regulars who came to check on him. Most every evening John and Joyce Kelley, who owned Kelley Motors in Sonora, stopped by to share a libation. Wild Turkey was Joe's favorite.

Son Joe, Jr. took over the ranch located outside Jamestown. Dad Joe, Sr. was known to slowly drive by just to make sure everything was well cared for. He had put much of his life into the place, and still felt an attachment to the years gone by and all the hard work that he put into the land.

When he was ninety, the highway bypass was put in, and his house was to be demolished. Caltrans moved him to a house at Phoenix Lake, where he lived a few months and died, December 12, 1985 at ninety.

Cattlemen of the era looked up to Joe Martin. He represented the straight-talking, tough, single-minded men who worked hard, and carved out a successful business. He led cattlemen into the modern era, and set an example of honesty and dedication in making a living from the land.

Joe Martin's Cow Camp, in 1980.
Photograph by Cate Culver.

SOURCES

Appel, Jim. Personal interview, 2013.

Brennan, Bob. Personal interview, 1 Oct. 2018.

Conners, Pam. "A Century or So of Land Use on the Central Stanislaus Watershed Analysis Area, 1848-1958," p. 218.

Dodge, Stacey Martin. Personal interview, 1 Oct. 2018.

Dyer, Richard L. Columbia College Library Oral History Series interview. 23 Sept. 1982.

Hamilton, Jack. Personal interview, 15 Jun. 2017.

"Joseph Martin, Sr. Obituary." *Union Democrat*, 13 Dec. 1985. p. 6.

Randall, Joanne Snyder. Personal interview, 2014.

Sardella, Johnny. Personal interview, 2015.

Terzich, Irving. Personal interview, 2013.

CHAPTER 39

Charles Sachse
A Man With Few Needs

Charles Sachse came to California from Germany, at twenty-two, to see the cowboys and the West. He found work as a farm laborer in the San Joaquin Valley, then in the mountains with the cattlemen. Sachse liked California so much he never returned to his homeland, but his German accent never left him.

Born February 27, 1859, he was a well-educated young man who had trained to make surgical instruments. Sachse lived in a cabin in the mountains above Cherry Lake and below Jawbone Creek. He had dug a water ditch from the creek, which ran down to his cabin and large vegetable garden. All the cattlemen knew and liked him.

In 1912, Sachse homesteaded property beside Ferretti Road east of Groveland, and owned a little house. He farmed a bit but favored being in the mountains with the cowboys, so the house and property fell into disrepair.

Sachse loved the West and the cowboy lifestyle. He worked for the cattlemen in and around Groveland. During the winters he was content to bunk on a porch or sleep in a barn. He was a man of few needs.

One fall, when Sachse was helping cattleman John Meyer round up his cattle below Horse Meadow near Yosemite, a snowstorm quickly blew into the high country. By late afternoon, cold and wet, Sachse made his way to the Meyers' cabin, where he built a fire as darkness fell. He waited for John to return and became alarmed when John failed to appear. He decided to take a lantern and start a search. He returned to the area where he had last seen John Meyer. There he found him, snow-blind

Charles Sachse with a buck he had just killed and tagged.
Photograph courtesy of Chris Robinson.

Charles Sachse in the mountains near his cabin.
Photograph courtesy of Chris Robinson.

and disoriented. Sachse led him back through the snowdrifts to the cabin, where he quickly kindled the fire and fixed a hot meal for his friend. Charles Sachse had saved John Meyer's life. The next day the storm had passed, so the men returned to get the last of the cattle. They were horrified to find all the cattle had frozen to death.

Sachse married briefly in his old age. The 1940 census shows him at age 81 and widowed, but nothing else is known of the marriage.

Sachse lived to be very old. John Meyer took care of him in his old age. The old, gentle man died at 91 on July 24, 1949. When Sachse died, his body was cremated. John Meyer paid some men to carry Sachse's ashes to the top of a rock landmark and sprinkle them in the area as a tribute to the old German. It became known as Sachse Monument, and noted as such on maps.

SOURCES
Anderson, Bob. Personal interview, 16 Nov. 2016.
California Death Index, 1940-1997 *Ancestry.com.*
De Ferrari, Carlo M. *The De Ferrari Family Memories of Times Past*. Tuolumne Heritage Publications. 2013. pp. 237-8.
Rosasco, Jean. Personal interview, 12 Mar. 2016.
Whittle, Donnie. Personal interview, 14 Aug. 2016.

CHAPTER 40

The Sheepmen
The Unwelcome Shepherds

Sheep passing through the forest ate much of the underbrush.
Photograph courtesy of the Tuolumne County Historical Society and Museum.

The first sign of a herd of sheep approaching was a slow-moving cloud of dust. It was a creeping wooly mass of bleating lambs, tinkling bells, and barking dogs. Herds traveled at a steady eight to ten miles per day. Herders yelled out instructions to the indispensable sheep dogs. Thousands of sheep passed through the foothills during their spring migration to the mountain meadows of the Sierra.

Neither the sheep herders nor their flocks were welcome in the mountains. While the Forest Service campaigned against allowing them on their land, cattlemen claimed they destroyed the lush grasses of the mountain meadows and trampled the soil. Yet they came. The moving of the sheep took place after lambs were old enough to move and the sheep had been shorn. Sheep graze very close to the ground leaving behind a land denuded of shrub or blade of grass. Once vibrant meadows eroded to an expanse of dust, until the fall rains returned.

The sheep business spanned half a century, from after the Civil War to well into the 1900s. It was a big business in early California and very profitable.

Feeding the sheep on government land was cheap. The herds would almost double in size every year because the ewes frequently had twins. The sheep were sheared in April and again in October,

Sheep with pack mules in 1899.
Photograph courtesy of the Tuolumne County Historical Society and Museum. (Gerald French collection)

and the wool brought a good price. In 1871, twenty-two million pounds of wool were processed at mills in San Francisco or shipped to East Coast mills.

As the business boomed and a labor shortage ensued, Frenchmen and Basques, Portuguese and Mexicans immigrated and hired on as sheep herders. Basques were historically reluctant to serve France and Spain in their colonial wars. So the young men left the country overnight in the 1870s, bound for America. The locals looked down on these foreigners and their invading bands of sheep.

By 1882 there were 13,932 sheep counted in Tuolumne County. Soon huge herds were devastating the mountain meadows, and conservationists became alarmed.

In a special message to Congress on December 3, 1901, President Theodore Roosevelt eloquently explained the scourge of the sheep. "The forest reserves must be set apart forever for the use and benefit of our people as a whole, not to the shortsighted greed of a few." The sheep ranchers became bitter over the policy that excluded them from grazing in the reserves. Eventually it became a criminal offence to pasture sheep in specified public lands of the Sierra.

Forest Supervisor Grant Taggart, a small nervous man, was frustrated by murky government rules and the uncertainty of how much authority the rangers had to arrest violators without permits. Sheep trespass cases took up a large part of Taggart's time. He had a staff of only eight rangers to patrol the forest reserves.

The situation became so desperate that on June 25, 1904, the Government Land Office sent Supervisor Taggart a letter instructing him to discourage the herders from entering the forest reserve with their sheep. The Land Office had no policy in place and could only offer these suggestions, "To unite bands of sheep and take them out by the most available route. Or to scatter them to break up the bands. Or to separate the sheepherders from their bands. Or remove the bells from the bell wethers and tie up the dogs whenever needful to handle the sheep better." To prevent the sheepherders from warning others, the rangers ordered them, after bedding down at night, to take off their pants and shoes, which the rangers then confiscated until morning.

With limited resources, the rangers were not able to patrol all of the federal reserve, and there

Herding sheep on Patterson Grade.
Photograph courtesy of the Tuolumne County Historical Society and Museum. (Fred Leighton collection).

A sheep herder coming from the Eastern side of the Pass, stopped by Brightman Flat Ranger Station in 1942. Young Shirley Spicer, daughter of the ranger aboard his burro.
Photograph courtesy of Jo Spicer Danicourt.

were many violators. A government report noted that despite restrictions, 54,645 adult sheep and 29,939 lambs crossed Sonora Pass in 1904.

By 1905, the General Land Office Commissioner held that the government had the right to insist on grazing permits for entrance to the forest reserves. The cattlemen cooperated and applied for grazing permits and followed the laws. The sheepherders, in protest, did not obtain grazing permits but did respect warnings to leave the reserves. Not being able to secure sufficient range elsewhere, eventually they moved into the Nevada rangelands.

It took years to regulate the size of the herds, but slowly they became more manageable. Sheep ranching declined in Tuolumne County. No longer did the herding of sheep, bells tinkling and dogs nipping at their heels, echo throughout the forest. The once thriving business sputtered to an end.

SOURCES

Ayers, Robert W. *History of the Stanislaus.* Feb. 1911. Stanislaus National Forest files.

Dillon, Richard H. *"Shepherds of Sonora Pass." Westways.* Auto Club magazine. Sep. 1965.

Douglass, William A. "Basque Sheepherding." *Amerikanuak! Basques in the High Desert.* 1995. Carson Valley Museum files.

Holland, John. *"The Great Sheep Chase." Union Democrat,* 20 Feb. 1997. p. 10A.

Lee, W. Storrs. "Mountain Meadows Churned Dust." *The Sierra.* (excerpt). Putnam, 1962.

CHAPTER 41

J.D. McCarty
The Sheepman of Eureka Valley

Thomas McCarty and his bride Agnes Dean, both Irish Catholic, came to California from New York via the Isthmus of Panama, arriving in San Francisco on New Year's Eve, December 31, 1852. Thomas had previously been to Calaveras County and decided this was where he wanted to mine for gold, buy ranches, and raise a family. Thomas homesteaded land at Log Cabin Creek near Copperopolis and raised a family of nine children. He operated a trading post and store and raised horses, cows and sheep.

His sons, Ransome Thomas, born in 1856, and Jackson Dean, born in 1858, carried on the empire that their father had built in his lifetime. The two McCarty brothers eventually dissolved their partnership, divided the livestock, and each purchased separate ranches.

Jackson Dean J.D. "Jack" McCarty bought the Alban Hettick Ranch in Salt Spring Valley in 1901. The ranch included the building, all the livestock, and the AH brand. The property had been a roadhouse and stage stop for teams in the 1880s.

Jack later bought the Dean Ranch, owned by his uncles, and also purchased the original Log Cabin Ranch from his brothers and sisters. In addition to raising sheep and cattle, Jack raised and bred horses. He was a great lover of horses, and at times his herd numbered seventy to eighty head. He always drove a fine span of horses, and enjoyed racing his horses in the Calaveras County Fair.

By the age of forty-four Jack had built up a sizable estate and decided it was time to marry and raise a family. In 1902, J.D., tall and handsome married twenty-three year old neighbor girl Helen Hunt. They raised a family of eight children.

Jack needed mountain pasture land for his sheep and explored the Sonora Pass area. He selected a flat on Eureka Valley for his summer headquarters. Jack then explored the Seven Pines trail above the flat, and followed Douglas Creek to view the

Jackson Dean McCarty.
Photograph courtesy of the Calaveras County Historical Society.

Jackson Dean McCarty.
Photograph courtesy of the Calaveras County Historical Society.

fished and swam in the Stanislaus River, just across the road. The McCartys made friends with Bill Nelson and his wife, who owned Douglas Station, just a short distance from the McCarty Sheep Camp. The McCartys were fun loving, and enjoyed visiting with neighbors and locals.

The road by the camp was busy with workers passing by who were building the Relief Dam, high above Kennedy Meadows. Long teams of mules, hauling freight to the dam site, stirred dust. The sound of the muleskinners snapping their whips, cracked through Eureka Valley. At the sound of an automobile, everyone stopped to take notice, visit with the driver, and ask questions about the car.

Tragedy struck in 1917 when Helen died in childbirth, leaving Jack McCarty with eight young children to raise. Jack was devastated to lose his dear wife. He never remarried. The older children also helped in caring for the younger ones. He continued

meadows near Red Peak, Sonora Peak, and Stanislaus Peak. He liked what he saw, and the area became known as the Red Peak allotment, which he claimed for his grazing rights. On the trail to the pasture he built a small storage shed to store salt and other supplies used by sheep herders, including camp tender Lupe Barrios, who worked for McCarty.

In 1910 J.D. began taking his 4,000 sheep up to his allotment. It took weeks of planning to pack the wagons with all the family's clothing, a large supply of food, and even furniture. Each night they stopped to camp with the sheep. These long trail drives took about ten days.

The family divided the year between their ranch in Salt Spring Valley in Calaveras County, and their High Sierra camp on Sonora Pass. In the summer the entire ranch family, including the ranch hands and cook, moved to the high camp where there was green grass for the sheep to graze. A caretaker was left behind at Salt Spring Valley to watch over the ranch.

The children loved summers in the mountains, in the fresh cool air away from the hot valley. They

Helen Hunt McCarty.
Photograph courtesy of the Calaveras County Historical Society.

The McCarty family in 1914, camped in front of their sheep wagons at their summer camp in Eureka Valley, near Douglas Station on Sonora Pass. Left to right are Agnes, Helen, Mrs. Helen McCarty, Clarice Lucille, George Blazer Jr., Jackson Dean McCarty with young sons Albert, Jackson and Cyril. *Photograph courtesy of the Calaveras County Historical Society.*

taking his sheep to the grazing allotment on Sonora Pass. His children loved the mountains and helped out when Jack decided they were old enough to lend a hand around the camp.

In the spring of 1920, Jack decided to build a dance hall across the road from his camp. Jack knew of an old dance hall down the road at Sugar Pine. He looked it over, admired the fine tongue-and-groove flooring, and made the owner an offer to buy the old building. The offer was accepted, and Jack hired two carpenters to dismantle the building and move it to Eureka Valley. By September, the carpenters had completed a fine twenty-by-forty-foot building, with shutters on the sides and a sharp inclined roof to shed the heavy winter snowpack. The *Union Democrat* newspaper reports on September 18th, "Probably it cost Mr. McCarty five hundred dollars besides his labor to have this pleasure house built. It is an investment without monetary returns, since the gentleman proposes to donate it to the use of the mountain visitors to hold dance parties. In order to make it more inviting he will next season equip it with a two-hundred and sixty dollar Victrola and the latest and best music, which will also be at the service of the dancers, gratis. The only rule that users of the hall must observe provides that no dancing will be

Storage shed on the McCarty allotment at Red Peak. *Photograph courtesy of the Tuolumne County Historical Society Museum. (Francis Nelson collection).*

permitted in hob-nail boots, and this will be enforced simply to preserve the fine floor from damage."

Jack McCarty as a young man had the wisdom to acquire land and build a fine ranch in Salt Spring Valley. He chose Sonora Pass for his mountain sheep camp, and he was well respected by the cattlemen, as well as other sheep ranchers.

When Jack's health began to decline, he moved to Stockton, where he was cared for by his daughter, Helen Stanaway. He died in 1935, after a three-month illness at age seventy-seven.

J.D. McCarty family sheep by Hayes Station on their way up toward the summer range up on Sonora Pass. *Photograph courtesy of Tuolumne County Historical Society and Museum. (Francis Nelson collection.)*

A herd of about three thousand sheep on the Patterson Grade, headed for the McCarty Sheep camp in 1920. *Photograph courtesy of Tuolumne County Historical Society and Museum. (Francis Nelson collection).*

SOURCES

Findagrave.com. Memorial #16675290

Fuller, William P., Judith Marvin, and Julia G. Costello. *Madam Felix's Gold*. Calaveras County Historical Society and Foothill Resources, Ltd., 1996.

Grace, Harry D., Forest Supervisor to Adelbert Nichols, Tuolumne County Supervisor. Letter, 4 Jun. 1965. Letter undoubtedly written by Robert E. Stokes. Stanislaus National Forest files.

Hiatt, Ella M. "Some Copperopolis Pioneers and Old Timers." *Las Calaveras* quarterly bulletin of the Calaveras County Historical Society, Volume XV, No. 2. Jan. 1967.

"Jack McCarthy Borne to Rest." *Calaveras Prospect,* 16 Nov. 1935.

"Observations in the Mountains." *Union Democrat*, 18 Sep. 1920, Front page.

CHAPTER 42

The Fishermen

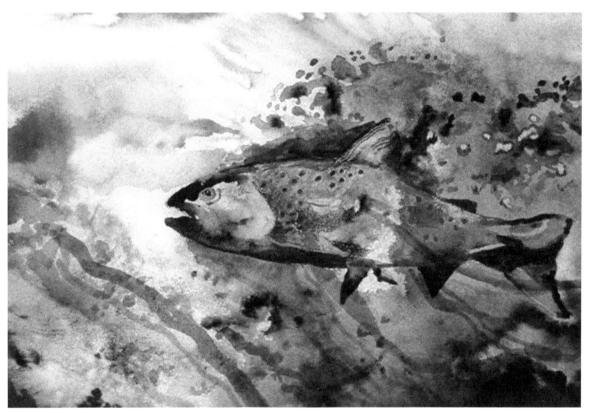

A Trout for George.
Watercolor painting by Cate Culver.

The Middle Fork of the Stanislaus River below Sonora Pass has a reputation for its numerous trout fishing holes, for both the fly and bait fisherman. The river and its little sister, the sparkling Clarks Fork, have attracted fishermen for years. Both rivers are accessible by car, so it is easy to just pull off the highway and walk to a fishing hole. Ice-cold, deep water in the thundering river gorges is filled with trout, as are the more quiet holes tucked under logs and behind boulders. It's a fisherman's paradise.

To fish the lakes requires riding a horse or hiking, with the exception of Leavitt Lake in Mono County, which is accessible by a high-clearance vehicle. Emigrant Basin at the Sierra crest holds many remote pristine lakes. Trails are marked and the lakes well stocked.

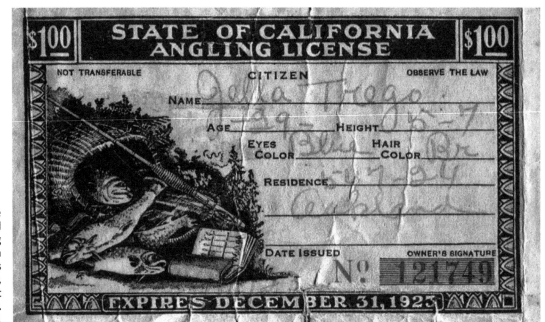

In 1913, the Department of Fish and Game began requiring a fishing license, which cost $1.00 for anglers eighteen years or older, and set the trout limit at fifty fish per day. *Courtesy of Janet Cornell.*

Howard Remick at left, with his father-in-law Will Barron in 1935, posing in the driveway of their Bone Springs cabin at Dardanelle. *Barron family photograph collection, courtesy of Bill Remick.*

Fishing pals ready to take on the Stanislaus River. Bets Frazier on the right, and friend Wanda Mohatt, in 1937.
Photograph courtesy of the Frazier family.

Rose Mitchell in 1940, at the bend in upper Kennedy Meadow. She owned the Kennedy Meadows Resort from 1945 to 1961. The Mitchells were cattle ranchers from Vallecito in Calaveras County.
Photograph courtesy of Jo Spicer Danicourt.

Ruth Caldwell fishing in upper Kennedy Meadow in 1954.
Photograph courtesy of the Cate Culver and the Caldwell family.

Young angler Connie Caldwell tries her luck in 1950.
Photograph courtesy of the Cate Culver and the Caldwell family.

Thundering water through the deep gorges of the Stanislaus River.
Cate Culver photographer.

Harold and Mary Wright pose with their breakfast catch in 1960.
Photograph courtesy of the Ruth and Edson Caldwell family.

High water in the gorge along the Stanislaus River.
Photograph courtesy of the Edson and Ruth Caldwell family.

John Balestra with his catch at Huckleberry Lake in 1928.
Courtesy of Chris Robinson photograph collection.

Outdoorsman Edson Caldwell displays his catch from Emigrant Lake in 1948.
Photograph from the Edson and Ruth Caldwell family collection.

Fishermen in camp with their catch, circa 1935. The car is a Model A Ford five-window coupe.
Photograph courtesy of Cynthia McCarrie.

Fishermen's catch at Fred Leighton's Yellowhammer Fish Camp.
Courtesy of the Tuolumne County Historical Society and Museum. (Fred Leighton collection).

Yellowhammer fishermen Zeke Goodwin (left) and Ed McMahon in 1922.
Courtesy of the Tuolumne County Historical Society and Museum (Fred Leighton collection).

At left, young outdoorsmen Zeke Goodwin fishing and deer hunting in 1922, with pal in center who is unknown, on the right is Ed McMahon, at Fred Leighton's Yellowhammer camp.
Courtesy of the Tuolumne County Historical Society and Museum. (Fred Leighton collection).

Fisherman Ed Burgson on the right, with unknown companion in 1945, at a lake in the Emigrant Basin.
Courtesy of Chris Robinson photograph collection.

Huckleberry Lake fishing trip, July 16, 1930.
Courtesy of the Tuolumne County Historical Society and Museum.

CHAPTER 43

Planting Trout
Stocking Mountain Lakes With Fingerlings

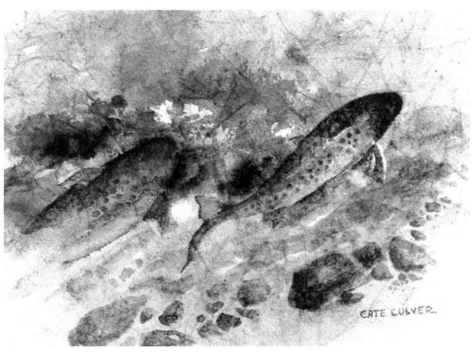

Two Trout.
Watercolor by Cate Culver.

The High Sierra contains many cold, clear lakes. Yet when early explorers and outdoorsmen dropped a line to catch dinner, not one nibble tested the hook. It was soon discovered that there were no fish in the granite-rimmed mountain lakes. Barren of fish-life, these high elevation lakes were enormous bathtubs of rainwater and snowmelt. No streams entered or drained these rock basins, so there was no way a fish could find its way up a stream into the deep pools.

Fishermen were eager to catch trout in the high mountain lakes. Eastern brook trout, natives of the East Coast, were particularly desirable for planting in the Sierra's landlocked lakes. Their eggs do not require flowing streams to propagate, and

can hatch in the clean gravel beds. Rainbow trout, natives of the Sierra, require fresh running water to spawn. A fisherman's favorite, the rainbow, is a fighter on the line, and takes flies as well as other bait and lures.

The smaller golden trout, a California native, is by far the most beautiful fish with its striking gold and orange colors. German brown trout arrived in Massachusetts from Europe in 1884, and by the early 1900s were introduced into California streams. The German browns, which grow large, are still plentiful and are the hardest to catch. The big browns hide under brush in quiet water or under logs, and are crafty fish that put up a good fight. They are a delicacy to eat with, a mild flavor.

Emigrant Lake surrounded by granite rock high in the Emigrant Basin remains a sport fisherman's delight.
Postcard from the Jerry and Cate Culver collection.

It took men with grit and dedication to pack into the wilderness and release fingerlings into the barren lakes. In the early 1870s, outdoorsmen began planting trout using the primitive methods of taking a bucket of fish from a stream and walking miles to toss them into a lake. Guy Scott, an early game warden, packed trout to lakes but met with no success. Others filled coal oil cans with fish and carried them for miles and released them in lakes. All these efforts failed.

On April 12, 1870, the newly-created State Board of Fish Commissioners established state fish hatcheries. In 1888, the large Sission Fish Hatchery near Mount Shasta was built. In 1908, the Sission hatchery shipped thirty cans of rainbow and Eastern brook fingerlings to a holding tank near Lyons Dam, up the mountain from Sonora. One to two inches in length, the young fish were transported by rail in a special sixty-foot-long car purchased from Southern Pacific Railroad. Locals from Sonora came for a look at the railcar. Designed with tubes filled with cold air, each can was aerated to keep the fish alive. The cans weighed one-hundred and forty pounds loaded. The temperature was kept at fifty degrees, which needed to be checked every thirty minutes

and ice added to the containers. Nine of the cans of the fingerlings were taken to Strawberry Lake, and thus the first trout from a fish hatchery arrived in Tuolumne County.

In 1883, a Bureau of Patrol and Law Enforcement was formed, and one of its duties was to plant fish in the remote lakes. On fish-planting days, two Patrol wardens were up at 4:30 in the morning to have their breakfast. A crew fed the stock and packed the animals. Initially, milk cans were used to carry the fish, but eventually twenty-five gallon "fish" cans were specially designed for transporting the young trout. The outside of the cans was covered with a heavy burlap fabric, which was kept wet and cool by the sloshing water in the fish cans. Stops were seldom made, as the movement of the animals was needed to aerate the water so the fish could have enough oxygen. If they needed to stop for the night, the fish cans were placed in a swiftly-moving stream to keep them cold and aerated during the layover.

Once the wardens arrived at the lake, it was a huge job to unload the heavy cans filled with fish and carefully release the fingerlings into the lake. Exhausted after unloading, they often spent the

Basin Creek Fish Hatchery in 1937 on the Tuolumne River. *Courtesy of the Tuolumne County Historical Society and Museum. (Fred Leighton collection).*

night. In the cool of the morning, the men gathered the stock and headed back down the trail.

Shortly after WWI, the Department of Fish and Game stepped up its distribution of fingerling trout in the California mountain streams and lakes. On June 7, 1926, the Basin Creek Fish Hatchery was dedicated on the North Fork of the Tuolumne River. A five-foot-high diversion dam was built on the creek. The fingerlings were primarily Rainbow trout and a few Eastern Brook. In 1954, a larger, more efficient hatchery was built at Moccasin Creek in southern Tuolumne County. In 1958, the small, older hatcheries, including Basin Creek, were closed.

The roads into the mountains had improved by 1937, and automobile transportation became faster and more reliable. The state abandoned the railroad cars and pack trains and transported the fragile fingerlings by truck.

The state experimented in 1946 with planting fish from airplanes dropping them into the high lakes. By the early 1950s, planting thousands of trout by airplane had become a common practice. The planes flew over the lakes at about eight hundred feet and dumped the fish from cans. Most of the planting was done in the spring, which gave the little fish a head start when the food and water conditions were good, and enabled the fish to grow rapidly. Amazingly, the little fingerling trout tossed

Overview of Basin Creek Fish Hatchery.
Courtesy of the Tuolumne County Historical Society and Museum. (Fred Leighton collection).

from planes had a high survival rate.

In 1926, three men who owned cabins at Bone Springs Summer Home Tract at Dardanelle started planning how they could plant fish locally. These men were all fishermen and neighbors who knew each other well. Each took on a phase of the fish-planting project. First under the direction of Frank Ralph, County Supervisor, men built a wooden holding tank. It was to be a new county trout-rearing tank. The dimensions were eight feet wide by sixteen feet long, and four feet deep. This tank was placed at Mitchell Terzich's cabin, which had ample water from his spring. A short flume brought water from the spring to the fish tank.

In June of 1926, thirty cans of fingerlings arrived and were placed in the wooden tank. It was maintained throughout the summer by Chauncey

Packing fingerling trout into the remote lakes in 1941. Cliff Mitchell at left, with Ed Burgson, who leads the pack train. Both were Emigrant Basin cattleman.
Photograph courtesy of Matt Bloom.

The water flume at the Mitchell Terzich cabin feeds water to a wooden holding tank for fingerlings.
Photograph courtesy of the Irving Terzich collection.

SOURCES

Hooper, George. "The Old Timers Didn't Wait for Fish Trucks." *Las Calaveras*. Calaveras County Historical Society, Vol. XLIV Jan. 1996 No. 2.

"It Arrives Here With Thirty Cans of Trout." *Union Democrat,* 14 Nov. 1908.

Lietritz, Earl. "History of California's Fish Hatcheries." Inland Fisheries Branch 1970. State of California Resources Department of Fish and Game. Fish Bulletin 150.

"Lyons Creek Chosen for Trout Tanks." *Union Democrat,* 22 Jun. 1907.

Magladry, Bill. *Fish Planting in the High Sierra.* Recollection from his private collection.

"Our Fish Repository." *Union Democrat,* 27 Jun. 1907.

Terzich, Irving. Personal interview, 2014.

Union Democrat, 4 Jul. 1908. Newspaper notation.

Wetmore, a Terzich relative. Ed Burgson, whose cabin was next door, packed the fingerlings in five-gallon milk cans, and transported them on mules to the local mountain lakes. Because of Ed's efforts in planting fish, the Forest Service named Burgson Lake, a small lake near Dardanelle Cone, after him.

The collective effort of the Department of Fish and Game and local outdoorsmen, brought sport fishing to the remote mountains where an outdoorsman could hike to an alpine lake, drop his line, and actually catch a fine limit of fish for dinner.

CHAPTER 44

The Deer Hunters

John Balestra poses with the big bucks shot in the Emigrant Basin area in 1930.
Photograph courtesy of Chris Robinson.

Mankind has embraced hunting in order to survive. The need to hunt evolved into a desire to hunt—more a sport than a necessity. Through lean times hunters fed their families. Hunting wild animals is regulated now by seasons, designated areas, and fees. Sonora Pass has a long history as a very good place to hunt.

Deer hunting season in the fall attracted great numbers of outdoorsmen. The back roads were filled with hunters' canvas tents and assorted hunting gear. Skill at hunting is often passed from father to son. As most outdoorsmen did not hunt alone, it was a great time of male companionship. Moreover, the companionship around the campfire the night before is a huge part of the sport. In the light of the fire,

they recounted past hunts, deer killed, and the ones that got away. Tales were often told of the hunters that got lost, rifles that jammed at a critical shot, and goofy things that happened when packing out a deer. The success stories sometimes became part of the plan for the next morning's hunt. Up at daylight, the hunters wolfed down a breakfast over the campfire, and set in motion plans for the hunt that day.

Much of the enjoyment for the hunter has been the pleasure of walking alone in the forest as quietly as possible, watching the sunrise, and hearing the birds flitter above in the trees, with delightful chirps. The rewards of being one with nature can fill the hunter with awe. It is not uncommon for a hunter to spot a buck, aim, and decide not to take its life.

Unknown deer hunter.
Photograph courtesy of Chris Robinson.

Deer hunters, left to right: Walt Strojan, Art Bjorge, Walt Arnold, Jack Arnold and Earl Arnold in 1948.
Photograph courtesy of the Art Bjorge family.

Deer hunting party in 1945. Cabin owners and their friends at Brightman Flat make plans for their annual hunt at Wheats Meadow near the Dardanelles. The group includes Frank Hendricks with his dog Paint, Albert Roen, Stanley Gatesman, Jack Erickson, Roger Erickson, Lee Prouty, Robert Carpenter, and Bill Cashman, the camp cook. They all used their own horses. Some would travel ahead and set up the camp.
Photograph courtesy of Robert Carpenter.

Hunters leaving Brightman Flat and headed for Bummers Flat, where they will set up camp and hunt. 1942.
Photograph courtesy of Robert Carpenter.

Hunters Frank Burgson and friend John Balestra, wearing the hat.
Photo taken on the back porch of Frank's Bone Springs cabin in 1938.
Photograph courtesy of Chris Robinson.

Hunter Zeke Goodwin in 1922 with his buck.
Courtesy of Tuolumne County Historical Society and Museum (Fred Leighton collection).

Frank Burgson with buck he packed in on horseback in 1945.
Photograph courtesy of Chris Robinson.

Photograph courtesy of Jim Prunetti.

Mabel Bjorge, with her trophy buck at Dardanelle Resort 1940.
Photograph courtesy of the Art Bjorge family.

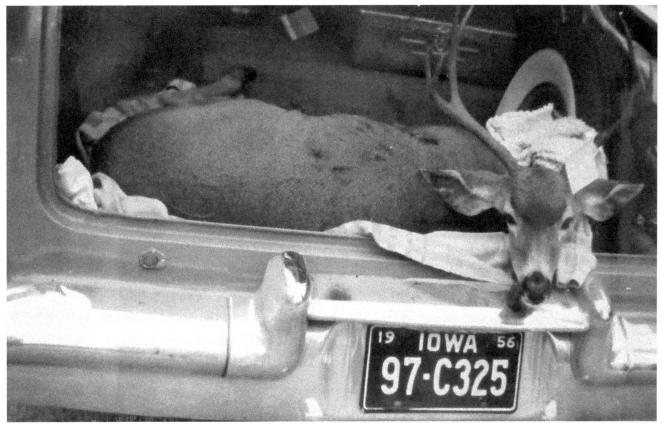

Hunters' success.
Wade Coffill photograph album, courtesy of Mildred Montgomery.

Five large bucks.
Wade Coffill photograph album, courtesy of Mildred Montgomery.

Deer hunters pride on the fenders of a 1941 Chevy.
Wade Coffill photograph album, courtesy of Mildred Montgomery.

Jim Bruin with his buck in 1926. Jim worked for Frank Kurzi as a wrangler at Kennedy Meadows, and also at the Pickering Lumber Company. Jim and his wife Celia lived at Tuttletown where Celia had a milk cow and processed the milk to make cream and butter. She was known for her delicious fresh strawberry short cake.

Photograph courtesy of Matt Bloom.

State lion hunter Charles Ledshaw, at left, with friend Ross Harry. A crowd gathered to view lions and a bear displayed in Sonora in 1930.
Photograph courtesy of Jerry and Ruth Howard.

Bear shot by John Snyder in the high country near at the base of the Dardanelles in 1942. It was estimated to weigh 500 lbs.
Photograph courtesy of the John Snyder family.

CHAPTER 45

Building Relief Dam
in the Wilderness

The incredible achievement of building Relief Dam high on the Middle Fork of the Stanislaus River for primary water storage is amazing by today's standards. Photograph taken in 1909.
Photograph courtesy of the Calaveras County Historical Society. (Lester Walker collection).

The West Coast city of San Francisco was a hub of activity, and proud of its modern electric streetcars. In the early 1900s, it became apparent that more streetcars were needed to serve its growing population. To add to the network, the city needed more electrical power. In the Mother Lode, Beach Thompson, president of the Jupiter Gravel Mining and Water Company, needed water and electricity for his gold mine in Angels Camp. The year was 1894, and he knew there was a fortune to be made in gold mining, if he had water to run a hydroelectric plant. Thompson, young and well educated, with a Master's degree in geology from Stanford University, was very knowledgeable in the design of electrical power plants, so he started investigating how to get water to his mine.

After studying the geology of the Sierra Nevada, Thompson decided that a large reservoir in the mountains above Angels Camp could be the answer to bringing power and water to the lower elevations.

He traveled the Sonora-Mono Road into the Sierras on horseback and rode the trail to Kennedy Lake, observing the granite rock formations and the watershed. Several miles farther, he located a natural

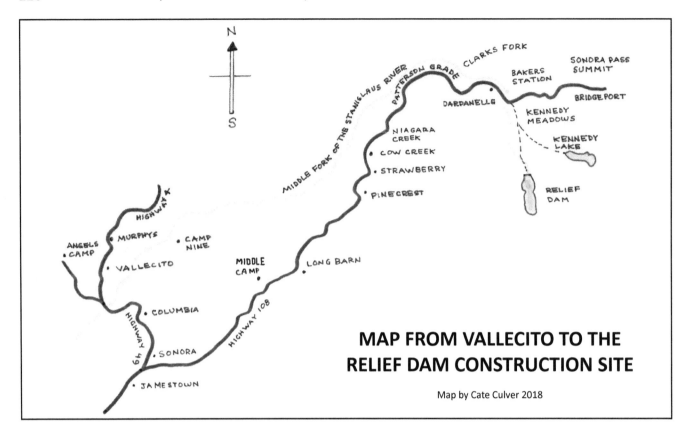

MAP FROM VALLECITO TO THE RELIEF DAM CONSTRUCTION SITE

Map by Cate Culver 2018

granite basin perfect for a reservoir. The location was rugged and remote, at an elevation of 7,229 feet above sea level. During the following years, with financial backing he started buying up water rights in the area.

The *Union Democrat* on September 23, 1905 announced, "A company headed by Beach Thompson, a promotor who is now in New York, talking over the water question in the west with eastern capitalists, seems to be striving to get in on the ground floor while admission prices are cheap. These gentlemen have filed for five water locations with the County Recorder during the fiscal week of November 2–9, 1905."

These water rights were bought for $10 each. Once Beach Thompson had acquired sufficient water rights, he formed the Stanislaus Electric Power Company. His holdings included Kennedy Lake and the surrounding Stanislaus River watershed. He planned to build a large dam, construct pipelines, and install an immense electric power plant on the Stanislaus River.

Employing capital raised from Boston-based capitalists, Thompson formed the Union Construction Company. By 1905, enough capital

had been raised to begin construction on the complex of dams and flumes and the powerhouse.

A large construction camp with the project headquarters at Vallecito in Calaveras County was established in 1906. It was named Camp Nine, and consisted of nearly twenty buildings. There was a warehouse for food, and another for electrical supplies, a carpenter shop, machine shop, the cook house with an ice plant, dining room, office, post office, two bunk houses, a clubhouse with a pool room and card table, and a reading room with magazines.

Mike O'Shaughnessy, a popular and powerful Irishman from San Francisco, was hired as the consulting engineer for the immense project. With O'Shaughnessy's name on the project, the plans moved quickly forward.

While the Sonora-Mono Wagon Road had a turnoff into Kennedy Meadows, there was no road from Kennedy Meadows to the Relief Dam site. There was just a trail five miles to the canyon where the dam was to be built. Originally called Mammoth Dam, later it was renamed Relief Dam because a relief party had arrived there to rescue the Clark-Skidmore emigrant train in 1852.

Primitive wagon road into the Relief Dam site. *Photograph courtesy of Calaveras County Historical Society. (Lester Walker collection).*

Mike O'Shaughnessy, center, the consulting engineer for the Union Construction Company that built the Relief Dam. Photo taken in 1909 at the Relief Reservoir camp.
Photograph courtesy of the Calaveras County Historical Society.

By 1905, the site for building the dam was being equipped for the influx of men coming to work on the project. A sawmill was set up and buildings were constructed. By 1906 the work camp at Relief consisted of four supervisors' houses, a warehouse, barn, blacksmith shop, cement house, doctor's office and quarters, commissary, dining hall, bunk houses, powder magazine building, office buildings, camp tents, potato shed, stable, and a barn for storing 200 tons of hay. The camp operated from April to October, when it started to snow and it became impossible to continue working.

It was a huge task to provide food for all the laborers at the camps and dam construction site. The task was compounded by the fact that the

location was so remote. Addison Mills Mitchell, a cattleman and businessman at Vallecito, started providing food supplies and beef to the workers at Camp Nine. After the contract with Camp Nine, the Mitchells expanded their business and became the contractor for supplying the Relief Dam project.

During this time, Mitchell obtained the lease for summer grazing at Kennedy Lake. These cattle, in proximity to the Relief Dam project, were easily slaughtered on site for fresh beef. When he hired Bensie Morales to be the butcher, Bensie brought his family with him and camped near the Kennedy's cabin.

Relief Dam construction camp with the reservoir canyon in the background.
Photograph courtesy of the Mitchell family. (Millie Krause collection).

Middle Camp.
Photograph courtesy of the Tuolumne County Historical Society and Museum.

Building at Camp Nine.
Photograph courtesy of the Mitchell family. (Millie Krause collection).

Bridge built to transport supplies to Relief.
Photograph courtesy of the Mitchell family. (Millie Krause collection).

Freight platform at Niagara Creek transfer station in 1906, used to transfer materials from the traction engines to the freight wagons.
Photograph courtesy of the Mitchell family. (Millie Krause collection).

The dining hall at the Relief Camp provided adequate meals prepared by Chinese cooks. The lodging for the workers was modest. However, this did not come with the job, and the workers had to pay out of their pockets for lodging and meals.

Hundreds of men were needed to work on the dam. Much of the work was backbreaking, unskilled labor. Men were packed into wagons and hauled up the mountain to work at the various camps and the dam itself. Many were young immigrants eager to get ahead and make a wage.

The Sonora-Mono Wagon Road was in poor condition. Taken over by the state in 1901, it was made a part of the State Highway system. However, there was no funding to keep the road in good condition. Parts of it were rutted so badly that large slabs of cedar bark were packed in the road to make it passable.

The State Department of Highways gave the Union Construction Company permission to work on the road as far as Baker Station, a distance of 38 miles, to get their workers up the mountain.

The *Union Democrat* on July 14, 1906 reported, "In July of 1906 the Union Construction Company had a force of 135 men at work along the eight miles of the road between Middle Camp and Long Barn. With the completion of this stretch, construction will in turn be pushed along to the summit of the Patterson Grade, where a sub-station will be installed. To this point traction engines will be run, and from there on to Kennedy's Lake the hauling is to be done by horses. The grading is being done, whenever

Mule team pauses while hauling pipe in 1905.
Photograph courtesy of the Tuolumne County Historical Society and Museum.

possible, with the latest and best plows, scrapers, etc. all heavier than any heretofore used in the county. With its complete equipment the present force can make rapid headway, but as the season advances and room is made, doubtless many more horses, men and machines will be added."

During the course of construction, there were many camps located along the Stanislaus River, such as the Storage Dam Camp, the Diversion Dam Camp, the Power House Camp, and the Transmission camps. All of these were connected by telephone. Much of the communication from camp to camp was done entirely by phone.

Mail service on horseback was available from Vallecito to the dam site. The *Union Democrat* reported on October 6, 1906: "Ralph Burden carried the mail between Cow Creek and Kennedy's Lake, distributing at various Union Construction Company camps en route. He rides thirty miles every day, but says that the swell cooking of the rangers at Cow Creek is enough to make the job worth holding."

One of the main supply camps was located on a back road west of Sugar Pine. It was called Middle Camp. Sugar Pine Railroad transported supplies to this location. Middle Camp was used for storing cement, steel reinforcement materials, and other equipment, and supplies for the construction of the dam, plus food for the mess hall. Not all supplies were hauled on the railroad, some came by long-line mule teams from Angels Camp and Middle Camp. It took one full day for a traction engine to haul a wagon filled with supplies from Middle Camp to Strawberry and then on to Niagara Creek, where the supplies were transferred to wagons. The traction engines damaged the road so it was constantly in

Relief Dam construction progress by 1907.
Photograph courtesy of the Mitchell family. (Millie Krause collection).

Mule teams hauling supplies to Relief Dam, stop at Cow Creek Ranger Station before heading over Patterson Grade.
Photograph courtesy of Ray Sardella.

Workers building the flume to carry water, take a break in 1905.
Courtesy of the Stanislaus National Forest.

In 1906, lowering the small narrow-gauge donkey engine, into the track.
Photograph courtesy of Calaveras County Historical Society. (Lester Walker collection).

Securing the engine on the tracks.
Photographs courtesy of Calaveras County Historical Society. (Lester Walker collection).

need of repair. Leaving Niagara Creek, they passed over the treacherous Patterson Grade, to Kennedy Meadows and up to the Relief Dam site. Only experienced men drove these freight wagons with their large mule teams.

While excavating the foundation rock for the dam, a deep depression was found in the bedrock. This was an unexpected situation. To build as they had planned might make the dam footing unstable. After much discussion, the engineers reversed the arc of the dam to the downstream side, to avoid the dam's unstable rock base.

At the completion of Relief Dam, it had a height of one hundred and sixty feet, and a varying width at the base of over two hundred feet. Concrete's ability to hold water was largely untested, and engineers took great care in Relief's design. The mesh of steel wires employed to reinforce the concrete facing of the dam was laid

Men quarrying the granite rock that will build the face of the dam.
Photograph courtesy of Calaveras County Historical Society. (Lester Walker collection).

Drilling the granite rock with a dry air-powered machine drill mounted on a tripod with weighted legs.
Photograph courtesy of Calaveras County Historical Society. (Lester Walker collection).

Huge laminated wooden gin poles move the granite blocks into place.
Photograph courtesy of Calaveras County Historical Society. (Lester Walker collection).

by hand as men worked from scaffolds. It was dangerous, tedious, hard work.

Using granite quarried on site, the elaborate cable-and-derrick system carried the massive boulders to the dam's face, where they were set in place and interlocked by hand. Huge derricks were built of laminated wood, strong enough to lift massive blocks of granite. Workers carefully filled spaces with sand and earth on the downstream side, and a five-foot thickness of mortar on the upstream side. Iron hooks inserted in the mortar provided an anchor for the network of steel reinforcing. The face was finished with concrete.

The plans called for a spillway. To accomplish this, workers blasted through the solid granite to form a spillway.

By October of 1906, the cold weather was becoming more severe every day, and the construction crew struggled in the wet slush of the snow. It became too much to bear, and one by one the laborers quit

Men being transported above the dam with booms moving rocks into place below.
Photograph courtesy of the Mitchell family. (Millie Krause collection).

in frustration with the demands of the job. Countless young men returned to Sonora with their pay. Unfortunately, many gambled it away in poker games, where money changed hands rapidly and the men had no plans for a job during the winter months.

In the summer of 1907, good progress was being made on the dam. The work force had risen to about 600 men. The *Union Democrat,* July 27, 1907 remarked, "Owen Leonard, Tuolumne County's Assessor, said that what he believed to be the largest free reading room in the world was discovered by him in a recent tax-collecting outing in the mountain districts. It is located at Camp 31, on the Union Construction Company's line, where men are congregated by the hundreds. In the evening he noticed that the surrounding country was studded with lights as though a big illumination scheme was in progress, but an investigation proved each to emanate from a hanging lamp suspended from the limb of a tree. Under each tree were grouped men engaged in reading books, magazines and newspapers. There were tons of reading matter in

sight, but as the vast place had no visible walls and only the sky as a ceiling the Assessor felt he might overstep his authority by trying to assess it."

Later in the year, a massive fire broke out at the dam site and the *Union Democrat* ran the story on October 5, 1907: "At an early hour, a Thursday morning fire destroyed property worth thousands of dollars at Camp Relief, where the Union Construction Company is building a massive dam for the Stanislaus Electric Company.

"Telephone messages received from Strawberry at noon today state that practically everything in camp, except the record books and papers, were fed the angry flames. The commissary store house, bunk houses, powder magazine, office buildings, camp tents, 200 tons of hay, tramways, cable, etc. were consumed. The burning of the powder house, which contained a ton of powder, was attended by a terrific explosion which was distinctly heard and felt in Strawberry thirty miles away."

This was a huge setback and disaster for the building of the massive dam. The camp had to close and discharge all the men for the winter. The company lost financial backing and had to reorganize to start work again in 1908.

The company brought in Ray Fulcher to take control as Superintendent of Construction. Ray was tall, lanky, and young. He was extremely capable, and familiar with the equipment and how the massive project would come together. He was

After the fire, in order to keep working in October of 1907, workmen resort to mixing concrete by hand.
Photograph courtesy of the Mitchell family. (Millie Krause collection).

Charles Elsbree holding rifles, and Ray Fulcher, Superintendent of Construction, returning from a successful deer hunt.
Photograph courtesy of the Tuolumne County Historical Society and Museum.

an engineer, diplomatic and good at working with people. Frequently, Ray would be on site and walk up to a man and say, "Take a blow, I'll run this derrick while you have a break," or relieve a man working hard loading cement. The men worshiped him. When Ray walked by, they would tip their hats and bow, much to his embarrassment. After dinner in the mess hall, Ray met with his foremen. He gathered them in a circle and discussed what needed to be accomplished the next day. He listened carefully to each man, asking what he needed and figuring out how he could resolve issues. He worked tirelessly to keep the operation running smoothly.

By July of 1908, a force of 280 men were on the site, rebuilding what was destroyed by the fire and working on the dam. Soon the work force increased to between 500 and 600 men. When operations ceased for the winter, the dam reached a height of 70 feet.

The *Union Democrat* on July 4, 1908 printed, "A dynamo has been sent to Relief. It will be operated for power from the saw mill and the entire place equipped with electric lights. When these are installed, a matter of a short time, work will be carried on at night as well as day."

The work was dangerous and several men died while the dam was being built. One hapless thirty-one-year-old laborer was killed when he jumped to avoid a snapped derrick rope and fell thirty feet to solid rock below. Another, only seventeen, was crushed by a falling boom from a derrick. One young man from Austria chose to not pay for food at the dining hall, and lived off the deer he shot. Eventually, he developed scurvy, became ill, and died under the care of company physician, Dr. Warren.

By October 17, 1908, Fulcher closed the operation for the winter. Prior to Fulcher's

Dumping granite rock fill on the back side of the dam.
Photograph courtesy of Calaveras County Historical Society. (Lester Walker collection).

leadership, work came to a conclusion in October, when disgruntled laborers could no longer endure the cold and wet conditions. Fulcher anticipated this problem and planned an orderly shutdown. Two caretakers remained on site for the winter. Much of the livestock, no longer needed, was brought down to Middle Camp, where it was sold.

By May 1909, the dam was one hundred and thirty feet high. The engineers kept calculating the height, and how much more the volume of water would increase if they added an additional ten feet, then another ten feet.

Work began again the next year. The *Union Democrat* stated on August 24, 1909, "The construction work on the Relief Dam is being carried on by a force of 500 men, which number is daily augmented. Over a hundred men were sent up Wednesday. Along the flume line and other points on the system three hundred additional men

are employed. Everything is moving without a hitch at the big dam under the direction of Ray Fulcher."

In September 1909, the Reverend Hugh J. Furneaux visited the camp and held church services at night around a huge open campfire, as there was no building large enough to accommodate the crowd. Everyone turned out to hear him.

In 1910, the engineers decided to raise the dam another ten feet. More laborers were hired, and brought the project to nearly completion. Eventually, the dam reached one hundred and sixty feet, but the financial resources of the Stanislaus Electrical Power Company were exhausted. At this stage, the Sierra San Francisco Company was organized to take over the facilities and the operation.

The construction lasted from 1906 to 1910 and produced Relief Dam, six bridges, 15 miles of wood flumes, and Sand Bar Diversion Dam, which had

Carts filled with cement from a chute are pushed along a ramp on the face of Relief Dam as men above attach steel reinforcements in 1907.
Photograph courtesy of Calaveras County Historical Society. (Lester Walker collection).

The immense mountain dam slowly fills.
Photograph courtesy of Calaveras County Historical Society. (Lester Walker collection).

Relief Dam spillway.
Photograph courtesy of Calaveras County Historical Society (Lester Walker collection).

an eleven mile long tunnel, a massive timber trestle, a powerhouse, and a transmission line. The system started delivering power to San Francisco in the fall of 1908.

When the dam was fully completed in 1912, the only structure needed was the dam tender's four-room cottage. The tender monitored water levels, water releases, dam safety, and watched over the company's camp, still fully equipped with construction equipment. By 1912, the San Francisco Electrical Power Company had spent over $10,000,000 developing its essential water and power system.

In 1919, Pacific Gas and Electric Company took over operation of the dam as part of its lease agreement for the Stanislaus hydroelectric system. From then on, all work on Relief Dam was conducted by the Pacific Gas and Electric Company.

The building of the dam was an amazing feat of engineering, planning, and the back-breaking work of ordinary laborers. Nestled in the remote Emigrant Basin of solid granite, the dam continues to withstand the test of time. With modern upgrades, the dam continues to operate to this day.

Ironically Beach Thompson, who started the building of the dam to transport water to his gold mine in Angels Camp, found little gold in his Jupiter gold mine.

Camp Relief dam and reservoir as seen August 1, 1909.
Photograph courtesy of Calaveras County Historical Society. (Lester Walker collection).

SOURCES

"Assessor Leonard Makes Discovery." *Union Democrat*, 27 Jul. 1907, P. 3.

"The Big Dam at Relief." *Union Democrat,* 4 Jul. 1908. Front page.

"Big Force at Work on Mountain Road." *Union Democrat,* 14 Jul. 1906. Bishop. Francis.

"Big Force at Work." *Union Democrat*, 24 Aug. 1909, P. 3.

"History of Relief Reservoir" Jul. 2011. (Shoup and Caruso 1989:35) Pacific Gas and Electric Company. Stanislaus National Forest files.

Joy, Charles R. "Calaveras County Goes Electric." *Las Calaveras* Quarterly Bulletin of Calaveras County Historical Society, Apr.-Jul. 1975.

"The Mysterious Disappearance of Windsor A. Keefer." *Las Calaveras* Quarterly Bulletin of Calaveras County Historical Society, Apr.- Jul., 1983.

"Relief is in Ashes." *Union Democrat,* 5 Oct. 1907.

Oral interview with Charles Arthur Dambacher. Interviewed by Joan Gorsuch in 1976. Columbia College Library Oral History series.

Mike Curtin interview, 3 Mar. 1982, with Pamela Conners. Stanislaus National Forest files.

"Water Rights Located." *Union Democrat,* 23 Sep. 1905, P. 2.

Fifteen spectacular miles of wooden flume were constructed down the Middle Fork of the Stanislaus to the Camp Nine forebay. Eight feet high and nine feet wide, an immense amount of lumber was required to build this flume. Maintenance was a major problem, particularly as time went on. Note rail on top, which facilitated a small rail car to travel for inspection and repair. Equally spectacular was the replacement of the flume in 1939 by eleven miles of tunnels blasted out of the bedrock.
Photograph courtesy of Calaveras County Historical Society. (Lester Walker collection).

CHAPTER 46

"Shorty" Harris
Caretaker of Relief Dam

Though he stood at just five feet tall in his bare feet, Shorty Harris enjoyed a giant reputation in the Dardanelle and Relief Reservoir area of the Stanislaus National Forest. He was a man who enjoyed the company of visitors even when he lived in secluded mountain cabins, and he loved a good tipple, which was occasionally to his detriment. Born Frank Harris in Michigan on August 21, 1856, no records survive to reveal what he did as a young man.

Around 1910, Shorty, at age sixty-six, was hired by Pacific Gas and Electric Company as a dam tender at the newly built Relief Dam, high in the Sierra Nevada Mountains, above Kennedy Meadows. He communicated by telephone with Pacific Gas and Electric. At their request, he released water from the dam. Shorty would measure the volume of water released by a weir situated downstream from the face of the dam. He also provided routine maintenance.

At Relief Dam, Shorty lived in the dam tender's cabin. This remote location at 7,000 feet in elevation meant he spent much of his time isolated from the company of others. Eventually Pacific Gas and Electric built a two-story cabin for him. This structure had living quarters on the upper level accessed by an exterior staircase, allowing him entrance even in the deepest snow. The ground level, used mostly for storage, was reached by an interior set of stairs. Pacific Gas and Electric provided him with a large, commercial-size wood cook stove.

His cabin was supplied with water from a nearby spring, which also provided drinks for thirsty hikers and horseback travelers. He was always pleased to have visitors and catch up on the latest news. Many remember his hospitality and delicious homemade doughnuts.

Shorty liked his bourbon whiskey, and it didn't take much to get him tipsy. He admitted to falling off one of the lower abutments of the dam and banging himself up pretty badly. He also fell down the interior cabin stairs after a few drinks and broke several ribs. That accident was in the dead of winter, so he was able to rest while his ribs healed.

He used a very short and narrow pair of wooden skis for winter travel. During the winter months, he ran a trap line for catching fox and snowshoe hares. The line made its way down to Dardanelle from the higher elevations at Long Valley and Eagle Meadow. For extra money, he would shovel snow off the roofs of Dardanelle cabins.

On March 13, 1920 The *Union Democrat*, reported, " 'Shorty' F.O. Harris breezed into town Thursday afternoon from his snowy home up at Relief, where he guards the big dam of the power company through the icy winter months. This is 'Shorty's' first visit to Sonora since early last fall, and he says going over the snow was not very good. He had with him $200 worth of pelts, for he amuses himself in the hills in trapping. He had a number of otters worth from $15 to $20 each, some martins [sic], that will bring an average price $15, and a number of coyotes. The latter he registered with the County Clerk, in order to get the county bounty. Shorty with his pelts under his arm left this Friday for San Francisco to dispose of them and

Shorty Harris, at left, in front of his cabin at Relief Dam. Blacksmith Will Barron at right.
Photograph courtesy of the Calaveras County Historical Society. (Lester Walker collection).

make a personal application to the Fish and Game Commission for a renewal of his trapper's license for next season."

During the 1920s and 1930s Shorty made occasional summer trips to lower elevations in order to obtain supplies. This was a period when a number of mountain cabins and resorts were built. He usually visited with many people along his route, and was recognized throughout the area. Making his way down the mountain, he stopped over at a Pacific Gas and Electric company house at Niagara Creek to spend the night.

Jim Appel of Dardanelle remembers, "I was born in 1929 and remember his summer camp at the southeast side of the Eagle Creek Bridge until

at least 1936. Shorty Harris did have a tent. As I remember, he also had pieces of canvas strung up to form a room-like area. I assume he had means to cook, a stove. I don't know. I don't know how many years he camped. In 1937, the new road bypassed his camp site at the old Eagle Creek Bridge. I was too young to know if many people visited him, I do know he was well known."

John Sardella, remembers, "I was packing in with a string of mules and crew of men to store emergency supplies at our Pacific Gas and Electric snow cabin. We stopped at Dardanelle, where my brother Reno Sardella had a small temporary pack station. The crew needed breakfast and Shorty Harris was the station cook. We all sat around

Young dam tenders soon after the dam was built. It is here that Shorty Harris would have operated these valves to release water from the reservoir.
Photograph courtesy of the Calaveras County Historical Society. (Lester Walker collection).

Relief Reservoir filling after dam completion in 1910.
Photograph courtesy of the Calaveras County Historical Society. (Lester Walker collection).

a table and watched Shorty cook us up a fine breakfast. We expected Shorty to sit and join us. However, he continued cooking eggs at the wood stove. They were scrambled, and he would flip them over and fry them and then flip them again and again. We watched perplexed as to who would want to eat these leather tough eggs. Then he suddenly flipped them off in the dirt. A dog rushed in and wolfed them down. Shorty said, 'the dog has to eat too.' We were pleased to see Shorty provide breakfast for the dog as well."

Shorty retired from Pacific Gas and Electric Company sometime in the late 1930s. Unable to continue life in the mountains, he settled into a small cabin located on Hope Lane in Sonora, where he lived out his life. He died November 6, 1945, at eight-nine. Shorty left behind no family members. He is buried at Mountain Shadows Cemetery in Sonora.

Jim Appel with "Shorty" Harris and dog Peggy, at their cabin at Buena Vista Summer Home Tract in 1932.
Photograph courtesy of Jim Appel.

This is the cabin where Shorty Harris, the dam tender, lived. The Relief Reservoir dam tender's cabin was located in a remote meadow at 7000 feet in the Sierra Nevada. The Forest Service tore it down in July 2011.
Mesa Technical Architecnical and Archaeological photography. Courtesy of Judith Marvin.

Shorty Harris's marker at Mountain Shadows Cemetery in Sonora, California.
Photograph courtesy of findagrave.com.

SOURCES

Appel, Jim. Personal interview, 2014.

Findagrave.com. Memorial #115220271.

"Francis S. Harris, 89 Succumbs To Illness." *Union Democrat,* 8 Nov. 1945. P. 4.

Sardella, Johnny. Personal interview, 2014.

Terzich, Irving. Personal interview, 2013.

Terzich, Irving. "Shorty Harris." *CHISPA,* Tuolumne County Historical Society Quarterly publication, Vol. 50, No. 1.

CHAPTER 47

Fred Leighton
Yellowhammer and the Check Dams

Fred Leighton was a man of engaging intelligence who cut a wide mark across Tuolumne County's mid-century history. His love of the mountains led him to create his own private domain tucked away among the lakes of Emigrant Basin. Leighton's observation of nature led him to spearhead building "check dams" to help propagate trout.

Fred Leighton was born in Arcata, California, on January 23, 1885, to John and Lizzie Shaw Leighton. Following Fred's birth the family moved to Tuolumne County, where they lived near Columbia. His father logged timber for the nearby mines.

Fred's first trip to the high country came as a result of his uncle Alvah Shaw's association with fellow cattleman John Rosasco. Shaw had recommended that Rosasco use the remote Emigrant Primitive Area for his summer cattle range, and, by 1896, Rosasco had built a cabin there. Introduced to Rosasco by his uncle, twelve-year-old Fred soon found himself on a cattle drive to the high country. The drive began at Rosaco's ranch near the Phoenix Power House, and concluded in Rosasco's grazing lands in the southern Emigrant Basin. Fred had offered to help because Rosasco promised he would have time for fishing. However, there was too much work involved, and a disappointed boy returned home, having never wet his line. Fred Leighton continued to help with other cattle drives. He loved the backcountry, and fishing and hunting with his uncle.

In 1903, Fred, at 18, decided he wanted a career in business and moved to San Francisco to attend Heald Business College. He boarded with

A young Fred Leighton.
Photograph courtesy of the Tuolumne County Historical Society and Museum. (Fred Leighton collection).

friends. Fate had a hand in ending Fred's business education. On April 18, 1906, a massive earthquake struck San Francisco. All Fred could think about was getting home. Unhurt, he made his way through the rubble to the ferry building and boarded a vessel to Stockton. From Stockton, he made his way to Tuolumne County.

Seeking employment, Fred found work at the Union Construction Company as a paymaster. This company was actively involved in the Relief Dam project. As company paymaster, he was required to visit the work site for two days at the end of each month. Traveling primitive dirt roads to this location, he assisted the resident company payroll clerk. He had returned to the high country where as a boy he had driven cattle.

In the summer of 1909, with his paymaster job about to end, romance entered Fred's life. He met and courted Edna Hales, the daughter of T.F. Hales, of Hales and Symons Company in Sonora, then primarily a hauling business. He married Edna, the boss's daughter, early in the morning of December 28, 1909, at her parents' home. The bride and groom boarded the evening train for San Francisco where they planned to live.

In 1913, they moved back to Sonora into a cottage next door to the Hales house. The Leightons became a popular couple in Sonora's social circles.

Fred accepted employment offered by his father-in-law at Hales and Symons. He started driving freight wagons and was later promoted to bookkeeper. Fred sat in a small office next to Irving Symons, who observed Fred's gift of gab and thought him lazy. Symons became so irritated with Fred's talkative nature that he sent young Fred out to collect unpaid bills, so he could have some peace. Despite irritating Symons, Leighton had a forty-eight-year career at the thriving business, becoming secretary-treasurer in 1962.

Cattleman John Rosasco's cabin built in 1896. It was destroyed by fire in October of 1921. Photograph from 1918.
Photograph courtesy of the Tuolumne County Historical Society and Museum. (Fred Leighton collection).

During the summer of 1917, at thirty-two, he returned to the Emigrant Basin with his wife for a two week camping trip. He was overjoyed to be in the mountains again, and eager to return at any opportunity. Fortunately for Fred, Edna liked the mountains as well.

Eventually, Fred returned to the Rosasco cabin with friends Bill Burnham, the owner of Burnham's Candy Store in Sonora; Karl Defiebre, who owned Karl's Place in Pinecrest and Tuolumne City; real estate agent Charlie Rudoruff; and Hi Pruett, who worked for West Side Lumber as a train conductor. They were all outdoorsmen who wanted a place to hunt and fish. Leighton was the youngest of the group.

Fred Leighton. Yellowhammer. September 1922. "We were building a new cabin to replace the old one which burned last fall. Hi Pruett and I spent 80 days peeling poles and building same, we needed shakes for the roof so Irving Symons and I with eight head of horses made a trip to Strawberry and packed in 24 bundles of shakes made by Ed Jenness. This picture was taken on our arrival in Yellowhammer. Irving Symons is standing near the horse, far right."
Photograph courtesy of Tuolumne County Historical Society and Museum (Fred Leighton collection).

Fred Leighton's remote Yellowhammer fishing and deer hunting camp.
Photograph courtesy of Tuolumne County Historical Society and Museum (Fred Leighton collection).

Yellowhammer Camp built by Fred Leighton, Hi Pruett, and Bill Burnham in 1922. The rock pile on the right is part of the fireplace from the old John Rosasco cabin. Zeke Goodwin and Ed McMahon put the shakes on the roof.
Photograph courtesy of Tuolumne County Historical Society and Museum (Fred Leighton collection).

In 1977 Fred was interviewed by historian Sharon Marovich, who writes in the Tuolumne County Historical Society's publication, *CHISPA*, "In 1919 he and a friend, Bill Burnham, obtained a U.S. Forest Service permit from Vic Wulff, Supervisor of the Stanislaus National Forest, to allow construction of a cabin at Yellowhammer, and a special grazing permit to pasture their saddle and pack horses in a nearby meadow."

Yellowhammer, named for a New Zealand bird, became Fred Leighton's high country kingdom, encompassing breathtaking scenery, alpine lakes, and lush meadows. They built a barn, corral, shower house, work table, cookhouse, two cabins, and an outhouse. This was a primitive camp with no road for vehicles. Visitors made the trip in on horseback across granite expanses.

Fred was very social and invited many guests throughout the years. The *Union Democrat* on August 23, 1940 reported, "Miss Mary Long, Mrs. Fred Leighton, Mrs. Millie Mitchell and daughter Kathleen of Vallecita [sic], Arthur Hender, Karl Defiebre, and the guide, Louis Faguerro, make up a party spending two weeks at Fred Leighton's camp at Yellowhammer."

Fred tried to keep the camp a secret. However, local cattlemen who had cow camps in the area knew him and would socialize with the Leightons, stopping by for news of the day and a bite to eat.

The only drawback to Yellowhammer was that the nearby lake fishing was generally poor. Other cattlemen and local sportsmen had attempted to plant fish in the backcountry lakes, hauling fingerlings in coal-oil cans or milk cans, and planting

Karl Defiebre and Dick Kronke in camp, 1937.
Courtesy of Tuolumne County Historical Society and Museum (Fred Leighton collection).

Fred, left, inspects the ten foot high Horse Meadow check dam. 1951.
Courtesy of Tuolumne County Historical Society and Museum. (Fred Leighton collection).

them. By summer, the streams feeding the small lakes went dry. Sometime after 1910, Guy Scott, a game warden, packed fish into a few other lakes, but there was no chance for propagation.

In 1920, Leighton and his friend Bill Burnham decided to dam up the outlet of the lakes to collect the water, so the rainbow and Eastern brook trout would survive.

Bill Burnham had a keen interest in sports, matched by his love of the outdoors, and hunting and fishing. He was one of the organizers of the Tuolumne Rod and Gun Club, a forerunner of the

In 1951, Edna Leighton and Mary Long give the beans a taste.
Courtesy of Tuolumne County Historical Society and Museum. (Fred Leighton collection).

Tuolumne Fish and Game Association. Bill was active in establishing Tuolumne County's first fish hatchery.

Fred and Bill were the perfect pair to find a solution to the previous failures to plant fish in Emigrant Basin. They worked on a lake near the Yellowhammer camp. The two men gathered rocks and packed dirt around the rocks to hold them in place, and built a small dam to raise the lake level a few feet. They were pleased with the result and named it Yellowhammer Lake. They constructed a second dam the following year at Red Can Lake, upstream from Yellowhammer. In 1925, they built a third dam at Fifty Acres Lake, which was re-named Leighton Lake. Fred called these "check dams" because they check the water flow. He also dammed the water outlet from the meadows so they retained more water during the summer, to improve grazing.

In 1939, his dam-building partner Bill Burnham died of a heart ailment at age sixty-one. He did not live to see their work completed.

Encouraged by his success in constructing the check dams, Fred actively promoted more construction. He created relationships with the Forest Service, the Department of Fish and Game, Tuolumne County Chamber of Commerce, the State Chamber of Commerce, Tuolumne County Fish and Game, and Tuolumne County Board of Supervisors. The $1,000 was raised for additional check dam construction. Two crews of seven men utilized this money in the summer of 1931 to build additional dams. The check dams increased fish spawning grounds, and soon the planting of fish produced

Bear Creek check dam built to be ten feet high.
Courtesy of Tuolumne County Historical Society and Museum. (Fred Leighton collection).

Fred Leighton at left; next is Bill Knell, and unknown man at Yellowhammer. Andy Weaver in front.
Courtesy of Tuolumne County Historical Society and Museum. (Fred Leighton collection).

Fred Leighton packing in supplies to his Yellowhammer Camp. He kept his camp private and did not want uninvited guests to appear. To accomplish this, he would sweep away any evidence of his horses passing over rocks.
Photograph courtesy of Tuolumne County Historical Society and Museum. (Fred Leighton collection).

satisfactory results. The mountain streams no longer ran dry. Fred and his friends continued building dams.

During the Great Depression, the Forest Service ultimately enlisted the help of the Civilian Conservation Corps to build dams in Emigrant Basin. They built an additional eight check dams. The final two dams were built in 1951 by the U.S. Forest Service and the Department of Fish and Game. A total of eighteen check dams were built throughout Emigrant Basin.

In 1975, when Fred's Yellowhammer domain became the Emigrant Basin Wilderness Area, the Forest Service allowed Leighton a lifetime use permit for his remote camp. Yellowhammer was Fred's mountain retreat throughout his life. Fred Leighton died in 1979 at age ninety-four.

In a *Union Democrat* article published on April 4, 1941, Game Warden Francis F. Johnson stated, "Now there is a surplus of fish in the mountain streams which in former years ran dry." Fred had succeeded in populating the high mountain lakes

with trout. In a broader sense, he had passed on a history of the area and fostered a renewed awareness of the environment not seen before. A historian at heart, Fred documented his life with a collection of newspaper clippings, correspondence, and priceless photographs, all methodically labeled and organized. He generously passed this treasure on to the next generation.

SOURCES

Bowman, Steve D. *Leighton's High Sierra Check Dam Legacy*: *A Photographic Journal*. Xlibris, 2006.

"Early Morning Wedding." *Union Democrat*, 1 Jan. 1910.

Marovich, Sharon. "Fred William Leighton." *CHISPA*, Tuolumne County Historical Society publication, Vol. 16, No. 3, Jan-Mar. 1977.

Ruoff, Leonard. Personal interview, 15 Dec. 2014.

Tuolumne County Historical Society publication *CHISPA*, Vol. 49 No. 3 Jan.-Mar. 2010.

"W.E. Burnham Succumbs to Heart Ailment."Bill Burnham Obituary in *Union Democrat*, 8 Dec. 1939. Front Page.

CHAPTER 48

The Tungsten Mines

Tungsten is a heavy metal that has a grayish-white color and looks much like quartz. It is brittle and hard. The ore is used as a filament for incandescent light bulbs. During WWII, it was in demand for hardening steel in battleships and other military equipment. For a short time, tungsten mining became an important economic windfall in Tuolumne County.

The first tungsten ore discovery in Tuolumne County occurred in 1941, high in the Sierra northwest of Dorothy Lake, within Yosemite National Park. It was a small claim six feet wide and sixty feet long. The deposits were examined by the United States Department of the Interior in 1942. The ore was determined to be of a sufficiently high grade, worthy of the expense to pack it out and get it processed. The claim was named "The Dorothy Lake" claim.

In the summer of 1943, supplies were hauled in, and the deposit was developed by the Metal Reserve Company under an agreement with the National Park Service. Transporting the ore out of Yosemite was no easy task because there were no roads. The ore had to be moved by pack mules. The closest pack station, ten miles to the north, was Kennedy Meadows, operated by Frank Kurzi. The government paid Kurzi and his best wrangler, Artie Scruggs, to haul the ore out. The ore was packed in canvas bags, loaded onto mule trains, carried down the steep granite mountains to Kennedy Meadows, and trucked out.

Thirteen years later, in September of 1956, another tungsten mine at Snow Lake was developed by L.W. Osborn, Emmett L. Dahl, a safety officer

Loading the mule train with bags of tungsten ore from the Dorothy Lake prospect.
Photographer unknown.

A compressor shack at the Dorothy Lake prospect.
Photographer unknown.

for West Side Lumber, and his brother Tom. The Dahls were from Tuolumne City. The brothers built a long, plain cabin overlooking Snow Lake. Tom's wife Frances came to the cabin in the summer to enjoy the mountain scenery.

L.W. Osborn was from Yerington, Nevada. His son-in-law, Willard Hanson, bulldozed a road from Leavitt Lake into the area to make the transport of ore easier. Trucks with a short wheelbase and four-wheel drive carried the ore down the road to an ore chute off highway 108 at the Leavitt Lake turnoff. From there, larger trucks hauled the ore to be processed and sold.

Emmett Dahl.
Courtesy of the Dahl family.

In the fall of 1954, Donald J. Whittle and his nephew Loren Whittle decided to go into the backcountry on a fishing trip. The Whittles, cattlemen from Angels Camp, packed out of Crabtree cow camp, where they had a summer cattle range. High above much of the tree line near Snow Lake, they noticed some white quartz-like rocks that were exceptionally heavy. Curious about what they might be, they loaded a few into their saddlebags.

The Dahl camp at the edge of Snow Lake.
Photograph courtesy of the McBride family.

That winter, Ray Whittle, Donald's eldest son, thought the rocks might have some value and decided to have them assayed. He met with Walter Finley, who lived in Arnold and worked at White

Mule pack train hauling out the ore in canvas bags.
Photographer unknown.

Pines sawmill. Walt was a knowledgeable assayer who performed a chemical test on the samples and determined them to be high-quality tungsten.

The news spread quickly throughout the Whittle family, and visions of mining and wealth dominated every conversation. The Whittle family formed a partnership. Seven of the Whittle men joined it, including cousin Daniel O'Toole, and assayer Walter Finley. The partners named it the High Sierra Scheelite Mining Company.

After further thought, the partners realized they would need an attorney to handle all the legal paperwork. For this job, the partners chose a longtime friend of the cattlemen, Virgil Airola, known in Calaveras County as "The Rancher's Attorney." Although Virgil never did any of the mining, he and his family were included as part of the outfit, and enjoyed trips to the mine.

Finley led the charge of excitement to see the site where the tungsten rocks were found. They started making plans. As soon as they could pack in through the deep winter snow, an expedition was formed. With much anticipation they returned to the discovery site on horseback, and showed Finley the promising area.

With the advice of assayer Finley, they planned twenty-two claims. The family patriarch, Joe Whittle, who was never actually there, affectionately called it the "High Lonesome Mine."

The claims were surveyed. Donald R. Whittle and Loren F. Whittle went to the Land Office in Sacramento and staked the claims. They patented the Jan Cavanaugh lode mine, which was anticipated to be the most promising. The claims encompassed twenty acres.

They started open cut mining in 1956, working on just the surface of the ground, using dynamite as needed. The partners bought a small rock mill and shaker table, powered by a generator. As the ore was crushed, the heavy tungsten separated from the quartz and limestone on the shaker table. The Whittles were able to process three-quarters of a ton of ore per hour.

The ore was hauled out in canvas bags by packers Ben and Odie Albertson, on mules three to four miles to connect with the road built by the nearby Montezuma Mine. It was loaded onto small trucks and hauled to be processed in Bishop.

Between 1955 and 1956, the miners realized it was feasible to build a road up the canyon through Horse Meadow to their mine. They needed a bulldozer, so they turned to Harry Whittle, the only relative with enough money to buy heavy equipment. Ray Whittle, a heavy equipment operator, engineered and built the primitive road, blasting his way through granite boulders. The road was narrow, with steep grades and many switchbacks. It crossed the summit at 9,700 feet elevation. The road could only be negotiated by vehicles with a short wheelbase and four-wheel drive.

The Whittles built a cabin on the Tamarack Claim, where trees blocked the snow sliding down the mountainside. The site was the warmest on the mountain and pleasant, except for the mosquitoes. A carpenter from Melones drew up plans for how the cabin was to be built. He cut all the lumber by hand, and instructed the Whittle men in assembling the cabin. That year Harry, Don, Donnie, and

Harry Whittle.
Photograph courtesy of Betty Whittle Garner.

Loren gathered at the mine with tools, and assembled the cabin.

The cabin was sixteen by thirty-two feet, with an upstairs sleeping loft, filled with single beds. A large cook stove was hauled in from the old ranch in Angels Camp, a sentimental touch from the days when the Whittles homesteaded in Calaveras County. The cabin was never locked. A small supply of food was left, should an outdoorsman ever need to take cover in an emergency. After it fell into disuse, the Forest Service tore it down in the 1980s.

In September of 1956, when the Whittle cowboys came to round up cattle, four of them continued on up the mountain to the mine. They packed in supplies, and Ray, Harry, Walt Finley, and Daniel O'Toole stayed for a month to work the mine. At the end of the month they brought out the ore and sold it for $8,000. The Whittle mine was the richest in the Emigrant Basin.

In September of 1967, they leased the mine to John Loring, a young mining engineer from San Francisco. Loring planned to expand the mine by

Remains of the Whittle tungsten mine.
Courtesy of the Stanislaus National Forest.

Horse Meadow.
Photograph courtesy of Chris Robinson.

tunneling under the open cut. Loring, a pilot, saw the advantage of building an airstrip to bring in supplies. A landing field was built in Horse Meadow, so planes could bring in people and supplies, saving visitors the long jolting truck ride up the mountain.

Once his plans were in motion, Loring was frequently on site, overseeing the mining operation. He was at the mine working with employee Al St. Onge when a plane with mechanical difficulties made an emergency landing at the airstrip. The owner of Columbia Airport, a great distance away, came in to repair the airplane.

Loring decided to hitch a ride and fly to the Columbia Airport. After taking off and flying up the canyon, the plane lost elevation. The pilot tried to turn the plane around but the airplane clipped a tree, killing John Loring instantly. The pilot crawled out of the wreckage unhurt.

Employee Al St. Onge radioed for help. The U.S. Marine Corps responded from their Winter Warfare Training Station at nearby Pickle Meadow. Later, they removed the crashed plane.

Disheartened, Loring employees tried to continue with the mine. However, without Loring's knowledge and leadership, and after spending approximately $75,000, the endeavor failed. That winter the government dropped the subsidized unit support price to $20 per twenty pound of tungsten concentrate. The mine closed. The Whittle family continues its ownership of the tungsten claims, and maintains their patent on the Jan Cavanaugh claim.

Forty-four tungsten claims were filed in Tuolumne County, of which forty-two remained valid in 1968. They were all located at the high elevations of the Emigrant Basin area. Despite their importance, the legacy of the tungsten mines has faded until hardly any trace of their history remains.

SOURCES

Airola, Ken. Personal interview, 20 Apr. 2017.

de Hart, Lisa, Stanislaus National Forest archaeologist. Personal interview, 24 Sep. 2018.

Cassinetto, Ben. Personal interview, 30 May 2016.

"Mineral Resources of the Emigrant Basin Primitive Area," *California Geological Survey Bulletin* 1261-G, pp. G53-G58.

United States Department of the Interior Geological Survey. Tungsten Deposits near Dorothy Lake, Yosemite National Park, Tuolumne County, CA. Series 44-88.

Whittle, Donnie. Personal interviews, 15 Sep. 2016 and 5 Feb. 2017.

CHAPTER 49

The Movies
Filmed on Sonora Pass

Hi Pruett of Tuolumne City offered the use of his tractor during the filming of *The Fighting Caravans*.
Photograph courtesy of the Tuolumne County Historical Society and Museum. (Leonard Ruoff collection).

When Hollywood filmmakers began venturing away from Southern California in search of new locations, they discovered the countryside surrounding Sonora. The scenery was diverse, and by the 1920s, a steady stream of motion picture companies were filming in Tuolumne County. One of the main attractions was the Sierra Railroad, which had steam locomotives and an assortment of passenger cars. It conveniently operated in nearby Jamestown.

All through the 1920s, motion pictures were filmed in the county. Sonora businessmen came to realize the boost the motion picture companies provided to the local economy and banded together to bring in more business. They formed the Sonora Motion Picture Cooperative Association. In 1937, the name was changed and the organization was incorporated as the Sonora Motion Picture Association. Its goal was to assist film companies in scouting suitable locations, hiring "extras," and arranging for lodging, meals, and other services.

One of the first movies to be filmed up at Sonora Pass was *The Virginian,* starring a very young Gary Cooper with Mary Brian and Richard Arlen, directed by Victor Fleming. Produced by Paramount Pictures, it was shot in May, and released in November of 1929. After making a few silent films, this was Gary Cooper's first talkie movie. Once the film was released, the movie association put on a big party for the crew and cast. A local cattleman donated beef for the barbecue, and even California's Governor James Rolph, known as "Sunny Jim," attended.

In 1930, Paramount Studios returned to the Pass to film *The Fighting Caravans,* a sappy Western based on a Zane Grey book, again with Gary Cooper. The plot revolved around a young frontier scout who guides a freight wagon train across the nation accompanied by his mountain men pals. Of course, there was a love interest, too.

Filming on Sonora Pass late into the fall, the 300 members of the film crew became alarmed as snow began to fall. They made their way down to the newly built Dardanelle Resort where they quickly erected their canvas tents for refuge from the snow. The crew tried to make the best of the situation and attempted to stay warm around campfires. All they could talk about was how long they would be stuck and how to get themselves out. Then an amazing event happened. Down the road came a herd of cattle. The cattle had also been caught in the storm while up in the high country at their owner's summer grazing allotment. The cattleman had gathered his herd and brought them down out of the storm, headed to his winter range at a lower elevation. The cattle herd cleared a pathway down the highway.

In 1935, *Robin Hood of the El Dorado,* the fictionalized story of Joaquin Murrieta, the folk hero bandit, was filmed at Douglas Flat in Eureka Valley. The plot, set in 1848 California during the Gold Rush, revolves around Murrieta's revenge on gringos who had killed his wife. The cast was led by Warner Baxter, much too old for the part, and Ann Loring as his love interest. J. Carrol Naish played Three Fingered Jack, with Bruce Cabot as the lawman.

William Wellman directed the movie for Metro-Goldwyn-Mayer. Muddled with eight writers and overly lavish costumes, the film was filled with the sentimentality of the era. No expense was spared to build the movie sets of the Mexican village, and multiple horse corrals. Filmed at Douglas Flat during July and August, the movie crew moved in and Douglas Resort came alive as headquarters for the movie. The Nelsons, owners of the resort, were happy to lodge the cast and crew. All their rental

Actor Gary Cooper shovels out the front of his tent while stranded at Dardanelle Resort during snowstorm. He was the lead actor in *The Fighting Caravans,* filmed in 1930.
Photograph courtesy of the Tuolumne County Historical Society and Museum. (Leonard Ruoff collection).

Wagon and teams from *The Fighting Caravans* stopped at Douglas Resort in 1930.
Photograph courtesy of Ray Sardella.

A visitor poses with actor Francis McDonald, in costume at the set of Joaquin Murrieta's hidden Mexican village at Douglas Flat.
Photograph courtesy of Jo Spicer Danicourt.

Actor Baxter Warner at left, in discussion with co-star Bruce Cabot.
Photograph courtesy of Jo Spicer Danicourt.

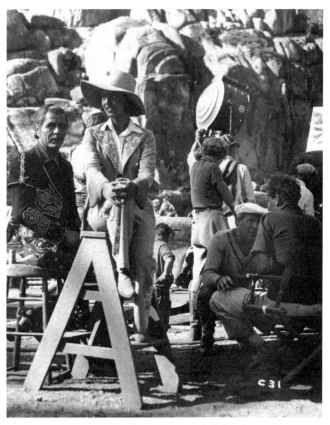

On location near Douglas Flat, *Robin Hood of the El Dorado* actors Warner Baxter and Ann Loring take a break.
Photograph courtesy of the Tuolumne County Historical Society and Museum. (Leonard Ruoff collection).

Filming at Douglas Flat, a movie camera is set up at left, preparing for a scene in *Robin Hood of the El Dorado* in which lawmen chase Joaquin Murrieta's gang.
Photograph courtesy of the Tuolumne County Historical Society and Museum. (Leonard Ruoff collection).

cabins were filled, while most of the crew stayed in a large tent erected at the river. A few members stayed at the nearby McCarty cabin. The restaurant operated at full capacity with cattleman Frank McCormick as the main cook. Frank Kurzi, owner of Kennedy Meadows Pack Station, provided the horses.

During the Great Depression, movie extras were always available. Director Wellman needed a shot of the lawmen chasing Murrieta's gang. It required a lot of men on horseback, riding full tilt. Wellman instructed the extras to ride very fast and if they fell off their horse, he would pay extra. When the cameras rolled, Wellman watched in amazement as all the riders fell off their horses. For the second take, he picked which riders would be paid extra. The movie was well received, despite an excess of scenes featuring men riding horses at a full gallop up and down Douglas Flat.

SOURCES
Bloom, Matt. Personal interview, 11 Aug. 2016.
Jensen,Larry. "Sierra on the Silver Screen." *CHISPA*,
    Tuolumne Counties Quarterly, Vol. 25, No. 3, Jan.–
    Mar., 1986.
Ruoff, Leonard. Personal interview, 15 Dec. 2014.

Mexican style house built on location.
Photograph courtesy of the Tuolumne County Historical Society and Museum. (Leonard Ruoff collection).

Movie set for the Mexican village in *Robin Hood of the El Dorado*.
Photograph courtesy of the Tuolumne County Historical Society and Museum. (Leonard Ruoff collection).

CHAPTER 50

For Whom the Bell Tolls

Something happened in the winter of 1941 that took Sonora by storm. With a population of just 2,500, the sleepy Mother Lode town was greatly impacted by the arrival of the Paramount Studios film crew that came to Sonora Pass to film the movie *For Whom The Bell Tolls*. News of the arrival of the large movie company was a breath of fresh air for the stagnant economy.

In 1940, Ernest Hemingway, famed American novelist, had just finished his book *For Whom The Bell Tolls*. It was an impressive work that some critics consider his finest novel. Typically Hemingway, the book was about manhood, love, and war. It is the story of an American man, Robert Jordan, fighting in the Spanish Civil War on a desperate mission to blow up a strategic bridge. He unexpectedly finds romance with a young woman named Maria, a behind-the-scenes guerrilla fighter. The book was an immediate best seller.

While writing the book, Hemingway knew it would be snapped up by Hollywood and made into a movie. It reportedly was sold to Paramount Pictures for $100,000, a great deal of money at that time. He visualized Gary Cooper and Ingrid Bergman playing the leading roles. Ernest Hemingway and Gary Cooper were great friends. Gregory Hemingway, Ernest's youngest child, remembered, "They really did like each other. You could tell by the resonance of their voices and the way their eyes smiled. There was never a rivalry between them." The two frequently met up at Sun Valley, Idaho to hunt and fish together from 1940 to 1961.

Sam Wood was recruited to direct the film. At fifty-eight, the seasoned filmmaker, whose work had been nominated for several Academy Awards, took on the task. Wood had a reputation for reliability, a no-nonsense approach, and the ability to finish a project on time and under budget. He selected Sonora Pass for filming the mountain scenes in the movie. Some of the basic background mountain scenes were filmed in 1941, and wrapped up on the historic day of December 7, 1941, when the Japanese attacked Pearl Harbor. The first twelve weeks were shot on Sonora Pass, the last twelve weeks were shot at the Paramount Studio in Los Angeles, California.

Once he had sold his novel to Paramount Studios, Hemingway insisted that Gary Cooper and

Ingrid Bergman, director Sam Wood, and Gary Cooper on location in 1942.
Photograph courtesy of Ruth and Jerry Howard.

Ingrid Bergman star in the film. Bergman desperately wanted the part of Maria, but was filming *Casablanca* and wasn't available. She, Humphrey Bogart, and Paul Henried all believed that *Casablanca* was a little picture and a waste of their time.

Wanda Spicer (at left) the local Ranger's wife, relaxes here with Vera Zorina on the Elliott cabin deck, which overlooks the Stanislaus River.
Photograph courtesy of Jo Spicer Danicourt.

Director Wood cast Vera Zorina in the role of Maria. The beautiful and noted Norwegian ballerina, theatre, and film actress was already under contract and available. Vera had her hair cropped for the part of Maria, and arrived on location. Hemingway was outraged that he didn't have his way.

Meanwhile, Ingrid met with Hemingway and his wife at a San Francisco restaurant. The author assured her she would get the part. As a girl, Ingrid had read everything Hemingway had written and was a bit star struck to meet him in person.

On preliminary scouting trips, director Wood found that many of the cast and crew, numbering nearly one hundred and fifty, could be housed at the Kennedy Meadows Lodge. He made arrangements with owner Frank Kurzi in the fall of 1940. Filming was to begin the following spring.

Unfortunately, in the fall of 1940 Kennedy Meadows Lodge burned down. Kurzi was devastated, but immediately started rebuilding the following

spring, in order to accommodate Sam Wood's movie crew. During construction, Kurzi arranged for some of the crew to stay in privately-owned cabins. Many were rather primitive and lacked electricity, but they had kitchens, bedrooms, and indoor plumbing.

In the spring of 1941, with the Kennedy Meadows Lodge still being rebuilt, the movie producers scrambled to find lodging for the large cast and crew. Douglas Resort had a few cabins for rent. Private cabin owner Colonel Harold Cloke let Gary Cooper stay in his cabin. Director Sam Wood stayed at Mrs. R.H. Raymond's cabin next door.

Dardanelle Resort, a larger operation, offered additional cabin rentals and a restaurant. Actors Akim Tamiroff, Vladimir Sokoloff, Misha Egan, Ted Mapes (Gary Cooper's double), and Bill Woods, a make-up specialist, all stayed at Dardanelle Resort.

Vera Zorina stayed at the Elliott's cabin Lot 50 at Brightman Flat Summer Home Tract overlooking the Stanislaus River. Katrina Paxinou, a supporting actress, was housed at the Ballantyne's cabin, Lot 51 next door. The ladies cooked meals together.

Dardanelle Resort.
Photograph courtesy of the Tuolumne County Historical Society and Museum. (Fred Leighton collection).

Nearby Brightman Flat Ranger Station had the only telephone in the area. Paramount arranged to tap into this telephone line to use as their communication center. It went down the mountain as far as the Strawberry Hotel. At Strawberry, Marie Sullivan Shell took the calls at her exchange and relayed them to Paramount in Los Angeles.

A large tent was set up on Brightman Flat, across the highway from the Ranger Station. This tent became Paramount's mountain headquarters. It had desks for Business Manager Syd Street, an affable executive, and Ed Tate, a large Dutchman

Filming on location on Sonora Pass in 1941.
Photograph courtesy of Jo Spicer Danicourt.

who was Chief of Operations. Tate rode his bicycle to the resort for meals. The tent also provided a place for locals to meet up for instructions, and production assistants to order supplies.

After a day of filming, the reels were transported to Modesto, where they were put on the night train to the studio. There they were developed and shipped back to Modesto, to be picked up on the 7 a.m. morning train and taken back to Dardanelle.

Paramount set up a large screening tent behind Dardanelle Resort. Every night the "rushes" from the previous day's filming were shown. The production crew would assemble to evaluate the shooting to see if they needed any retakes.

Every Tuesday, Saturday, and Sunday evening Paramount Studios showed one of their newly-released feature films in the tent. This was a huge hit with the locals who came from campgrounds and

cabins to enjoy the movies. There was no admission charge. Paramount asked that a contribution be made to their USO donation box. The United Service Organization was a non-profit service organization that provided entertainment for service men.

By August, director Wood became frustrated with Vera Zorina. Vera's hair would not cooperate and the director noticed she often walked too much on her toes. If a scene required her to jump across the stream, she was always concerned that she might hurt her legs. Paramount agreed to terminate her contract and Vera was dropped. When Vera was replaced by Ingrid Bergman, she threatened to sue Paramount. The matter was arbitrated, and she received a cash settlement.

Bergman had achieved recognition for the movie *Intermezzo,* released in 1939. When she came on board to film *For Whom The Bells Tolls,*

Casablanca had not been released yet, so she wasn't a Hollywood box office star; however, once released, *Casablanca* became a hit, boosting everyone's profile. It was nominated for eight Academy Awards, and won three.

Danny Selznick, a member of the famous Hollywood family that produced numerous films, remarked about Bergman, "God, she was beautiful! There was no one I have ever met, of any age, of any generation, that took one's breath away at every meeting the way she did. And she was just completely unselfconscious."

Bergman was a joy to work with as she was even-tempered, sincere, always prepared, and she only needed minimal makeup. At twenty-six, she was a natural beauty who was a cameraman's dream. She could be shot from all angles and was radiant in her youthful beauty. She was an instant sensation with her short haircut and was emulated by young women in the 1940s. Bobbed hair became the rage.

Cooper was a well-established film star by the time he was forty. He had just finished filming *Pride of the Yankees*, a film about Lou Gehrig. It was directed by Sam Wood and nominated for eleven Academy Awards. Gary Cooper was quite familiar with Sonora Pass. In 1929, when just beginning his career, he had filmed *The Virginian* in the area. In 1931, he starred in *Fighting Caravans*, filmed on Sonora Pass. He was pleased to return to the familiar mountains and continue working with Sam Wood.

Bergman and Cooper first met on location at Kennedy Meadows. In her autobiography, Ingrid recalls, "I thought he was the most underplaying and natural actor I ever worked with. Gary Cooper made me blush. I hate to admit I was very attracted to him." Other people who worked with Gary remarked that he was unbelievably handsome, gentle, courteous, and always well dressed. Likewise, Gary Cooper said of his co-star, "She was so completely natural, not fussing with her hair or makeup."

Ingrid's new haircut for the part of Maria required way too much fussiness for her. She wrote, "I had a hairdresser who followed me around like a shadow and rolled up my hair every minute of the day in little bobby pins, then combed it out before each shot. But of course the poor women who had their heads done in the Maria cut in the morning found that after two hours it fell down again and they looked like little rats."

Actor Mikhail Rasumny at left, visits with Gary Cooper and Ingrid Bergman. The cabin in the background, which overlooks the Stanislaus River, is where Bergman stayed.
Photograph courtesy of Jo Spicer Danicourt.

During the filming, Ingrid stayed at the Elliott's cabin, Lot 50 at Brightman Flat Summer Home Tract, just as Vera had. Her longtime friend, language coach Ruth Roberts, shared the cabin with her. Greek actress Katrina Paxinou was housed in a cabin next door. The three ladies took turns cooking dinner and enjoying meals on the deck overlooking the Stanislaus River.

In her autobiography, Ingrid commented, "We had such fun up there in the Sierra Nevada mountains in that summer of 1942. Yes, the war was on, and we hadn't forgotten it. The climate was incredible. We chilled in the morning, sweated in the afternoon sun, and froze at night.

On location near the summit of Sonora Pass, the day before Pearl Harbor was attacked, December 6, 1941. Lunch break, as people are lined up at a table and carrying food trays to sit at a table in the background.
Photograph courtesy of Tuolumne County Historical Society and Museum.

"Then of course there was that poor horse. In the closing scene in the picture, the guerrillas have to race to safety across an open gully, under enemy fire. Gary Cooper races across last of all, his horse stumbles, falls on Gary, and breaks his leg. Well, there weren't many horses in Hollywood who could do this without really breaking your leg. But they had sent up a special horse who could do the trick. Trouble was he was brown, and all through the film Gary had been riding a dapple-gray. So our make-up men painted the brown horse dapple gray. But the horse didn't care for his new color at all. He was so dejected that he refused to act. For twenty-four hours he just stood there hanging his head looking sorry for himself. Then at last he did his trick, and as soon as they washed the paint off he was all right again. All the cast understood his feelings."

Kennedy Meadows owner Frank Kurzi, anxious to make a few dollars while building the new resort, had about eight tent cabins built. They were constructed behind the resort, with merely a canvas fitted to a wood frame and a wood floor, just enough for a place to sleep comfortably and house some of the film crew.

Meanwhile, Kurzi had no shortage of customers at his saloon, which had survived the fire. At last, among the activity and confusion of film employees everywhere, Kurzi opened for business on July 4th. Throughout the rest of the year, the resort was awash with Paramount employees, and the Kurzis recouped their losses.

Lottie Pedro, who ran the laundry room, had her fourteen-year-old niece Patricia "Pat" Wright visiting for the summer. Lottie, who loved children, frequently would have her nieces and nephews stay with her at the resort through the summer season. They loved it. Pat recalls, "One day while working with my aunt in the laundry room a film assistant brought in a wet jacket to dry. It was Gary Cooper's jacket he wore in the movie. Up on the Pass, they got caught in a downpour and the jacket got soaked. It was leather with a sheepskin lining. Lottie wasn't so sure what to do with the wet leather, and carefully hung it over the back of a chair to dry. I was star-struck by Gary Cooper and kept eyeing the jacket on the chair. Soon temptation overwhelmed me and I grabbed the heavy jacket and put it on. Huge and heavy over my little body, I danced around the room chanting, 'I have Gary Cooper's jacket, I have Gary Cooper's jacket'. Aunt Lottie laughed at me in amusement." To this day, Pat looks back on her days at Kennedy Meadows in 1941, remembering the moment she felt the glamour of a movie star. Pat also added, "Gary Cooper while at Kennedy Meadows liked to take his shirt off and pose for photographs with lady tourists wearing his sleeveless T-shirt."

At the Que de Porka, a local landmark on the highway, Sam Wood needed cameras set up above the landmark to film shots of army tanks descending the Pass. Getting the camera equipment onto the granite rocks and through the chaparral was a

The Que de Porka landmark.
Cate Culver postcard collection.

The Sonora Inn was used as the movie headquarters.
Photograph courtesy of the Tuolumne County Historical Society and Museum.

GARY COOPER'S FALSE TEETH

Gary Cooper arrived as usual at the Sonora Inn for breakfast and his assignments for the day. The assistant director had made special arrangements for a man from the studio to accompany Cooper on location, for this one day only, and was pleased to see Cooper arrive.

Oddly, Cooper held his hand over his mouth and mumbled to the director that he could not work that day. The director became agitated and asked why not? Cooper removed his hand to reveal that he had no teeth. He explained that during his previous night of drinking he had taken out his false teeth and set them on the bar. Later he could not find them.

After a brief discussion, Frank Bigelow, the local mortician who provided a limousine for Paramount dignitaries, commented that he had several buckets of false teeth back at the mortuary. Cooper found a set that fit and worked that day!

Source:
Interview with Leonard Ruoff in 2015. He was hired as a truck driver for Paramount Studios.

challenge. The crew anchored cables on top of the landmark rocks, then they engineered pulleys to hoist the camera equipment up from the roadbed. In doing so, they removed the sign "Que de Porka" that hung over the road labeling it. The sign was never replaced.

Down the mountain, the Sonora Inn was the main movie headquarters. Assistant directors held meetings every morning over breakfast and coffee so that everyone could receive their work assignments. The inn was packed with movie personnel while the movie was in production.

The Screen Actors Guild ruled that all cast and crew members be provided a hot meal every five hours. Sometimes they were able to eat at various resort dining halls, although much of the time they were on location.

When the crew was on location, the Screen Actors Guild required an ambulance, fire truck, and law enforcement present at all times. Deputy Sheriff Miller Sardella made himself available much of the time. Frank Bigelow, the mortician, provided a combination ambulance and limousine service.

Sonora residents made use of the opportunity to make some extra money. They creatively came up with ways to get hired by the film company.

Paul Frances was an example of such ingenuity. He owned a luncheonette in Sonora and saw a business opportunity to provide hot meals for the production company while it was on location. He rigged up a trailer equipped to burn charcoal, allowing him to cook hot meals anywhere. He became a vital resource, serving large groups on location in the mountains.

There was a need for transportation from Sonora to various locations up the mountain. Charlie Stone from Copperopolis had the school bus contract. He was able to provide bus service from Sonora to filming locations on Sonora Pass.

George Williams, a Sonora trucker, realized an opportunity to provide dressing rooms for the cast while out in the wilderness. Using a large panel truck, he partitioned the inside, creating two dressing rooms and arrived wherever he was needed.

To support the production crew, much of the equipment was rented from businesses in Sonora. Truck drivers were hired to transport equipment from Sonora to various locations.

Terry Millard Mee recalls, "We moved to Sonora in June of 1941. Daddy Russ Millard owned a Diamond T produce truck, and used it for hauling building supplies, and planned to start a

Russ Millard and his grocery truck in 1941.
Photograph courtesy of Terry Millard Mee.

nursery business. He offered his truck for hire and immediately Paramount Studios had him haul the new technicolor equipment up to Dardanelle. His truck was used for the scene where the big army trucks come creeping down the grade from the Que de Porka and get blown up. Only ours didn't get blown up. They spray painted it a washable army green. He brought home pieces of fake papier

The Confidence Inn.
Photograph courtesy of Tuolumne County Historical Society and Museum.

mache rocks that had come rolling down the hill as props. We were greatly amused by those chunks of material, which I still remember. Yes, the movie industry probably paid enough to mostly support our beginning nursery business during the War. We were very thankful for the job."

During the filming of *For Whom The Bell Tolls*, the Confidence Inn was a busy watering hole, located between the filming on the Pass and headquarters at the Sonora Inn. Many of the cast and crew were regular customers, including Gary Cooper. The bar had a back room with a couch and table, where patrons could stay overnight if they were unable to safely drive home. Phil Tomosovich, who built the Confidence Inn in 1926 as a general store and saloon, was a gold miner and bootlegger from Stent. Phil and Gary Cooper had become friends when Cooper was filming *The Virginian* in 1928.

Sam Wood admired a sunset from what is today's Donnell Vista. He had his heart set on using a sunset looking down the canyon as the opening shot of the movie. The crew referred to it as Paramount Point. For a week, his camera crew went to the overlook and filmed the sunset. None of them were like the first he had seen, and he eventually gave up on the idea.

Despite its three-hour length, *For Whom The Bell Tolls* became a 1943 box office hit and grossed $11,000,000. It was nominated for nine Academy Awards, including Best Picture, Best Actor, and Best Actress. Only Greek actress Katrina Paxinou won an Oscar for her portrayal of Pilar. Hemingway hated the film.

Many locals in Sonora have relatives who watched the filming or were extras. The movie was a national sensation. It brought fame to Sonora and to many locations on Sonora Pass.

Gary Cooper in costume, on location at Sonora Pass, while filming *For Whom the Bell Tolls* in 1942.
Photograph courtesy of the Tuolumne County Historical Society and Museum.

SOURCES

Bergman, Ingrid and Alan Burgess. *Ingrid Bergman: My Story,* Delacorte Press, 1980.

Bloom, Matt. Personal interview, 11 Aug. 2016.

Chandler, Charlotte. *Ingrid Bergman: A Personal Biography,* Simon & Schuster, 2007.

Danicourt, Jo Spicer (Forest Ranger's daughter, who circulated a local newsletter during the filming, called *Pine Whispers*). 2015.

Day, Pat Wright. Personal interview, 28 Oct. 2016.

Hollywoodsgoldenage.com. *For Whom The Bell Tolls.*

Janis, Maria Cooper. *Gary Cooper Off Camera: A Daughter Remembers,* Abrams, 1999.

Lemon, Robert. *The Road Genealogist,* blog post on Blogger. com.

"Lost Men Return Safely; Resort Accidently Burned." *Union Democrat,* 27 Dec. 1940, Front page.

Mee, Terry Millard (daughter of a truck driver), email interview, 7 Jan. 2016.

Ruoff, Leonard (truck driver for Paramount), Personal interview, 2015.

CHAPTER 51

The Forest Service
Keepers of the Land

On February 22, 1897, President Cleveland proclaimed thirteen new forest reserves in the West, known thereafter as the "Washington's Birthday Reserves." Establishing a forest reserve would control and protect vast primitive areas. The Stanislaus Forest Reserve encompassed 820,000 acres of government land, with a large portion of land on the east side of the Sierra. It extended from the Merced River to the Mokelumne River, and from the east side of the Sierra Nevada to the foothills of the San Joaquin Valley. It was wild acreage, thick with conifer forests, rivers, creeks, lakes, and meadows, intermixed on a foundation of granite. The Sonora-Mono Wagon Road was the only passage into the reserve by wagon. Trails cut to Wheats Meadow, Mill Creek, Clarks Fork, Eagle Meadow, and Kennedy Lake provided access by horseback. Cattlemen, sheepherders, trappers, and lumbermen moved in. Water developers scouted for possible dams.

Grant I. Taggart became Forest Supervisor in May 1902. He was the first supervisor to make any improvements since the creation of the forest reserves. Taggart was a small, elderly, nervous man. Little is known about previous supervisors, except that they set up a tent near Strawberry and performed their administrative duties.

The Department of the Interior was very strict in regards to sheep. They were not permitted on the reserve. All the bands of sheep had to be escorted through reserve land by a ranger, and prevented from grazing. When the sheep and their herders were caught on reserve land, they were driven back to Sonora, then delivered to the U.S. Marshall in

Sign at Sonora Pass Summit.
Photographer Cate Culver, 2017.

San Francisco. They pled guilty and were fined $1,000 dollars.

After a few months in his new position, Taggart raised the rangers' salaries from $60 per month to $75. Taggart lived in Sonora, where he directed his force of six rangers. Taggart and his rangers were primarily concerned with fire, and sheep and cattle grazing. The job was political, and it was always tempting to give favors to relatives and cattlemen. By 1906, he left the Reserve and went on to become a special agent in the Oakland Police Department for twelve years. Taggart lived to be ninety-six years old.

In 1902, during Taggart's reign, the Forest Reserve Manual was published. It was a small, red, leather-bound book. Each ranger was required to know its contents and follow its directives.

Taggart's replacement was S.N.L. Ellis, a pudgy fellow who entered the Forest Service about 1901,

J.C. Wells, and Robert Ayers (right), at the Cow Creek Station in 1911.
Courtesy of the Stanislaus National Forest Service.

Ranger Wells in 1902, patrolling the West Walker River area.
Courtesy of the Stanislaus National Forest Service.

in order to watch over his cattle in the mountains. Ellis was middle-aged, dignified, easygoing, and well mannered. Unfortunately, Ellis lasted only until Thanksgiving of 1907 when he was ousted for hiring incompetent cronies and his relatives, and making a mess of the timber sales.

In 1905, the management of the forest reserves was transferred from the Department of the Interior to the Department of Agriculture. The U.S. Forest Service was formally established on July 1, 1905, replacing the Bureau of Forestry. An act on March 4, 1907, changed the forest reserves to the National Forest.

The USDA Forest Service—The First Century, by Gerald W. Williams, Ph.D., has a description of the test to become a ranger. "Beginning in the summer of 1905, the new Forest Service required that applicants for the forest ranger position (now under Civil Service rules) take practical and written field examinations. The written test, although not highly technical, was quite challenging. Questions were asked to determine an applicant's knowledge of basic ranching and livestock, forest conditions, lumbering, surveying, mapping, cabin construction, and so on. The field examination, held outdoors, was also quite basic. It required applicants to demonstrate practical skills such as how to saddle a horse and ride at a trot and a gallop, how to pack a horse or mule, how to 'throw' a diamond hitch, accurately pace the distance around a measured course, compute the area in acres, take bearings with a compass and follow a straight line. In the field examination's early years, the applicants were also required to bring a rifle and pistol along with them to shoot accurately at a target. At some ranger examinations, the applicants were required to cook a meal, then EAT it! The applicants, as well as the rangers themselves, were not furnished with equipment, horses, or pack animals—they were required to have them for the test and for work, at their own expense. The pay was $60 per month."

Robert W. Ayres became the Stanislaus Forest Supervisor from 1908 through 1919. The job became a huge challenge, as its responsibilities increased to oversee dams, Special Use Permits, and timber sales.

In 1931, the Forest Service established the Emigrant Basin Primitive Area, holding 97,000 acres of mountainous country, lying north of Yosemite National park on the headwaters of Cherry Creek and the Stanislaus River. This area was set apart as a true wilderness, to preserve for the use and enjoyment of everyone. No road building or permanent structures were allowed. However, the grazing of livestock was permitted and controlled by allotments.

The Forest Service feared a northward extension of Yosemite National Park. To generate public support for the Stanislaus National Forest, it established summer home tracts. Tuolumne County also urged the Forest Service to add taxable improvements on public land.

Outlying stations were primarily used for rangers on patrol. A one-room cabin was built at Wheats Meadow in 1910, measuring fourteen by sixteen feet, plus a four-stall barn to stable the horses and mules. A small one-room station cabin was erected at Iceberg Meadow in 1912.

The first Ranger Station was established at Cow Creek in 1903, followed by another in 1927, at Brightman Flat. The Civilian Conservation Corps built another at Pinecrest in 1934, on a spacious lot behind the east end of Pinecrest Lodge, at the corner of Highland Way and Lakeshore Drive. It was a one-bedroom residence with a small office, woodshed, a four-bay garage, and two tent platforms for extra employees. This building was occupied in 1948 by Jack Reveal, the new District Ranger, his wife Arlene, and their two boys.

The old residence and four-bay warehouse was moved to the new Ranger Station complex, during the summer of 1949. A new Summit District office

Pinecrest Peak fire lookout station in 1935.
Photograph courtesy of Bill Zurnstein.

Ranger Station at Pinecrest in 1934.
Courtesy of the Stanislaus National Forest Service.

was opened at the intersection of Highway 108 and Pinecrest Road. This location offered fire permits, fishing and hunting licenses, and general information. Two old tent cabins were also moved to the site to accommodate summer help. This area formerly was Reno Sardella's Pinecrest Pack Station.

The District Ranger job consisted of meeting with other rangers, helping with their problems, visiting each organization camp and getting acquainted with the staff, visiting the summer home tracts, hiring fire lookouts and trail crews, visit grazing allotments, taking supplies to the Pinecrest Peak lookout, watching for unlawful Christmas tree cutting, and talking with tourists to exchange thoughts and ideas. The job was overwhelming. In 1948, the District Ranger's job had two forestry aides: Johnny Spicer at Brightman and Cow Creek, and George Weaver at Pinecrest. From June until October, George and Johnny each got a helper.

However, it was the rangers' wives who held down the stations. They greeted visitors, answered the telephone, collected the mail, kept the station looking tidy, and maintained a working relationship with the locals. For all this, they received no pay and never enough credit.

The rangers laid out campgrounds, kept buildings maintained, burned slash piles, supervised trail crews, shod horses, dumped garbage, and solved any problems that arose. Everyone worked a forty-hour week, but the District Ranger's job was never-ending, and overtime was unheard of.

In his recollections, District Ranger Jack Reveal mentioned how drinking was a way of life for men who spent many hours alone in the high country. He said it was especially true for the cattlemen and the forest rangers. In the Forest Service, it seemed to go along with the job. Alcoholism was widely accepted, and became part of their social activities. Many had a bottle tucked under a seat or in a saddle bag. Meetings were deliberately held at a bar, and stops were made for a short drink at a friend's cabin.

Reveal stated that, "Hardly a season went by without someone reporting that ladies in one of the camps appeared to be in the business of 'entertaining' men. Although there were a few suspicious circumstances, to my knowledge no hookers ever set up a business in a campground, not even in Pinecrest during the Tri-Dam days. But there was an often-told story going around in the Forest Service about a happening some years before. According to the story—even by then almost a legend—a ranger phoned Forest Supervisor Jess Hall, saying that he had some undesirable women in a campground and asked what he should do. Jess was said to have replied, "Well, get rid of them and get some desirable ones."

In the winter of 1949, the Forest Service began issuing twenty-year permits for summer homes. This replaced the original ninety-nine year leases permits. The old-timers didn't trust the bureaucrats, and were unsettled over the new arrangement. Some thought the Forest Service was intent on doing away with the cabins.

Another problem with the Forest Service was that supervisors often hired their incompetent relatives. This practice led to conflicts and proved to be disastrous. Many supervisors had also been cattlemen and made decisions that favored the cattle industry, which also caused friction.

By the late 1950s, the Forest Service cooled on its concept of recreational residences, and felt the land should be available to all the public. The last cabin tracts in California were surveyed in 1958. Cabins are now mostly passed down in families, and rarely sold.

Without the foresight of the early conservationist, the forest would have been carved up into private land holdings. Our rugged, awe-inspiring Sierra would have not been preserved. Fortunately, it has been saved for generations to come.

SOURCES

Ayers, Robert W. "History of the Stanislaus" Summit District, Stanislaus National Forest. Feb. 1911.

Conners, Pam."A Century or So of Land Use on the Central Stanislaus Watershed Analysis Area, 1848-1958." 1993 Summit District, Stanislaus National Forest.

Reveal, Jack, District Ranger. "Contributions to" *A History of the Summit District: Recollections of the Years 1948-1960,* First Draft. Summit District, Stanislaus National Forest. San Diego, CA. 18 Apr. 1984 (District Ranger Report).

Williams, Gerald W., Ph.D. *The USDA Forest Service — The First Century.* Revised Report. Apr. 2005. FS-650.

United States Government Office memorandum to John L. Spicer, Forestry Aide from the District Ranger, job assignments, 1948. Stanislaus National Forest files.

Courtesy of U.S. Forest Service.

CHAPTER 52

Cow Creek Ranger Station

The newly-built ranger station in 1906.
Photograph courtesy of the Tuolumne County Historical Society and Museum. (Francis Nelson Collection).

The Sonora-Mono Wagon Road passed through a flat area six miles above Strawberry Lake called Cow Creek. Deep in the forest, along the road between Cow Creek and Leland Creek, was a small building used as a freight agent's cabin. Jonathan Florentine Ralph consistently hauled supplies from Sonora to Bodie from 1875 to 1881. His first night's stop was at Cow Creek. He built a ten- by twelve- foot dwelling with a sugar pine shake exterior. Inside it had a small cast iron stove, a dirt floor with a rug, a bed at the back, and counters and shelves. Ralph could comfortably stay in the cabin for his regularly scheduled overnight stop. He fenced the nearby meadow for the mules.

Once Ralph no longer ran his freight wagon, the dwelling stood empty.

By the turn of the century, the rangers assigned to Cow Creek used the abandoned cabin for shelter. It soon became obvious that a new ranger station was needed. The old building remained until the Forest Service burned it down in the fall of 1926.

Under the administration of Supervisor Grant Taggart, the Department of the Interior appropriated $65 to build the Cow Creek Ranger Station. Ranger Paderson Y. "Bud" Lewis was assigned to oversee the ranger station's construction, and selected a site near the old station agent's cabin on the south side of the Sonora-Mono Wagon Road.

Cow Creek Ranger Station, 1906, manned by Ranger Johnny Tyler. Teamsters hauling supplies to Relief Dam stop for a rest.
Photograph courtesy of the Tuolumne County Historical Society and Museum (Francis Nelson Collection).

Begun in 1902 and completed in the summer of 1903, the ranger station was a two-story structure, layered on the outside with sugar pine shakes. It was a sturdy structure, built primarily of poles and rough-sawn boards. There was a spacious room that included a fireplace built from river rocks, and a kitchen. A beautiful, polished, red manzanita railing built by Bud Lewis, led to a large sleeping loft above. The bathroom was installed off the back porch. Another porch went all around the front and one side of the building. The steps up to the front porch were carved from a huge sugar pine tree, and created an impressive entrance.

Ranger P.Y. Lewis used the building as his headquarters, accompanied by Taggart's son, Ranger Charles Taggart. A four-stall barn, rail fencing, and a blacksmith shop were built between 1907 and 1912. Across the road, they had a vegetable garden and successfully grew potatoes. They planted Timothy grass for grazing livestock, and enclosed it with a split-rail fence.

There were no other access roads into the forest for the rangers to perform their duties. Trails

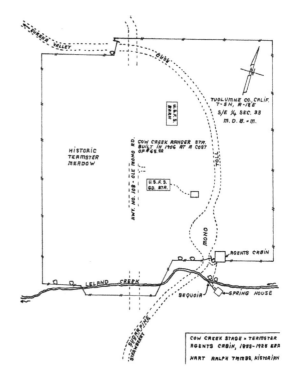

had to be cut wide enough for a saddle horse and pack animals. In the fall of 1903, the rangers built a bridge across the Middle Fork of the Stanislaus River to access Hell's Half Acre, below the Cow Creek camp.

The barn at Cow Creek Ranger Station, built with sugar pine shakes.
Photograph courtesy of the Ray Sardella family.

Cow Creek Ranger Station in the 1920s.
Photograph courtesy of the Ray Sardella family.

After the station was built, there was constant activity on the wagon road in front of the station. The noise of mule teams, freight wagons, and tractor engines filled the mountain air, as teamsters hauled equipment and supplies up to the new Relief Dam, being built above Kennedy Meadows. It was a time of great commotion, with teamsters stopping by to take a break and exchange news.

In 1922, the Forest Service started surveying lots for a summer home tract around the ranger station. The site was chosen because it was flat, near the road, and had abundant water. By 1925, seventeen lots were under the Special Use Permit by cabin owners.

In 1933, upgrades to the station included new red linoleum floors, the interior was painted gray, and a garage was added outside. The ranger station got a telephone and a switchboard. Usually, it was the ranger's wife who handled the telephone calls. One ranger built a primitive desk to use for business purposes. Visitors had given the rangers various items, including a Victrola and a Singer sewing machine. Cabin owners and campers would gather at the ranger station in the evenings and dance as the Victrola played music. Children in bed upstairs looked down through the cracks in the floor and watched the dancing that went on all night.

Fire Guard Ray Castilo and his wife Alma were stationed at Cow Creek for several years. They planted two ten-inch-high sequoia trees in front of the station in 1935. The trees came from what is now Calaveras Big Trees State Park. They thrived and grew to be enormous trees. Unfortunately, these two trees no longer exist to mark the station and have most likely been cut down or removed for lumber.

John Spicer on steps of Cow Creek Ranger station in 1947.
Photograph courtesy of Jo Spicer Danicourt. Sign reads: Stanislaus National Forest Cow Creek Station. Maps, Information and Camp Fire Permits.

Cousins visit the Spicer family at the Cow Creek Ranger Station in the summer of 1943.
Photograph courtesy of the Jo Spicer Danicourt family.

In November of 1950, the headquarters moved to Pinecrest. Although the Cow Creek station was abandoned and fell into disuse, it stood for fifty years, sturdy against all the heavy snow and wind from winter storms. The Forest Service tore down the Cow Creek Ranger Station in 1967. Sadly, all the old furniture, letters, and business correspondence inside were lost. Later, the Forest Service regretted tearing down the station, and wished the old building could have become a museum complex. Gary Hines, The Summit Ranger District Public Information Specialist, spearheaded a plan to reconstruct the site for an Interpretive and Information complex, displaying historic artifacts, but the plans for this vision were never developed.

Guard station in 1960.
Courtesy of the Stanislaus National Forest Service.

SOURCES

Ayers, Robert W. *History of the Stanislaus.* Summit District, Stanislaus National Forest files. Feb. 1911.

Charles A. Taggart Obituary. *San Francisco Chronicle*, 30 Jun. 1967.

Conners, Pam. Wanda Spicer interview. 30 Jul. 1986. Summit District, Stanislaus National Forest oral history files.

Hines, Gary and Bashford York. Wanda Spicer Interview, 10 Mar. 1983 by Summit District, Stanislaus National Forest files.

Personal Letter to Supervisor Harry D. Grace, from Ray Castilo, Oct. 10, 1967. Summit District, Stanislaus National Forest files.

Reveal, Jack, District Ranger. "A History of the Summit District: Recollections of the Years 1948-1960," Summit District, Stanislaus National Forest.

Snow, S.B., Regional Forester. Memorandum for Forest Supervisor. 28 Jun. 1933. Summit District, Stanislaus National Forest files.

Tambs, Hart Ralph. "Cow Creek's Historic Freight Agent's Cabin." Unpublished recollection. 1994. Summit District, Stanislaus National Forest files.

CHAPTER 53

Brightman Flat Ranger Station

There is no firm date as to when the first ranger station was built at Brightman Flat. It was actually known as a "guard station," to guard against forest fires. The station had several outbuildings, as seen in the older photographs and maps. The early rangers brought their families for the summer, and were considered part of the community, as they socialized with local cabin owners and campers. They attended functions at the Dardanelle Resort, and were known personally throughout the area. Rangers provided a safety net for people visiting the area, because in an emergency the rangers were there to help.

District Ranger Pete Kenney lived with his wife Ann and their family, at the larger ranger station built in 1933 by the Civilian Conservation Corps. This main station had a residence, a small office, and a tent platform. Across the highway, partly hidden by a granite outcropping, a four-stall barn and corral were also part of the station. The barn was damaged by snow in 1982, and was dismantled in 1983. Kenney spent the summer on horseback, riding from Lake Alpine to Hermit Valley and over to Yosemite, checking on grazing permittees. He took two pack mules and went twice each season. While Kenney was gone, Johnny Spicer took care of all the duties at Brightman Flat. Pete Kenney retired in 1947.

The Spicers moved to the Brightman Flat Station in the summer of 1938. Wanda was twenty-nine and Johnny was thirty-three. The Spicers married in 1920 and had two daughters, Betty Jo and Shirley Ann. They moved to Tuolumne County from Modesto in 1934, during the Great

Brightman Flat Ranger Station June 1927, known as "The Office."
Photograph courtesy of the Stanislaus National Forest Service.

Depression. Johnny found temporary work at Douglas Flat during the filming of *Robin Hood of the El Dorado.* Here he worked as a water pumper to keep the dust down while the cameras rolled. They moved that winter to Sonora, and Johnny found odd jobs to make ends meet. In the summer of 1935, he took the Forest Service exam and was hired. By 1937, the family moved to the Cow Creek Ranger Station. After one year at Cow Creek, they moved to the Brightman Flat Station at Dardanelle. He worked there for twelve years as a Fire Guard.

The Spicers lived in an old ranger station building called "the Office," located west of the new station, and north of the creek. It was about 16 by 16 feet, with the interior painted gray. It had a screened sleeping porch at the rear, although the Spicer girls usually slept outside. The Spicer family

Brightman Flat Ranger Station in 1929.
Photograph and map courtesy of the Stanislaus National Forest Service.

lived on site during the summer months. Sometime after the Spicers moved to Pinecrest, the building was intentionally burned down by the Forest Service.

The Spicer girls were well known throughout the Dardanelle area. When Paramount Studios arrived to film *For Whom The Bell Tolls* in 1942, the girls were star-struck and enjoyed having Hollywood stars at their doorstep. The eldest daughter Jo was a teenager when she started her own little newspaper called "Whispering Pines," with the help of her little sister, Shirley, as cub reporter. They watched the movie personnel at the headquarters set up in a tent across from the ranger station. The girls enjoyed all the activity and a summer of special memories.

After Pete Kenny retired, Jack Reveal became the District Ranger, but Johnny Spicer had expected to be promoted to that position. Instead, in 1950 he was moved to work at the Pinecrest Ranger Station and continued to split duties between Pinecrest and Brightman.

By 1952, work had begun to realign and replace the dangerous Patterson Grade, which was

a five-mile stretch of road from Niagara Creek to the Clarks Fork intersection. It was legendary for its cliff-hanging edges and narrow roadway. The new section was built above the old road and would take four years to complete. It required drilling, and blasting dynamite to take out trees, roots, and granite outcroppings to build the new roadbed. Blasts echoed throughout the canyon walls all summer.

It was on a September day that John Spicer was headed to the Ranger Station at Brightman Flat to prepare for deer season. He and his wife Wanda

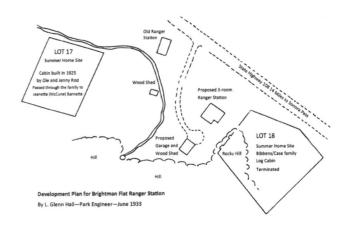

Development Plan for Brightman Flat Ranger Station
By L. Glenn Hall—Park Engineer—June 1933

Forest Aide Johnny Spicer and unidentified forestry official in the late 1940s.
Courtesy of Bill Zurnstein.

were stopped by flagman Bill Avila in a caravan of fifteen cars headed up the grade. The flagman gave the go ahead to follow his truck as he guided them through the blasting area. Suddenly, without warning, dynamite exploded, raining huge rocks down on the caravan of cars. Drivers honked their horns, but it was too late, and seventy dynamite charges could not be stopped.

The foreman, Jimmy Lester, made his way down to the disaster. The road was a fog of dust as he went from car to car. Lester came upon a sedan with its rear end flattened by a thousand-pound boulder. The occupants were shaken, but unhurt. He proceeded on to the next car, which had a smashed top where a rock had penetrated the roof. It had smashed the driver's ankle, and his wife suffered a fractured collar bone. Further down the road was Spicer's Forest Service truck, smashed through the driver's side by a seventy-pound, diamond-shaped boulder. It killed Spicer instantly. Sitting beside him, his wife Wanda was badly scraped on her left side by the rock as it passed though the cab. Dr. Paul Noeling of Angels Camp

John Spicer.
Photograph courtesy of Kenny Mitchell family.

was in the convoy, and rushed to the Spicer truck, but saw there was nothing he could do. The doctor proceeded down the road to give first aid to others. There was an inquest, and flagman Bill Avila was let go from the construction crew. The foreman, Jimmy Lester, fell to pieces. His good crew filled in for him and got the job done.

After Johnny Spicer was killed, Dutch Salazar and his wife Ruth moved to Brightman Flat Ranger Station and took over Spicer's duties. They remained there for seven years. Dutch was well liked, and they both enjoyed their new location in the mountains. Dutch died of cancer seven years after taking Spicer's job.

The station still remains, but has not had a ranger for many years. It is now used intermittently by summer fire crews. Iris once planted by a ranger's wife still bloom around the station's sign out front.

AUTHOR'S NOTE
Spicer Reservoir, off Highway 4, is not named after Johnny Spicer or his family.

SOURCES
Barnett, Jeanette. Personal interview, 2013.
Conners, Pam. Wanda Spicer Interview, 30 Jul. 1986. Summit
      District, Stanislaus National Forest oral history files.
Duncan, Judy. Personal interview, 2013.
Nelson, Francis. "A Personal Account of the Accident." 1 Feb.
      1996. Courtesy of the Tuolumne County Historical
      Society and Museum.
"One Dead, 3 Hurt In Sierra Road Blast." *Union Democrat*, 23
      Sep. 1954, Front page.
Reveal, Jack USFS District Ranger. "A History of the Summit
      District: Recollections of the Years 1948-1960."
      Summit District, Stanislaus National Forest files.

Brightman Flat Ranger Station built in 1933.
Photograph courtesy of Jo Spicer Danicourt.

Wanda Spicer, wife of Johnny Spicer in 1947 in front of the Brightman Flat Ranger Station.
Courtesy of Jo Spicer Danicourt.

The Spicer family at Brightman Flat in 1943. Shirley standing with her mother Wanda. Fire Guard John Spicer and daughter Betty Jo kneeling.
Photograph courtesy of Jo Spicer Danicourt.

CHAPTER 54

The Bennett Juniper
The Largest Living Juniper Tree in North America

Young visitors recline against the massive tree trunk.
Photograph courtesy of the Tuolumne County Historical Society and Museum.

High in the Sierra, at 8,400 feet, the dirt is thin and the winds sweep across the land, rattling the skunk cabbage in the fall. There, the Bennett Juniper has endured for centuries.

The tree is located off Eagle Meadow Road and stands as the largest juniper tree in North America. Despite its great age, the first record of an encounter with the tree only came about in the late nineteenth century. The Bach brothers, twins Albert D. and Rudolph C., ran sheep in the area. While passing with their flock of sheep, they stopped by the huge tree and carved their initials in the giant: "A.D.B. & R.C.B., 1878."

Basque sheepherders spoke of the great tree in the 1920s. It stands alone, and was probably an early landmark among the sheepherders in the area.

But it wasn't until California naturalist Clarence Bennett viewed the tree that it was given recognition. He was passionate about this species of Western Juniper, *juniperus occidentalis*. Bennett traveled the Sierra Nevada range, studying and documenting trees, especially the larger specimens.

Curious about the redwood trees he had read about in science and travel books, he explored the coastal mountain ranges to see them for himself. Then his attention turned to the junipers, and he began to study and document juniper trees ranging

80 ft high
circumference 57½ ft
The Bennett Juniper
ft Oldest living Juniper
Stanislaus Nat'l Forest. Tuolumne C
Calif.

The Bennett Juniper memorialized on an old postcard.
Postcard from the Cate Culver collection.

from Oregon to Mexico. For more than forty years, he explored and gained knowledge about these trees. Soon he became fascinated with the older and larger junipers.

In the basement of his home in Hillsboro, a suburb of San Mateo, Bennett set up a shop with electric saws, planes, sandpaper, and polishing wheels. He began collecting dead limbs and counting the rings. Here he examined the juniper specimens to learn more about how they grew and aged, and scrutinized them under magnifying glasses, carefully labeling each tree branch.

In his search to find the oldest and largest living juniper, he returned to the Stanislaus National Forest, where he had seen many large trees and

spoke with locals about juniper trees. In 1932, Frank Burgson, a Tuolumne County outdoorsman, took Clarence Bennett to Long Meadow to view a huge tree, located on private land owned by cattleman Joe Martin Sr.

After viewing the magnificent tree, Bennett concluded that his search had ended, that at last he was in the presence of the oldest and largest juniper on earth, eighty-seven feet high and fifty feet in circumference.

Frank Burgson the outdoorsman who led Clarence Bennett to view the huge juniper tree.
Photograph courtesy of Chris Robinson.

To document the age of the giant tree, Bennett bored eight holes around the base of the tree with a hollow bit. The cores were one foot in length, and taken in equal distances around the trunk. The rings were counted. Then the average number per foot was multiplied by the trunk's radius in feet. Bennett proudly determined the tree to be 6,000 years old. In 1940, the tree was recorded in the American Forestry Association's book of record trees.

In 1948, Jones Lumber Company built the first logging road, a distance of seven miles, from

Highway 108 to Joe Martin's cow camp. In 1949 it was extended three miles to Long Valley, and on to Haypress Meadow, about three miles farther. This was the first road into the area. Previously, anyone desiring to see the tree had to travel by foot or on horseback.

In the early 1950s, locals realized the tree needed to be officially recognized and protected. A Bennett Juniper Tree Association was formed, and the land surrounding the tree was named the Martin Memorial. About ten years later, on October 10, 1962, Joe Martin Sr. offered the tree to the association. This set in motion a formal recognition and naming of the world record tree.

The Sonora Pass Lion's Club then organized the funding and dedication of the tree. Because the tree was in such a remote location, the club members carefully planned the event. It was due to their efforts that the important occasion was a great success.

The dedication took place on a cool afternoon on September 15, 1962. A crowd of eighty people

Cabin owner and frequent visitor, Ruth Caldwell, walks to view the tree in the fall.
Cate Caldwell Culver photograph.

At left is Tan Boone, maker of the monument, Clarence Bennett, center, and cattleman Joe Martin, displaying the special cake.
Photographer unknown. Pony Express issue, Oct. 1963. A monthly historical publication.

joined the ceremonies, with Clarence Bennett proudly in attendance. Dr. Helen Anspach gave the invocation. Ruth Clarke, a soloist, led the assembly in the singing of the Star Spangled Banner, and the music penetrated the mountain contours as never before. The American flag was saluted, giving a solemn, patriotic grounding to the event. The ceremonies then closed with a benediction. All the guests enjoyed lavish refreshments, highlighted by a special cake. It was three-feet square, made by George Wingo of Sierra Belle Bakery in Twain Harte, and pictured the great tree and its marker.

Clarence Bennett died five years later on June 4, 1967, in San Mateo at age eight-three. Despite the fame the tree has achieved, little is actually known about Bennett. The tree lives on for centuries, for humankind to view in reverence.

Bennett and the Sonora Pass Lion's Club decided that the Bennett Juniper should have a stone marker to stand the test of time. The boulder for the monument was selected from the Hess estate property.

Tan Boone, in the stone memorials business, thought the rock was syenite; however, a chemist disagreed and said it is andesite. The polished face is flecked with white quartz crystals. The stone was so hard that Tan Boone could not surface it with his equipment. He hauled the five-and-a-half ton boulder to Madera County, to cut off a three-inch slab for a facing, and to have it polished. Inscribed on the face are the measurements of the tree, and the names of the Board of Directors, with credit to J. M. Boone and Sons Memorials.

In 1978 the Bennett Juniper Tree Association, concerned about protecting the tree, donated the juniper and three acres surrounding it, to the Nature Conservancy, a national conservation group that specializes in habitat protection.

Two years later it was passed on to the Save-The-Redwoods-League. In 1988, Ken Brunges, then a college student, was hired to be the caretaker.

In 2015, Ken explained that a small spring discovered on the hillside above the juniper provides the tree with year-round moisture. Other junipers are only fed by summer thunderstorms and snowmelt. Therefore, the Bennett Juniper may not be as old as Bennett had determined. Marmots have burrowed under the tree and brought out some dead wood. It was taken for carbon dating and determined to be 2,000 years old.

Unfortunately, the marker, wider at the top, was set in place without a foundation. It sits askew in the dirt propped up by rocks at its back. Ground squirrels also undermine it. Despite its lack of a foundation, no doubt the stone monument will survive for centuries.

Clarence Bennett unveils the stone marker.
Photograph courtesy of the Tuolumne County Historical Society and Museum.

Tourist Maren Bell visits with tree caretaker, Ken Brunges, reading the monument. A side view of the stone marker in 2015 reveals how askew it sits without a proper foundation. The Bennett Juniper is in the background at right.
Cate Culver photograph 2015.

SOURCES

Brunges, Ken. Personal interview, 2015 and 2018.
"Stories of Pioneers and Old Trails." *Pony Express,* November 1962 issue, p. 5.
"Stories of Pioneers and Old Trails." *Pony Express,* Vol. XXX, No. 5, No. 353 October 1963 issue.
Terzich, Irving. Personal interview, 2016.

Ken Brunges, the Keeper of the Tree

In 1988 Ken Brunges was a student majoring in Natural Resources Management at Columbia College when he was hired by the Save-the-Redwoods League for a seasonal summer job.

Ken explained, "I am the resident naturalist to explain the tree to visitors, the resident 'watchdog' to protect it, and the resident caretaker to repair erosion damage and make improvements to the property to prevent future problems."

When he first took on the job, he found the tree roots exposed from the activity of sightseers. Alarmed, he used a shovel and pick to dig topsoil from the area, and hauled it to the base, repacking the exposed roots. Now the tree is fenced for protection.

"Frequently at day's end, I walk down and sit by the tree and just feel it," Ken said. He keeps a pair of binoculars at hand and is an avid bird watcher. Ken regularly views bald eagles, red-tailed hawks, and other raptors that soar overhead in search of rodents.

About 1,500 visitors arrive every season, traveling the dusty dirt road twelve miles from Highway 108. The former logging road passes through thick forests of Jeffery pines, aspens, and fir trees, climbing to an elevation of 8,400 feet. In a passenger car the trip is slow going. It crosses two streams and includes breathtaking vistas of the High Sierra.

Ken explains that ninety-five percent of his visitors have come before, and return with someone who has never seen the tree. He has a visitor nearly every day.

The naturalist's camp has a solar panel that provides energy to power lights and a radio. In his

Ken Brunges in his tent.
Cate Culver photograph 2015.

outdoor kitchen, he cooks on a Coleman propane stove. All his water is hauled in from his home in Columbia, and his girlfriend brings him supplies. Brunges spends much of his idle time walking the mountains and viewing wildlife, or just relaxing on his small porch, reading.

Ken's summer tent camp.
Cate Culver photograph 2015.

AUTHOR'S NOTE:
I interviewed Ken Brunges in 1995 and 2018. I asked Ken about the minimal signage directing the public to view the tree. The road is a long way into the backcountry, and there are only two signs on the road. Ken explained, "We want the tree to be viewed by people who really have an interest in seeing it, not just as some roadside attraction."

My History Heroes

The Sources

Jo Spicer Danicourt

Jo came to the area as a young girl when her father, John Spicer, was the local Forest Ranger. She lived with her family at the Ranger Station at Brightman Flat in the early 1940s. Jo shared with me her enjoyment of old photographs, and has given me copies from her own collection. She had a fine memory of the early days, and was extremely helpful in recalling the past. She recalls when the movie *For Whom The Bell Tolls* was filmed on Sonora Pass. Many of the cast and crewmembers stayed at Dardanelle, and Jo got to know them all. With her little sister Shirley as cub reporter, managing editor Baird Whaley, and detective reporter Charlotte Verdi, they produced a small newsletter they named *Pine Whispers*. Copies were valuable to recreate the goings-on at Brightman Flat and Dardanelle in 1941. In 1979, Jo and her husband Harold bought a cabin at Brightman Flat. The Danicourt cabin was lost in the Donnell Fire of 2018.

Jo Spicer Danicourt, 2011.

Stacey Martin Dodge

Stacey's grandfather was Joe Martin, Sr., a prominent cattleman in Tuolumne County who ran herds at Eagle Meadows. Many times, I have driven Eagle Meadows Road and passed by the old buildings at the Martin Cow Camp. Then at last, I got to meet a member of the Martin family. Stacey met with me at length over lunch, and recalled her grandparents Joe and Jesse very well, sharing a few details about their personalities and interests beyond their label of being cattle ranchers. Stacey brought Bob Brennan, the current owner of Martin's Cow Camp, who also had many recollections of the people on Sonora Pass. It was one of those meetings where we would start to leave, and then want to share just one more bit of history with each other. So much fun! Bob brought an extremely nice copy of an historic photograph of the cow camp.

Stacey Martin Dodge, 2018.

Pat Perry

Pat is the City of Sonora historian and has been since 1985. She knows about everything in Sonora and has a lot of connections. She got on the phone for me to ask people questions and introduced me to people who know a great deal of local history. She is also a good teacher, introducing me to the Recorder's Office and explaining how to look up information. Pat and I share a love of history, and always enjoy each other's company. She was my editor for *CHISPA*, the Tuolumne County Historical Society's quarterly publication. I wrote about my childhood at our mountain cabin, and called it "Daughter of Dardanelle."

Pat Perry, 2014.

Leonard Ruoff

Born in Sonora in 1921 to a German pioneer family, Leonard has been of great help, with his fine memories about the film industry on Sonora Pass. His father Henry sold real estate and was president of the Sonora Motion Picture Association. His mother Hazel Rudoruff was also from an established pioneer family. Leonard was a young boy when *Robin Hood of the El Dorado* was being filmed at Eureka Valley. He worked as a "call boy," waking up the cast and crew. Leonard was especially helpful with information about the filming of *For Whom The Bell Tolls,* as he was frequently on location. Leonard drove a truck for Paramount Studios. He was present when Gary Cooper showed up for work missing his teeth, and told me the details!

Leonard Ruoff, 2016.

Pat Wright Day

Pat was a huge help with information about Lottie Pedro, of Kennedy Meadows fame. Pat's mother Isabel Vergara Wright, was Lottie's sister. Pat remembered Lottie very well. Possessed with an amazing memory, Pat was knowledgeable about much of the early days of Kennedy Meadows and the Kurzis. She shared with me her photographs of Lottie from her old black and white photograph album. And she fed me lunch!

Pat Wright Day, 2016.

Donnie Wright

Younger brother of Pat Wright Day, Donnie was also helpful with information about Kennedy Meadows. When he was a young boy in 1940, he sold worms to the fishermen. Donnie, born in 1932, is also was knowledgeable about the Veraga family and told me more about Lottie's husband Manuel and what a skunk he really was. Donnie and his wife Phyllis own a cabin at Kennedy Meadows and have helped me with much of the detailed history. He gave me a jar of his homemade cured olives!

Donnie Wright, 2016.

Chris Robinson

Chris, born in 1945, spent his boyhood summers with his great grandfather Frank Burgson at his cabin at Bone Springs. These memories have instilled in him a love of the area's history. Chris also has an interest in old photographs, and was kind enough to share with me his extensive collection inherited from his grandfather Ed Burgson. It is a fabulous record of the life of hunting and fishing on Sonora Pass in the 1930s and '40s. Best of all, Chris has given me encouragement to write this book, and spurs me on with helpful reference books from his private collection.

Chris Robinson, 2015.

Alice Foletti Hardin

Alice, born in 1923, is from a pioneer family that settled in Sonora. Her father, known as "Swiss" Foletti, built one of the first cabins at Bone Springs in 1928. He was known for his fine work as a stonemason, building several walls and fireplaces for cabin owners, and the bridge abutments at Clarks Fork. Alice shared with me many black and white photographs from her family album. They were a large part of the Italian community at Dardanelle, and socialized a lot with other Italian neighbors. The Folettis were fun loving and popular. The Folettis were avid mushroom hunters.

Alice Foletti Hardin, 2015.

Irving Terzich

Irving was born in Sonora in 1916 where his father Mitchell Terzich owned a soda works in Sonora. Irving was their only child. His father built one of the first cabins at Bone Springs in 1916. I had known Irving all my life, as he was a cabin neighbor. However, we only recently become friends when I started to write the history of Sonora Pass. When I began doing research people would say, "Go ask Irving, he would know." And much of the time he *did* know a wide variety of people and events. Plus, he recalled names and how families were related. Irving wrote a history of his childhood at the Bone Springs summer home tract, in *CHISPA*, a Tuolumne County Historical Society publication. Amazingly, at age 99 Irving was great at email. So, during the winter, I would email him an old photograph and he frequently would reply and tell me more about the history surrounding the photo. He was also good at dissecting an event and making sense of something I would never have figured out, opening my eyes to its history. He was amazing!

Irving Terzich, 2014.

June Terzich

Born in 1925, June remains helpful with the history that husband Irving also recalled. Frequently, when I walked over to the Terzich cabin to talk history with Irving, he would call to June to help him recall a name or a place. They were a history team.

June Terzich, 2016.

Judy Benedix Duncan

Born in 1940, Judy had grandparents who built a cabin at Brightman Flat in 1921. She visited as a baby, and later her parents also bought a cabin. As a teenager, Judy had a horse named Star and a Saint Bernard dog. On horseback, she freely roamed the corridor from Dardanelle to Douglas with her dog. She visited people along her route and made lifelong friendships. Judy is one of those friendly people, who "knows everybody." Her husband Glen Duncan was also helpful, and recalled history of the area. Judy has been a stalwart supporter of my history writing efforts, and has introduced me to many of her friends in the area, whom I then interviewed.

Judy Benedix Duncan, 2015.

Jeanette McCune Barnette

Jeanette was born in 1930 and often visited her grandparents, Ole and Jenny Rod, at their Brightman Flat cabin. She has many fond memories of her early days there as a child. The Rod cabin was built in 1925. Jeanette and her husband Ken Barnette bought the family cabin in the mid-1960s. A lifelong Brightman Flat cabin girl, Jeanette has a fine memory for people's names, families, and places. If she doesn't have an answer for me, she phones a relative to get information. Although nearly blind, she lets me look through her old family photo album, and shares anything I'd like to add to my photograph collection. Jeanette lost her cabin in the 2018 Donnell Fire.

Jeanette McCune Barnette, 2016.

Jim Appel

Jim, born in 1931, has a cabin at Buena Vista summer home tract, overlooking the Stanislaus River. His father, Robley Appel, built the cabin in 1926 with used lumber hauled from San Francisco. Jim has been at the summer cabin all his life. An antique car enthusiast, he has been a great help to me in identifying old automobiles in my photograph collection. He also knew old-timer Shorty Harris, and shed some light on history about Shorty. Jim lost his cabin in the 2018 Donnell Fire.

Jim Appel 2015

Janet Cornell

Janet, a former schoolteacher, was one of my supporters in the history project from the beginning. The first time I visited her cabin, she took me to meet her neighbors at Brightman Flat, and explained that we were on a history quest. Her family was at Brightman Flat very early on, and Janet has shared her old photographs with me. She explained that in the early days, owners arrived with just one load of lumber to build a small cabin. They slept in a tent cabin, which had canvas sides and roof. The cabin they built was used mostly for storage. Janet also shared with me copies of *Pine Whispers,* from 1941, written by teenager Jo Danicourt, about Dardanelle when they were filming *For Whom The Bell Tolls.* These were a special resource in writing the chapter on that movie.

Janet Cornell, 2016.

Chuck Knowles

Chuck was born in 1932, and as a young man worked as a hired hand for Reno Sardella. He shared with me many stories of those early days and insights into the Reno Sardella family. Chuck worked as a farrier most of his life, and knew many of the cattlemen. Chuck has an amazing memory with lots of details of peoples' names and dates and background information. He is also a nationally-known artist, whose oil paintings of horses and mountain landscapes tell a story. Chuck gave me permission to use his art in my book.

Chuck Knowles, 2016.

Donnie Whittle

Donnie, born in 1929, is member of the pioneer Whittle family of Angels Camp. The Whittles were cattlemen who ran their cattle at Crabtree and Wheats Meadow. He helped me with information about the local cattle industry. He proudly declares, "I never drew a wage for a job." Donnie was very knowledgeable about the Whittle tungsten mine in Emigrant Basin. He explained its history, how tungsten was mined, and showed me prized ore samples. He has a keen memory for people's names, dates and places, as well as a broad knowledge of local history. He and wife Nancy have been a pleasure to interview.

Donnie Whittle in 2017.

Janice Scruggs

Janice was born in 1925, and, accompanied by her cat Lucy Long Tail, shared her memories of working for the Sardellas at the front desk at Kennedy Meadows Resort. She also described the lives of the employees, and the people who came to the resort year after year. She explained how Artie broke and trained horses, and about their life together. I also met her son Jim Scruggs and his wife Karen who were especially helpful filling in the details of dates and events in Artie Scruggs' life.

Janice Scruggs in 2017.

Kenny Mitchell

From the Mills Mitchell family, longtime cattlemen of Vallecito in Calaveras County, Kenny, born in 1933, grew up at Kennedy Meadows Resort, as his parents owned it. Kenny and his wife Dora were helpful in explaining the early history of the resort and with many aspects of early Sonora Pass history. They also shared with me the Millie Krause photo album of the building of Relief Dam.

Kenny Mitchell, 2017.

Bennie Cassinetto

I met with Bennie at his home in Knights Ferry, with his sister Mary Jane. He showed me his historic wine cellar, and shared some wine with us. Bennie's mother was a Sardella. During his early years, Bennie worked for his uncle Reno at various pack stations. Bennie helped me understand the business of packing people into the wilderness, and the Sardella family history. He shared with me a photograph of Joe Ghoirso, and explained about Joe and the cattlemen. His sister Mary Jane also welcomed me into her home and shared old family photographs of the Sardellas.

Bennie Cassinetto, 2016.

Elvira Miller

I had been collecting information about Elbert Miller, the grocery peddler, when someone told me to go see his wife Elvira. I could not imagine that she was still alive, but she was very alert at 93 years of age. She shared photographs of the vegetable wagon, and told me more about her husband Elbert. Elvira has been a great resource, since she traveled the area with Elbert and knew a lot of people. She also recalled some personal stories about selling produce at Dardanelle, and moonlight horseback rides. I interviewed Elvira several times, and spoke with her at length in her home. She lived alone and welcomed a visitor. Nothing got by Elvira, as she recalled many experiences from her past. She has been a great resource, and lives just a few blocks from my house.

Elvira Miller, 2017.

W.C. Koch

I met W.C. Koch in the parking lot of the Dardanelle Store. I could see he was an older gentleman, and I learned that he had been coming to Dardanelle for many years. I arranged to meet him at his trailer that evening and talk history. He was a friendly man who welcomed me to the outdoor picnic table by his trailer, after a hard day of work. He and Cindy Fleischer, owner of the resort, are cousins. She had hired W.C., a contractor from Oakdale, to make repairs on the extensive winter damage. Although W.C. was not quite old enough to recall much of the history I was interested in, he did work as a teenager for cattlemen delivering hay, and recalled a few of the men, telling me about some of their history. He looked over my photograph collection with great interest. When W.C. mentioned he would tear out and completely rebuild the resort's back porch, I told him that I had heard several years back about a wine cellar under the porch. He allowed me to go through the fenced off area and have a look at the cellar, going inside and exploring how it was built, marveling at its size.

W.C. Koch, 2017.

Billie Lyons

I didn't know who Billie was until I became aware of her great Facebook page, Mother Lode Memories, where she posts old photos on a daily basis. The photographs are from the Tuolumne County Historical Society and Museum's collection, where she is the archivist. When I visit the Historical Society to do research, Billie, a history nut, is always eager to dig through information, answer questions, and find photographs. She is a gem who gave me encouragement to write this book. She declared it was a cross between a textbook and a coffee table book, and I like that.

Billie Lyons, 2018.

Dick Norquist

Dick attended The Jack Hazard YMCA camp as a boy, and later as a leader. Dick arranged for me to meet Jason Poisson, the current manager of the Jack and Buena Hazard Foundation, the organization operating the camp. He brought his older brother Tom to the meeting, and I interviewed Tom as well. However, it was Dick who explained the spiritual underpinnings of the YMCA, and how going to "Y" camp had such an impact on young lives. He spoke of all the activities and the staff with great fondness, and how those past years had influenced his life. I learned new things about the organization and what it actually did for youth.

Dick Norquist, 2018.

Matt Bloom

I met Matt Bloom at the end of a long day, and asked him if he had any Kennedy Meadow history, old photographs and such that he would share. I followed his long stride to his office, where he handed me a box of materials and said I could take it home to look through it for a couple of weeks. He didn't know me well, so I was amazed that I had this whole box to root through. The box did have some photos of value, and a few papers of interest. However, it was his gracious offer of help that impressed me. He is always patient to answer my questions and direct me to resources. Matt has given me guidance on Kennedy Meadows history and in the chapters "The Making of a Wrangler" and "Artie Scruggs."

Matt Bloom, 2017.

Bill Airola

From a pioneer cattle family, Bill and his wife Delores live on their ranch with views of oaks and rolling hills. They gave me a warm greeting, a seat by the fire, and a cup of tea. On their dining room table, they had laid out old family photographs for me to copy and use in my book. Bill explained much of the Airola family history. Bill practiced as a veterinarian for many years. However, his cattle business needed his full attention, so he gave up his work as a veterinarian. He has great knowledge and expertise about the business, and he explained what it was like to be a modern-day cattleman, and the obstacles of more and more regulations.

Bill Airola, 2017.

Cindy Fleischer

Cindy comes from the Benedix family, who have been at Dardanelle for several generations, and has an interest in local history. When Dardanelle Resort came up for sale, she felt obligated to take it on and continue its place in history. It has been a difficult project, but she perseveres. She has supported my efforts to learn about Dardanelle Resort. At my request, Cindy gave me my first tour of the upstairs. She allowed me to take her photograph collection off the restaurant walls and out of their frames to photograph them for my collection.

Cindy Fleischer, 2016.

Jack Hamilton

Jack, born in 1930 at Shaw's Flat, and his wife Glenna greeted me at their home on Longeway Road in Sonora. We talked on the porch, overlooking the chicken coop and vegetable garden. A fifth generation Sonoran, he told me his great grandfather Joaquin Morris hauled vegetables over the Pass to Bodie in the early days. The trip took seven days. Jack, a butcher and a carpenter, worked for Wade and Louise Coffill, building their house in Mono Village. He told me what he could remember about the Coffills. He was also good friends with Lou and Marjorie Sweet, who owned the Dardanelle Resort at the time, where he helped with the maintenance. So from Jack I learned about the Sweets.

Jack Hamilton, 2017.

Renalda Salyers

I first met Renalda at her cabin at Brightman Flat. I explained that I was writing a book about Sonora Pass, and planned to have a chapter on Kennedy Meadows. Could she tell me about her grandparents, Reno and Gerry Sardella? With ease, she told me her family history, including dates when great grandparents were born. I was amazed. I started taking notes and filled several pages. This information was the foundation of my chapter on Kennedy Meadows. I met with Renalda a second time at her home. At my request, she had unearthed old boxes of family photographs, and had them spread about the kitchen table. She generously shared with me any photograph I wished. She lost her cabin in the 2018 Donnell Fire.

Renalda Salyers, 2018.

Bill Coffill

Bill's uncle Wade Coffill owned Dardanelle Resort in the 1940s and '50s. However, Bill did not visit the area much, because his family owned a cabin at Pinecrest. Bill enjoys history and willingly shared with me his knowledge about the early days at Pinecrest. He also shared his postcard collection with me.

Bill Coffill, 2015.

My Angels
The Editors

Rob Gordon

I first met Rob at the Tuolumne County Historical Society office where I had gone to do research. He is the one to see for help with looking through their materials and resources. I showed him my progress on this book, and soon he was helping me search for more information. I could see he had an interest in my writing project. Rob is familiar with Sonora Pass and has spent time at Cow Creek. So, in Rob, I found a kindred spirit who knows Sonora Pass and has an interest in its history. In May of 2017, I got up the courage to ask Rob if he would be my editor. He said yes! Rob is a writer, and has encouraged me with my progress of becoming an author. Rob has supported me through this project, giving me valuable guidance and thoughtfully editing every chapter.

Rob Gordon, 2017.

Suzanne Murphy

I joined the writers group at Manzanita Writers Press in Angels Camp, and I met Suzanne, who had a background as a teacher and wrote poetry. Suzanne, a member of their editing staff, was familiar with Sonora Pass, and was willing to help me with punctuation, sentence structure, and in general, teaching me to be a better writer. Later, I chose the press to publish this book. Suzanne offered to meet with me on a weekly basis to read my chapters. She was dedicated in helping me write this book. We met over twenty times. Every week I pushed myself to have a chapter ready for Suzanne. She was a wonderful teacher, and we both looked forward to each meeting to visit, get some editing done, and finish another chapter. I could not have written this book without her.

Suzanne Murphy, 2018

Alan Haack

At the Tuolumne Museum, I gave a lecture about writing my book. Afterward, Alan greeted me and complimented me on what a great presentation I had given. Alan told me how much he had enjoyed it and that I am a natural storyteller. He has longtime family roots in Tuolumne County. In the 1920s, his grandfather Jack Brophy developed Long Barn, bringing in wells, laying out streets, and selling lots. Alan's family had a cabin at Pinecrest in the 1940s. He learned to ski at Dodge Ridge, and spent summers at Camp Jack Hazard near Dardanelle. He has hiked and explored the Sierra for years, especially along the Walker River. Alan lives near Standard, California. Alan offered to give the book a last editing from someone who would be a fresh eye to the project. I found him to be an excellent editor, and enjoy his friendship.

Alan Haack, 2018.

Index

A

About the Author

Cate Culver makes her home in the California Sierra foothills. After her twenty-five-year career in Oakland and Sacramento as a graphic artist in advertising, she and her husband Jerry relocated to Mountain Ranch, where she pursued her passion for painting and capturing the natural grace and power of the California region. Recently they have moved to Tuolumne County.

The family summer cabin of Cate's childhood, located at Dardanelle on Sonora Pass, inspired her to write her first book. *The Untold History of Sonora Pass and Its People: 1860 to 1960* chronicles the fascinating hundred years of development along Sonora Pass, and the unforgettable people who put their stamp on the land.

Cate served as Calaveras County's historian for eleven years, developing her skills for meticulous research. As a graphic artist, Cate designed every page in the book, and included a sprinkling of her art. Combined with her natural curiosity and primary source interviews, she brings life to the towering beauty of the Sonora Pass, and honors the intrepid spirit of its people.

Cate Culver
Photograph courtesy of Lynne Jerome.

Author at work with her cat, Basket, in her lap.
Photograph by Jerry Culver.

CPSIA information can be obtained
at www.ICGtesting.com
Printed in the USA
BVHW021402170721
612224BV00014B/118